# The Goddess and the Sun in Indian Myth

In analysing the parallels between myths glorifying the Indian Great Goddess, Durgā, and those glorifying the Sun, Sūrya, found in the *Mārkaṇḍeya Purāṇa*, this book argues for an ideological ecosystem at work in the *Mārkaṇḍeya Purāṇa* privileging worldly values, of which Indian kings, the Goddess (Devī), the Sun (Sūrya), Manu and Mārkaṇḍeya himself are paragons.

This book features a salient discovery in Sanskrit narrative text: just as the *Mārkaṇḍeya Purāṇa* houses the *Devī Māhātmya* glorifying the supremacy of the Indian Great Goddess, Durgā, it also houses a *Sūrya Māhātmya*, glorifying the supremacy of the Sun, Sūrya, in much the same manner. This book argues that these *māhātmya*s were meaningfully and purposefully positioned in the *Mārkaṇḍeya Purāṇa*, while previous scholarship has considered this haphazard interpolation for sectarian aims. The book demonstrates that deliberate compositional strategies make up the Saura–Śākta symbiosis found in these mirrored *māhātmya*s. Moreover, the author explores what he calls the "dharmic double helix" of Brahmanism, most explicitly articulated by the structural opposition between *pravṛtti* (worldly) and *nivṛtti* (other-worldly) *dharma*s.

As the first narrative study of the *Sūrya Māhātmya*, along with the first study of the *Mārkaṇḍeya Purāṇa* (or any Purāṇa), as a narrative whole, this book will be of interest to academics in the field of Religion, Hindu Studies, South Asian Studies, Goddess Studies, Narrative Theory and Comparative Mythology.

**Raj Balkaran** teaches at the School of Continuing Studies at the University of Toronto, Canada. He is also the host of "New Books in Hindu Studies", a podcast channel on the New Books Network, and the author of *The Goddess and The King in Indian Myth* (Routledge, 2019).

**Routledge Hindu Studies Series**
**Series Editor:** Gavin Flood, Oxford Centre for Hindu Studies

A RECOGNISED INDEPENDENT CENTRE OF THE UNIVERSITY OF OXFORD

The *Routledge Hindu Studies Series*, in association with the Oxford Centre for Hindu Studies, intends the publication of constructive Hindu theological, philosophical and ethical projects aimed at bringing Hindu traditions into dialogue with contemporary trends in scholarship and contemporary society. The series invites original, high quality, research level work on religion, culture and society of Hindus living in India and abroad. Proposals for annotated translations of important primary sources and studies in the history of the Hindu religious traditions will also be considered.

**Caitanya Vaiṣṇavism in Bengal**
Social Impact and Historical Implications
*Joseph T. O'Connell, edited by Rembert Lutjeharms*

**Vedic Practice, Ritual Studies and Jaimini's Mīmāṃsāsūtras**
Dharma and the Enjoined Subject
*Samuel G. Ngaihte*

**The Legacy of Vaiṣṇavism in Colonial Bengal**
*Edited by Ferdinando Sardella and Lucian Wong*

**Salvation in Indian Philosophy**
Perfection and Simplicity for Vaiśeṣika
*Ionut Moise*

**The Goddess and the Sun in Indian Myth**
Power, Preservation and Mirrored *Māhātmyas* in the *Mārkaṇḍeya Purāṇa*
*Raj Balkaran*

For more information about this series, please visit: www.routledge.com/asian studies/series/RHSS

# The Goddess and the Sun in Indian Myth

## Power, Preservation and Mirrored *Māhātmyas* in the *Mārkaṇḍeya Purāṇa*

**Raj Balkaran**

Routledge
Taylor & Francis Group
LONDON AND NEW YORK

First published 2020
by Routledge
2 Park Square, Milton Park, Abingdon, Oxon OX14 4RN

and by Routledge
605 Third Avenue, New York, NY 10017

First issued in paperback 2022

*Routledge is an imprint of the Taylor & Francis Group, an informa business*



*British Library Cataloguing-in-Publication Data*
A catalogue record for this book is available from the British Library

*Library of Congress Cataloging-in-Publication Data*
A catalog record has been requested for this book

ISBN 13: 978-1-03-240017-4 (pbk)
ISBN 13: 978-0-367-33805-3 (hbk)
ISBN 13: 978-0-429-32202-0 (ebk)

DOI: 10.4324/9780429322020

Typeset in Times New Roman
by Wearset Ltd, Boldon, Tyne and Wear

**For Satya, for lighting up my life**

tat savitur vareṇyaṃ
bhargo devasya dhīmahi
dhiyo yo naḥ prachodayāt

We meditate on the supreme splendour
of that divinely enlivening Sun;
May he illumine our minds.

*Ṛg Veda*, 3.62.10

# Contents


*List of illustrations* viii

*Foreword* ix

GREG BAILEY

*Acknowledgements* xi

Introduction: the turning tide of scholarship 1

1 Synchronic strategy: transcending diachronic dissection 5

2 Mirrored *māhātmyas:* Saura–Śākta symbiosis in the *Mārkaṇḍeya Purāṇa* 34

3 The story of Saṃjñā: Mother of Manu, threshold of tradition 68

4 Mapping Mārkaṇḍeya: Synchronic surveillance of *The Mārkaṇḍeya Purāṇa* 99

Conclusion: paragons of preservation – Goddess, Sun, King 131

*Bibliography* 143

*Index* 153

# Illustrations

## Figure

2.1 The *Mārkaṇḍeya Purāṇa* solar family tree 36

## Tables

1.1 Sections of the *Mārkaṇḍeya Purāṇa* 8
1.2 Historical Strata of the *Mārkaṇḍeya Purāṇa* 10
2.1 Parallels between *Devī* and *Sūrya Māhātmyas* 37
2.2 The structure of the *Sūrya Māhātmya* 38
2.3 The Manu-intervals (*manvantaras*) of the *Mārkaṇḍeya Purāṇa* 55
2.4 The royal dynasties (*vaṃśānucarita*) of the *Mārkaṇḍeya Purāṇa* 56
2.5 *Sūrya Māhātmya* episode chart 65
4.1 *Mārkaṇḍeya Purāṇa* Exposition Guide 107
4.2 Expositors of the *Mārkaṇḍeya Purāṇa* 110
4.3 Birds in the intermediary sections of the *Mārkaṇḍeya Purāṇa* 117
4.4 Birds throughout the *Mārkaṇḍeya Purāṇa* 118
4.5 Birds in the final section of the *Mārkaṇḍeya Purāṇa* 118
4.6 Birds in Section I of the *Mārkaṇḍeya Purāṇa* 121
4.7 Backstory of the Birds 121

# Foreword

*Greg Bailey*

Raj Balkaran has already established himself as one of the foremost scholars of the Purāṇas with his work on the *Devī Māhātmya*. The *Mārkaṇḍeya Purāṇa*, in which this text occurs, also contains another set of chapters, which Balkaran has rightly considered to be a *Sūrya Māhātmya* or "text of glorification to the Sun god", a text which has scarcely been mentioned by earlier scholars. It is to this text that the present volume directs its attention, and in exploring this *māhātmya*, he also shows how thematically interconnected it is with the *Devī Māhātmya*, if not with the *Mārkaṇḍeya Purāṇa* as a whole.

He contextualizes the *Sūrya Māhātmya* within the broad context of sun worship beginning from the *Ṛg Veda* and traces the few hymns to the Sun found in the third book of the *Mahābhārata* and in certain manuscripts of the *Yuddhakhaṇḍa* of the *Rāmāyaṇa*. In Chapter 3, he also gives a new interpretation of the well-known myth of Sūrya–Saṃjñā–Chāyā, and relates this directly to the main theme of the *Devī Māhātmya* where "Both mythologies bespeak powerful feminine divinities whose efforts restore order in the face of peril and both bespeak the danger which results when fiery figures, though required to preserve our world, exceed safe bounds" (XXX [116]). In doing so, he presents valid criticisms of Doniger's structuralist interpretation of the myth – emphasizing a contrast between good and bad mothers – where versions of the myth coming from texts over one and a half millennia are afforded equal validity. Rather, Balkaran interprets this myth, with its lengthy antiquity, in terms of the principle themes of the *Mārkaṇḍeya Purāṇa*, which inform the meaning of this myth in that text.

Above all, the incorporation of the mythology of the Sun in the *Mārkaṇḍeya Purāṇa* contributes to the theme of the preservation of the ordered world as is also so strongly reflected in the avatāric function of the *Devī Māhātmya*, the myths where kings play exemplary roles and the narratives of the *manvantaras*, the latter very much tied into the *Devī Māhātmya*. And this, in turn, leads into his ongoing discussion throughout the book of *pravṛtti* and *nivṛtti* as contrastive *dharma*s providing a confirmatory interpretative frame to the more explicit themes found in each of the myths.

Above all, *pravṛtti*, with its emphasis on affirmation of the world of society, ritual and kingship, aligns centrally with the principle emphases of both *māhātmya*s found in the *Mārkaṇḍeya Purāṇa*. *Pravṛtti* and *nivṛtti* are already treated in a more formal sense in Chapters 24–42 of this Purāṇa, but, as the present book demonstrates so admirably, their propositional and contrastive aspects are fully developed in the case studies such as the *māhātmya*s and the other parts of the *Mārkaṇḍeya Purāṇa* dealing with the *pañcalakṣaṇa*. This is not just the usual conflicting behaviour between irascible ascetics and non-ascetics, especially nymphs, but instances of royal figures having to come to terms with the *nivṛtti* attitude of detachment that is not consistent with the preservation of an ongoing society. In the final analysis, he offers the insightful opinion that: "The MkP might therefore be said to represent a means to pacify the extent to which pravṛtti dharma attains an accursed hue, viewed through the lofty lens of nivṛttic ideology" (p. 167).

If this treatment of some of the principal themes of the two *māhātmya*s and the other parts of the *Mārkaṇḍeya Purāṇa* were all this book contained, it would be enough in itself. Yet, it goes further than this in offering us new insights into how to read the purāṇa genre as a whole. As in his earlier work on the *Devī Māhātmya*, Balkaran urges Purāṇic scholars to go beyond the very strong historicism which has dominated this field since Wilson's translation of the *Viṣṇu Purāṇa* was published in 1840. This historicism has tended to see individual Purāṇic narratives as interpolation laid upon interpolation, with some larger guidance provided by the *pañcalakṣaṇa* theory. It refuses to countenance the possibility of a given Purāṇa being read in its own terms, especially with the guidance given by frame narratives, the interaction between reciters and interlocutors and the intertextual connections the interlocutors bring with them, especially in relation to the *Mahābhārata*. In this book, four types of frames are developed in Chapter 1, frames reinforcing the synchronic reading of the *Mārkaṇḍeya Purāṇa*, not just of the two *māhātmya*s the author offers to the reader. What he suggests provides very useful methodological signposts for the readers of any Purāṇa.

In short, this book offers valuable exposition of the *Sūrya Māhātmya*, shows its continuities with the *Devī Māhātmya*, demonstrates the importance of *pravṛtti* and *nivṛtti* as hermeneutical devices for reading the *Mārkaṇḍeya Purāṇa*, and offers a long overdue new approach for reading the Purāṇas.

# Acknowledgements

I'm very grateful to the two main ladies in my life,
Amrita and Satya, for their unwavering love and support.

I am very grateful also to Noah, the loveliest of sons,
from whom I've learned a great many things.

I feel beyond blessed to have received the mentorship and care of Krishan Mantri, without whom I could not begin to be the man I am today.

I deeply appreciate Joyce Rollick,
for her wisdom, skill and friendship.

A special thanks also goes to Amanda Iliadis
for her excellent research efforts towards this work.

I would like to express my gratitude to the
Social Sciences and Humanities Research Council of Canada
whose generous support enabled me to lay the foundation for both
*The Goddess and the King* and *The Goddess and The Sun.*

I am also thankful to the Routledge team,
who have been the gold standard of professionalism
every step of the way.

# Introduction

## The turning tide of scholarship

The *Goddess and the Sun in Indian Myth* is a natural progression, and direct evolute, of my previous contribution to the Routledge Hindu Studies series: *The Goddess and the King in Indian Myth*. To say that these works are companions would be an overstatement; yet, while *The Goddess and the Sun* is ultimately a stand-alone work, it stands squarely on the shoulders of *The Goddess and the King*. This current work is the germination of a seed planted in the closing paragraphs of *The Goddess and The King*, as follows:

> That the work of the making of the Manu equally entails the theme of preservation as with the work of our grand Goddess, it is perhaps not surprising that the sovereign of the universe would appoint the lord of an age in the form of the Manu Sāvarṇi … The Manu Sāvarṇi, along with the current Manu Vaivasvata, are offspring of the Sun, which the DM reminds us of in its opening lines. The themes of sovereignty and preservation are not only equally implicated in the myths of the Sun occurring in the MkP, these myths are concentrated in a tripartite narrative whose structure parallels that of the DM, which I have tentatively dubbed the *Sūrya Māhātmya*.
>
> (Balkaran 2019, 152–3)

This book explores the manner in which the structure and content of the *Sūrya Māhātmya* mirrors that of the *Devī Māhātmya* (the subject of *The Goddess and The King*), and, ultimately argues for an ideological ecosystem at work in the *Mārkaṇḍeya Purāṇa* privileging *pravṛtti* (over *nivṛtti*) dharma and the cosmic function of preservation, of which Indian kings, the Goddess (Devī), the Sun (Sūrya), Manu and Mārkaṇḍeya himself are paragons.

*The Goddess and the King* was spawned by asking "why are the exploits of the Goddess comprising the *Devī Māhātmya* (DM) framed by an encounter between an exiled king and a forest-dwelling sage?" Upon the completion of that work, I have since embarked on an enframement odyssey, asking after why the frame of the DM was framed by the mythology of the Sun, and indeed why DM and *Sūrya Māhātmya* (SM) find themselves in the *Mārkaṇḍeya Purāṇa* (MkP) at all. With respect to the research question spawning *The Goddess and The King*, I argued that text very consciously encodes what I call the dharmic

DOI: 10.4324/9780429322020-1

double helix – Brahmanism's paradoxical allegiance to both world-affirming *pravṛttic* and world-denying *nivṛttic* religious impulses – while emphatically privileging the sanguinary strand of that ideological double helix, celebrating the office of Goddess and Indian king in the name of preservation. *The Goddess and the Sun* charts the extent to which the *saura* authors take their lead from their Śākta counterparts, foregrounding the *pravṛttic* work of kings in their homage to the Sun.

Beyond featuring the discovery of the SM, and the manner in which the SM is modelled after the DM, *The Goddess and The Sun* demonstrates that the *pravṛttic saura–śākta* symbiosis interlacing these two *māhātmya*s of the MkP contribute to, and draw from, an ideological ecosystem that emphasizes the cosmogonic function of preservation. This emphasis is explicitly articulated in the ideology of *pravṛtti* religion, honouring royal power and the penchant of kings to preserve social and moral orders. The royal work of *pravṛtti* – wielding power for the preservation of moral and social order – is embraced by the Goddess, Manus (whose discourses frame her glories), the Sun, the lineage of kings (whose discourse cradles his glories), and is represented by Mārkaṇḍeya himself, the sole being preserved across cosmic dissolution.

While the trends advancing our current epoch of scholarship will necessarily be clearly discerned only from some future time – perhaps decades from now, empowered by the acumen of hindsight – we can nevertheless discern a very important shift afoot with respect to the scholarly study of Indian myth. While the World Sanskrit Conference has been meeting triennially since its inception in 1972, 2015 marked the first year when Purāṇic Studies was granted its own section (previously, it was lumped in with papers on the Sanskrit epics). As expressed in the Preface to the Purāṇa proceedings of the following World Sanskrit Conference at 2018:

> The purāṇas themselves betray an acute awareness of their own dynamism, i.e., their penchant to respond to religious change across time. Apropos of their object study, the theoretical and methodological approaches to this very important genre showcased in this volume bespeak an evolution in Indological scholarship. It seems we have officially moved away from the stringent historicism that has dominated the field thus far. This volume commemorates this important rite of passage: it is a testament of the disintegration of that dominion in favour of receiving the purāṇas in a manner befitting their position as the dynamic life-blood of Indian tradition itself.
>
> (Balkaran and Taylor 2019, vi)

*The Goddess and The Sun* serves to advance this trend of transcending the methodological pitfalls of our predecessors in encountering Indian myth. I take the Sanskrit texts I study herein at face value, attentive to the presence of highly conscious compositional strategies at play by the time of their final redaction. Diachronically composed no doubt, we can nevertheless retrieve great insight in accepting that the contents of these texts belong there, and with good reason.

I privilege the thematic trends one discerns in viewing the MkP as a whole over the temporal trends one discerns while slicing and dicing it for historicist or philological aims.

## 0.1 Chapter outline

### *0.1.1 Synchronic strategy: transcending diachronic dissection*

This chapter surveys scholarship on the *Mārkaṇḍeya Purāṇa*, along with Sanskrit sources on Sūrya including the *Mahābhārata*, *Rāmāyaṇa*, the Purāṇas and the *Sāmba Upa-Purāṇa*. It goes on to articulate a synchronic strategy for studying the Sansk.

### *0.1.2 Mirrored* **māhātmyas***: Saura–Śākta supremacy in the* **Mārkaṇḍeya Purāṇa**

This chapter examines myths of Sūrya (the Sun) in the *Mārkaṇḍeya Purāṇa*, including Sūrya's family (Saṃjñā, Chāyā, Yama, Manu, Śani and Tapatī), and his relationship to the Vedic gods Brahmā, Aditi and Viśvakarman. It argues for regarding these myths as *māhātmya* literature, since they parallel the much more famous *Devī Māhātmya* which glorifies the Hindu Great Goddess, Durgā. This chapter demonstrates a Saura–Śākta sectarian symbiosis at play in the compositional strategies producing these Sanskrit texts. It also discusses the way in which these texts both privilege the duty of the Indian king, pravṛtti dharma, and the cosmic function of preservation.

### *0.1.3 The story of Saṃjñā: mother of Manu, threshold of tradition*

This chapter analyses the very important Vedic myth of the goddess Saṃjñā. She is the wife of Sūrya (the Sun), and the mother of Manu. Her story is heavily implicated in the *Devī Māhātmya*, which glorifies the Hindu Great Goddess, Durgā. This chapter first debunks Wendy Doniger's problematic interpretations of this myth cycle, then goes on to deepen discussion of the Saura–Śākta sectarian symbiosis at play in the *Mārkaṇḍeya Purāṇa*. This chapter then uses Indian astrological material (Jyotiṣa) to provide insight into the connection between Vedic mythology and the ritual timing of the autumnal Navarātrī Goddess festival (Durgā Pūjā).

### *0.1.4 Mapping Mārkaṇḍeya: synchronic surveillance of the* **Mārkaṇḍeya Purāṇa**

This chapter probes the *Mārkaṇḍeya Purāṇa*'s rich frame to shed light on thematic currents spanning the text. It shows why the *Mārkaṇḍeya Purāṇa* is fertile ideological soil for both the *Sūrya Māhātmya* (glorifying the Sun), and the *Devī Māhātmya* (glorifying Devī, the Hindu Goddess). It ultimately suggests an ideological ecosystem at work in the *Mārkaṇḍeya Purāṇa*, predicated on pravṛtti dharma and the cosmogonic imperative of preservation as exemplified in the work of Indian kings, the Goddess (Devī), the Sun (Sūrya), and Mārkaṇḍeya himself. It also touches on important intertextuality between the *Mārkaṇḍeya Purāṇa* and the *Mahābhārata*.

### *0.1.5 Conclusion: paragons of preservation*

This chapter discusses the Sun as Preserver in other Sanskrit narratives, such as the *Rāmāyaṇa*, the *Mahābhārata*, and his relationship with epic and Purāṇic characters such as Yudhiṣṭhira, Karṇa, Yama and Rāma. It discusses the extent to which Indian kings, the Goddess (Devī), the Sun (Sūrya), Manu and Mārkaṇḍeya himself are paragons of the cosmic function of preservation befitting the pravṛtti dharma ecosystem constituting the *Mārkaṇḍeya Purāṇa*.

# 1 Synchronic strategy

## Transcending diachronic dissection

In researching the glories of the Goddess housed in the *Mārkaṇḍeya Purāṇa* (MkP), I couldn't help but notice the parallel laudation of the Sun, also housed in the MkP. I used the word 'houses' purposefully: these laudations are 'at home' there. These 'interpolations' are more akin to renovations than intrusions. In making sense of why those glories of the Goddess should be mouthed by Mārkaṇḍeya (the narrator of the *Mārkaṇḍeya Purāṇa*), I inadvertently ended making sense of why the glories of the Sun are also housed here. The MkP is marked by an ethos of preservation, represented by Mārkaṇḍeya's own biography, and embellished in the tales of the Goddess and the Sun therein. It is the ideology of kings.

The life sap of the Purāṇa is an ideological ecosystem predicated on the privileging of the function of preservation, explicitly articulated in *pravṛtti dharma*. As summarized in *The Goddess and The King*:

> Sanskrit narrative literature thus overwhelmingly celebrates these two divergent figures: the ascetic and the king. The ancient Indian king upholds society (stationed at its very centre), while the ancient Indian ascetic shuns society (poised at its periphery). As such, the former is a paragon of worldly pursuits, while the latter serves as the epitome of all things other-worldly. The dichotomy between the ideologies of kingship and asceticism might be understood as distinct expressions of power: the king wields *outer* power, which he employs to control others and regulates the mundane world, while the ascetic commands *inner* power, which he hones through ardent control of self and rejection of the world. Furthermore, *ahiṃsā* (non-violence) is the imperative of the ascetic, while kings are required to implement force in protection of subject and state. Yet each of these figures – ascetic and king alike – is venerated as a virtuoso of his respective realm. Their interaction comprises a literary trope that encapsulates a lasting ideological tension within the Hindu world: the tension between the divergent duties of (world-denying) renouncers and (world-affirming) householders, synthesized as *pravṛtti* and *nivṛtti dharmas* by the time of the MBh.
>
> (Balkaran 2019, 28)

DOI: 10.4324/9780429322020-2

While works such as the *Sūrya Māhātmya* (SM) and *Devī Māhātmya* (DM) symbolically encode the *pravṛtti–nivṛtti* complex – most palpably in the exchanges of forest hermits and exiled kings – the MkP does better than that: it is explicit in its discussion of these ideologies (MkP 24–42). Greg Bailey observes that while the *Mahābhārata* (MBh) is traditionally where we look to see this formulation, the presentation there is not as systematic as what we see in the MkP, and "as such these chapters constitute one of the few extended self-conscious treatments of the subject" (Bailey 2005, 19). These ideologies "might have been contrastive, not just complementary, even though there is the possibility they could have been both depending on which text one reads" (Bailey 2005, 17). Having said that, *pravṛtti* would most certainly have been the religion of the masses, and, intriguingly, the apex of those masses and paragon of pravṛtti – the Indian king – would have been presentative of necessarily encapsulating both strands, while of course privileging the world-facing *pravṛtti*. It is the king who protects the ascetics, and engages in ascetic means to derive the necessary blessings to protect the world. As Bailey notes:

> chapter 24 contains a whole set of rules prescriptive of kings and the accompanying restraints appropriate for a king who must of necessity hold within himself both pravṛtti and nivṛtti values. Whilst the former are dominant, the latter are reflected in 25,11–15; 29, verses which stress how much the king must conquer his emotions as a prelude to impartiality.
>
> (Bailey 2005, 4)

This book argues that while explicit only in this section, this ideological bent is implicit throughout the MkP, foundational to an ecosystem marked by this very same tension, always tilted towards *pravṛtti* as evidences in the glorifications of Goddess and Sun, and the biography of Mārkaṇḍeya himself.

*The Goddess and the King* was spawned by asking 'why are the exploits of the Goddess comprising the *Devī Māhātmya* framed by an encounter between an exiled king and a forest-dwelling sage?' Crucial to my findings is that encounters between an exiled king and a forest-dwelling sage serve as a narrative motif encapsulating opposing ideals. I have argued that text very consciously encodes what I call the dharmic double helix (Balkaran 2019, 35–53) – Brahmanism's paradoxical allegiance to both world-affirming *pravṛttic* and world-denying *nivṛttic* religious impulses – while emphatically privileging the sanguinary strand of that ideological double helix, celebrating the office of Goddess and Indian king in the name of preservation (Balkaran 2019, 60–87). *The Goddess and the Sun* charts the extent to which the Saura authors take their lead from their Śākta counterparts, foregrounding the *pravṛttic* work of kings in their homage to the Sun. Moreover, it argues that these two *māhātmya*s interface with an existing, complementary, emphasis on *pravṛttic* preservation innate to the MkP.

I have in effect discovered that there exists *two māhātmya*s in the *Mārkaṇḍeya Purāṇa*: in addition to the much more famous glorification of the Goddess (the *Devī Māhātmya*), there exists a mirrored *māhātmya* glorifying the Sun (the *Sūrya Māhātmya*). While the first telling of the myth of the Sun and his family occur as a stand-alone segment (MkP 77–78), the second telling of the sequence of events between the Sun and Saṃjñā (MkP 106–108) occurs as part of a conglomeration of tales embellishing the virtues of the Sun, casting him as a supreme primordial power even above the gods themselves. Remarkably, the MkP dedicates a nine-chapter episodic trilogy to lauding the majesty of the Sun (see Pargiter 1904, 553–87, Chapters 102–108), which I refer to herein as the *Sūrya Māhātmya* (SM).

To my knowledge, nothing has been written on this compilation of solar myths in the MkP, save for general remarks in passing, which refer to sectarian materials lauding about the Sun in the MkP. For example, there is no mention of a *Sūrya Māhātmya* in Jan Gonda's discourse on *māhātmya*s in his Sanskrit Medieval Literature section of his edited series *A History of Indian Literature*. With respect to works which praise the Sun, Gonda makes mention only of Mayūra's early seventh-century Sūrya-Śataka (see Gonda 1977, 251, which, interestingly enough, was contemporary with Bāṇa's Caṇḍī-Śataka, see Gonda 1977, 250), along with a praise of the Sun "attributed to a certain Sāmba" from mid-eighth century onwards (see Gonda 1977, 252). He furthermore refers to a *Sūrya Gītā* in one lone sentence as follows: "The Surya-Gita must belong to the comparatively late works of this genre because it has undergone the influence of Rāmānuja's Viśiṣṭādvaita philosophy" (Gonda 1977, 276). Gonda notes that while *māhātmya* literature often centres on places of pilgrimage (i.e. *tīrtha*), it can of course centre on "the figure of a god and the spread of his cult rather than the sanctity of a particular temple city or place of pilgrimage. A well-known instance is the Devī-Māhātmya" (Gonda 1977, 281). Therefore, since this conglomeration of myths details various exploits of the Sun, it is too elaborate to be called a *stotra* or *stava* (and indeed includes within it four such *stotras*), and lacks the requisite structure to be termed a *gītā* (indeed, there is an existing *Sūrya Gītā*), I deem *māhātmya* as the most apt appellation for the scope of these acts glorifying the Sun.

## 1.1 Diachronic dissection of the *Mārkaṇḍeya Purāṇa*

It is no wonder the SM has henceforth not been named as such: scholars of the Purāṇas have been too busy slicing and dicing these texts for historicist and philological reasons – as if each patch were more important than the quilt they collectively knit. While Eden Pargiter translated the entire Purāṇa into English in 1904, he was heavily under the sway of the he legacy of Purāṇic scholarship inaugurated by H.H. Wilson, one which condemned the Purāṇas as sectarian Brahmanical corruptions of some long-lost pristine non-sectarian texts (Balkaran 2019, 7–13). This very bias occluded Pargiter's ability to register the glaring similarities in the SM and DM, despite the fact that the DM emphatically declares at its very outset (and again at its conclusion, just so there is no ambiguity), that it shall elucidate the rise to power (as Manu) of the son of the Sun. Likewise this bias remained trenchant throughout the generations of

Pargiter's own scholarly heirs; in the subsequent scholarly generation, Winternitz (1972), too, notes the prevalence of solar mythology in the MkP (Winternitz 1972a, 560), yet makes no connection between the presence of that mythology and the DM or the MkP at large. Two scholarly generations past Pargiter's publication, even once the DM began receiving detailed scholarly attention in its own right, Agrawala (1963) condemns the connection between the DM and the *manvantara* discourse of the MkP as "obviously very flimsy" (Agrawala 1963, 832), which is again echoed verbatim twenty years later (1986) by Ludo Rocher (Rocher 1986, 195). As late as 1992, Nileshvari Desai undertakes a focused study on the MkP – titled "Ancient Indian Society, Religion, and Mythology as Depicted in the Mārkaṇḍeya Purāṇa" (Desai 1968) – in which he notes that "in the MKP much material on religion is available, particularly regarding the Devī, Dattātreya and Sun" (Desai 1968, 109). Yet, he too, preoccupied with mining the Purāṇa for ancient historical and cultural data, fails to survey the narrative fabric of the text as a whole, and thus fails to register the glaring interrelations between the mythologies of the Goddess and of the Sun, both in content, in form and in function, with respect the MV section of the MkP. Wendy Doniger, too, in her penetrating survey of Indian myths, including the myths of the MkP, partakes in this legacy of fragmentation, recapitulating its biases even into 2014 (Doniger 2014). This pervasive legacy must be addressed so as to embolden subsequent generations of scholars to embrace as purposeful the seeming madness of cross-generational Purāṇic assemblage. Amid the dizzying frame narratives and only seemingly intrusive interpolations lay profoundly insightful thematic continuities, which account for which tales wind up within which compilations, precisely clinched within which extrinsic narrative frames.

Banerjea, who first edited the work and upon whose edition English translation of the MkP Dutt (1896) and Pargiter (1904) relied, as early as 1855 classified the content of the MkP into five sections, as per Table 1.1:

In the words of Eden Pargiter:

> The Purāṇa is clearly divisible (as Dr. Banerjea noticed) into five distinct parts, namely: 1. Cantos 1–9, in which Jaimini is referred by Mārkaṇḍeya to the wise Birds, and they directly explain to him the four questions that perplexed him and some connected matters. 2. Cantos 10–44, where, though

*Table 1.1* Sections of the *Mārkaṇḍeya Purāṇa*

| *Sections* | *Cantos* | *Expositor* | *Interlocutor* |
|---|---|---|---|
| I | 1–9; 137 | The Birds | Jaimini |
| II | 10–44 | Sumati-Jaḍa | Father |
| III | 45–81 | Mārkaṇḍeya | Krauṣṭuki |
| IV | 82–92 | Medhas | Suratha |
| V | 93–136 | Mārkaṇḍeya | Krauṣṭuki |

> Jaimini propounds further questions to the Birds and they nominally expound them, yet the real speakers are Sumati, nicknamed Jaḍa, and his father. 3. Cantos 45–81: here, though Jaimini and the Birds are the nominal speakers, yet the real speakers are Mārkaṇḍeya and his disciple Krauṣṭuki. 4. Cantos 82–92, the Devi-mahatmya, a pure interpolation, in which the real speaker is a ṛṣi named Medhas, and which is only repeated by Mārkaṇḍeya. 5. Cantos 93–136, where Mārkaṇḍeya and Krauṣṭuki carry on their discourse from Canto 81. The 137th canto concludes the work; it is a necessary corollary to the first part.
>
> (Pargiter 1904, iv)

This fivefold division of the Purāṇa was implicated to bolster claims regarding the historical development of the text; for example, it is based on this dissection that Pargiter regards the DM section as a "pure interpolation" (Pargiter 1904, iv). The scholarly trajectory established by this diachronic thrust has proven most influential over the decades. Winternitz, for example, follows Pargiter in taking as the oldest the parts of the Purāṇa where Mārkaṇḍeya is the narrator proper (instructing his pupil Krauṣṭuki), that is, 45–81 and 93–136 (Winternitz 1972a, 559, n. 2). He does so on the basis that neither Viṣṇu nor Śiva take centre stage in these sections but rather, the Vedic gods Agni and Sūrya are glorified therein, and the text also includes a number of myths of the sun god. He, of course, fails to register that the persona of the Sun crafted in the MkP, as the primal cause of creation and face of immortality, is a vastly different entity from the figure we see in Vedic myths, where the Sun is the archetypal mortal bar none, enduring birth and death on a daily basis, marked by dawn and twilight. Winternitz dates these presumably most ancient sections (again following Pargiter) to 300 CE or earlier. The conclusions about the dating of all five strata of the text are reinforced by the work of R.C. Hazra who writes that "the above conclusion about the date of the chapters under discussion agrees remarkably with the view of Pargiter" (Hazra 1975, 13). He therefore cites Pargiter as follows:

> The *Devī-māhātmya*, the latest part, was certainly complete in the 9th century and very probably in the 5th or 6th century A.D. The third and fifth parts (i.e. chaps. 45–81 and 93–136 respectively), which constituted the original Purāṇa, were very probably in existence in the third century, and perhaps even earlier; and the first and second parts (i.e., chaps. 1–9 and 10–44 respectively) were composed between those two periods.
>
> (Hazra 1975, 13) Originally quoted in (Pargiter 1904, xx)

Table 1.2 provides a snapshot of the tripartite diachronic scheme laid out by Pargiter and subsequently reinforced by the work of Winternitz and Hazra:

Despite the obvious value of the legacy bequeathed by Pargiter to scholars such as Winternitz and Hazra, this trajectory has precluded examining the work on its own terms, as a synchronic whole; in pursuit of historical data, much has

*Table 1.2* Historical Strata of the *Mārkaṇḍeya Purāṇa*

| *Strata* | *Expositor* | *Interlocutor* | *Pargiter-Hazra Dating* | *Sec.* | *Cantos* |
|---|---|---|---|---|---|
| I | Mārkaṇḍeya | Krauṣṭuki | third century CE or earlier | III | 45–81 |
| | | | | V | 93–136 |
| II | The Birds | Jaimini | Between Strata I and III | I | 1–9; 137 |
| | Sumati-Jaḍa | Father | Between Strata I and III | II | 10–44 |
| III | Medhas | Suratha | fifth–sixth century CE | IV | 82–92 |

been missed regarding the craftsmanship at work to render the text in its current form. Even if one were to dismiss the 'persona' of the text as in some way 'false', is an understanding of the textual mechanics and religious function of the persona not of scholarly value?

In his volume on the history of Hindu Indian literature, Winternitz asserts that "neither Purāṇas nor the Tantras make for enjoyable reading" (Winternitz 1972b, 606), a stance which he bolsters on the following basis:

> They are work of inferior writers, and are often written in barbarous and ungrammatical Sanskrit. On the other hand neither the literary historian nor the student of religion can afford to pass them by in silence; for during centuries and even at the present time these writings are the spiritual food of millions of Indians.
>
> (Winternitz 1972b, 606)

Winternitz exhibits a palpable ambivalence; his elitist sensibilities prevent him from embracing the Purāṇas as respectable literature and yet his scholarly sensibilities prevent him from dismissing them as impertinent. Even in the face of prejudice whereby they are deemed barbarous, the Purāṇas nonetheless succeed in conveying their vitality and influence in the religious lives of countless millions. Let us note that Winternitz regards them as unenjoyable *because* he considers them inferior in style. Yet, it becomes clear from subsequent comments that he certainly is not unmoved by their content. He remarks, for example, of the MkP that it is one of the most important and most interesting, "probably one of the oldest works of the whole Purāṇa literature," but proceeds to qualify this with, "yet even this Purāṇa is no unified work, but consists of parts which vary in value and probably belong to different periods" (Winternitz 1972a, 559). Value, for Winternitz, was squarely a function of antiquity, a notion propelled by the perception that absence of unification within the work was to be attributed to corruption of the work by means of interpolation. This attitude has been largely implicated in the scholarly trend to identify and emphasize various chronological strata within the MkP.

In spite of his bent towards denigrating Purāṇa, Winternitz was nevertheless quite taken with the story of Vipaścit, despite its relative youth compared to the most ancient and therefore, in his view, most valuable strata of the MkP. The touching episode details Vipaścit's devotion and self-sacrifice through which the inhabitants of hell were released and sent to heaven. While Winternitz justifies his affection for the episode on the basis of its literary style in addition to its content, one might speculate that the redemptive elements of this episode would certainly not be lost on a Christian audience. He, therefore, refers to this episode as "one of the gems of Indian legend poetry" (Winternitz 1972a, 562) and goes so far as to reproduce an English synopsis of the tale so as to share it with his readers (Winternitz 1972a, 562–4).

Upon conclusion of his rendition of the Vipaścit episode, he comments that "in language and style this splendid dialogue reminds one very much of the Sāvitrī poem of the *Mahābhārata*" (Winternitz 1972a, 564). While Winternitz separately notes that it is Mārkaṇḍeya who comforts Yudhiṣṭhira in the MBh, with regard to Draupadi's fate, by telling him the story of Sāvitrī or Pativratāmāhātmya "the song in praise of the faithful wife" (Winternitz 1972a, 397, n. 4), he is unable to make the connection between the story of Sāvitrī and the story of Vipaścit, both being placed in the mouth of Mārkaṇḍeya, for such a connection would necessarily be coincidental, void of intentionality. It appears beyond the intellectual vista of early scholars such as Winternitz that the mechanics of "interpolations" could be anything but haphazard in nature or else he would surely have been able to perceive that, given the affinity between the story of Sāvitrī and the story of Vipaścit, the assemblers of the latter would have intentionally accorded it to the expositor of the former. Despite his esteem for the Vipaścit episode, he quickly adds that "but just as in the great epic the most absurd productions of the priestly literature stand by the side of the most beautiful poems, as also in our Purāṇa" (Winternitz 1972a, 564). One gets the sense that for Winternitz, imbibing from the wellspring of Purāṇic lore simultaneously posed both as an enjoyable indulgence and a hazardous habit direly in need of remedy. There is a pronounced ambivalence at play during the first century of Western Purāṇic scholarship as expressed by the sentiments of Winternitz, inherited by Pargiter, and inherited by Wilson before him. The stringency of this ambivalence, commingling both reverence and distaste for Purāṇic literature, commands great intrigue: it suggests that the battles and bents of men such as these cannot but comprise a Purāṇa of its own, replete with triumphs and failings, and demons in need of annihilation.[1]

Eden Pargiter takes his cue from Wilson regarding the general character of the MkP. He, therefore, quotes Wilson's words in the introduction to his translation of the MkP as follows:

> This Purāṇa has a character different from that of all the others. It has nothing of a sectarial spirit, little of a religious tone; rarely inserting prayers and invocations to any deity; and such as are inserted are brief and moderate. It deals little in precepts, ceremonial or moral. Its leading feature is narrative; and it presents an uninterrupted succession of legends, most of which when ancient are embellished with new circumstances, and when new partake so far of the spirit of the old, that they are disinterested creations of

> the imagination, having no particular motive, being designed to recommend no special doctrine or observance. Whether they are derived from any other source, or whether they are original inventions, it is not possible to ascertain. They are most probably, for the greater part at least, original; and the whole has been narrated in the compiler's own manner; a manner superior to that of the Purāṇa in general, with exception of the *Bhāgavata*.
>
> (Pargiter 1904, iii)

Pargiter and Wilson privilege the MkP not only because of the calibre of its narration (which in their view is second only to the *Bhāgavata Purāṇa*), but on the basis of its scant "insertion" of prayers and invocations to specific deities. It is most peculiar that they perceive a distinction between these "religious" creations and the "leading feature" of the Purāṇa: narrative. First, one wonders how these scholars dissect the sectarian sections (presumably those lauding the Sun and the Devī) from the narrative of the MkP when these sections themselves exist in the form of narrative; they are not comprising merely hymns or incantations but rather, they narrate entire episodes. Second, one wonders how "disinterested" the non-sectarian "creations of the imagination" in the MkP really are. As Hazra summarizes, although the MkP

> is generally true to the old definition of the Purāṇa of five characteristics, it contains a few chapters on topics dealing with hells (*Naraka*), chap. 15 with the results of actions done (*Karma-vipāka*), chaps. 28–29 with the duties of the castes and Āśramas, chaps. 30–33 with funeral sacrifices, chap. 34 with customs in general (*Ācāra*), and chap. 35 with eatables and non-eatables.
>
> (Hazra 1975, 8–9)

Hence, the MkP is "one of the oldest and most important of the extant Purāṇas" (Hazra 1975, 8), not because of the absence of religious ideologies, but because, in part, of its vibrant encapsulation thereof (Desai 1968). Given the primacy of narrative in the encapsulation and dissemination of religious ideologies, one is hard pressed to maintain the position that the "non-sectarian" fabric of the Purāṇa "deals little in precepts, ceremonial or moral" (Pargiter 1904, iii), for even when the ideologies do not take centre stage as with the sections Hazra points out to us, they are assumed to be within the world of the text and those assumptions are inevitably transmitted to its hearers.

While Pargiter endorses Wilson's summation of the overall quality of the MkP in writing that "the general character of this Purāṇa has been well summed up by Prof. Wilson in his preface to his Translation of the *Viṣṇu Purāṇa*" (Pargiter 1904, iii), he is sure to clarify that Wilson's description "hardly applies to the *Devī-māhātmya*" (Pargiter 1904, iii). Pargiter is referring to the overall absence of sectarian spirit for which Wilson lauds the work. Despite the fact that the DM is by far the most popular and most practised (ritually and devotionally) tributary of the MkP, it is viewed as the assemblage's most sectarian and most recent appendage, both attributes which oppose the grain of Wilson's pronouncement on the MkP as "one of the oldest and most important of the extant Purāṇas" (Hazra 1975, 8). Pargiter writes:

> The Devī-māhātmya stands entirely by itself as a later interpolation. It is a poem complete in itself. Its subject and the character attributed to the goddess show that it is the product of a later age which developed and took pleasure in the sanguinary features of popular religion. The praise of the goddess Mahā-māyā in Canto 81 is in the ordinary style. Her special glorification begins in Canto 82, and is elaborated with the most extravagant laudation and the most miraculous imagination. Some of the hymns breathe deep religious feeling, express enthusiastic adoration, and evince fervent spiritual meditation. On the other hand, the descriptions of the battles abound with wild and repulsive incidents, and revel in gross and amazing fancies. The Devī-māhātmya is a compound of the most opposite characters. The religious out-pourings are at times pure and elevated: the material descriptions are absurd and debased.
>
> (Pargiter 1904, vi–vii)

We perceive in Pargiter the very same stark ambivalence inherited by Winternitz, as detailed above. The DM's "interruption" of the MkP continues to vex and perplex scholars even in our present age of study. It is so trenchant a legacy that Ludo Rocher mentions it in his very first line introducing his discussion of the MkP: "the Mārkaṇḍeya [Purāṇa] consists of 137 adhyayas; the purana proper is interrupted by the thirteen chapters (81–93) of the Devīmāhātmya" (Rocher 1986, 191). He again reiterates its status as an "interruption", writing a bit later in his discussion that the MkP "proper is interrupted by thirteen chapters (81–93) which form the Devīmāhātmya" (Rocher 1986, 193). He later more fully unpacks the DM's mismatched status as follows:

> Even though the *Devīmāhātmya* has, more often than not, been recognized as an originally independent composition, its date and the date of the Mārkaṇḍeya [Purāṇa] have, in most cases, been examined simultaneously. The general idea is that the māhātmya is a later work which, at a certain moment, has been inserted into the already existing purāṇa. As indicated earlier, the description of the consecutive Manus is interrupted after chapter eighty, and resumes in chapter ninety-four with the same interlocutors, Mārkaṇḍeya and Krauṣṭuki; the interruption occurs on account of the eighth Manu, Sāvarṇi, an incarnation of king Suratha who, after hearing the exploits of the Devī becomes a worshiper of the goddess. This "obviously very flimsy" connection implies, then, that the purāṇa is older than the māhātmya.
>
> (Rocher 1986, 195)

Let us keep in mind that the assemblers weaving the narrative of the DM into that of the MkP (along with those responsible for transmitting these works) would surely be equally (if not more acutely) aware of the texture of the work and would have registered the distribution of its material; yet, to my knowledge, it is only we scholars at the Western academy who seem to take issue with the DM's status as proper to the MkP. The distinction of a "sectarian" versus "non-sectarian" spirit as advanced by Wilson and Pargiter above is not one that the assemblage itself supports, much less takes issue with. The Purāṇa appears oblivious that the presence of the DM might be an interruption to the section of the MkP where it is found. Nor are we in possession of traditional commentators who experience any angst that the contours of the Goddess should peek out from the fabric of the text. If there is a "spirit" at play, which has guided the hearts and hands of the assemblers of the MkP including the DM, it is of an artistic, rather than sectarian, variety. It manifests in thematic motifs residing within the mansion of the MkP, to which ample attention was paid by these assemblers, in an effort to accordingly adorn and furnish their architectural expansions of this abode. Now that we are familiar with the manner in which the MkP has been traditionally dissected into five constituent historical creations, let us trace the themes which cut across these strata, humouring the hermeneutics of framing argued in this study. What might we find when looking at the manner in which the work as a whole is framed? This very theme is pursued in Chapter 4, "Mapping Mārkaṇḍeya".

## 1.2 Solar sources

Veneration of the Sun, in one form or another, has played an integral role at every historical juncture of Indian religion, to which the textual records attest. That this was the case from Vedic is amply evidenced by the many Vedic hymns to Sūrya, the divinity ascribed to the solar orb itself. In the words of Farquhar, prominence of Sūrya worship "may be partially gauged by the supremacy of the Gāyatrī among Vedic prayers" … prescribed as evening and morning prayer for all twice-born men to this day (Farquhar 1920, 151). Yet, we only see for the first time in the MBh a full-fledged Saura cult. For example, Yudhiṣṭhira is met with 1,000 Sun-worshippers upon leaving his chamber in the morning (MBh VII.82.14–16). Yet, what we see in the Saura myths of the *Mārkaṇḍeya Purāṇa* is most remarkable, even comparison to the considerable solar laudation we find in the great epic. Mārkaṇḍeya eulogizes Sūrya as the eternal, supreme spirit pervading all things (brahman), indeed the self-existent source of all, on whom the ascetics desirous of emancipation meditate. Let us examine the existent to which we see glimpses of this solar vision in other Sanskrit texts.

### *1.2.1 The Sun in Vedic sources*

As evidenced through millennia of Sanskrit religious literature, each epoch of Indian religion is marked by some sort of solar veneration.[2] That the Sun is an important deity to Vedic religion[3] cannot be overstated. This is perhaps unsurprising for a nomadic culture heavily dependent upon the forces of nature – and ultimately the Sun – for survival. Moreover, that the daily rising and falling of this celestial orb would capture the religious imagination of any culture hardly needs justification, particularly as a heavenly counterpart to the sacrificial fire so crucial to Vedic religion. The following hymn from the *Atharva Veda* in fact explicitly equated the Sun with the sacred fire:

> A Golden Eagle thou hast soared with light to heaven.
> Those who would harm thee as thou fliest skyward.
> Beat down, O Jātavedas, with thy fury. The strong hath feared:
> to heaven mount up with light, O Sūrya (Atharva Veda 19.65).
>
> (Griffith 1895)

In the Vedic literature alone, we see a preponderance of solar deities, variously grouped over time, undoubtedly the result of some silent syncretism between Aryan and non-Aryan solar veneration. Take, for example, the Ādityas (Srivastava 1972, 116–22), an uncertain grouping of solar deities, first including Mitra, Aryamān, Bhaga, Varuṇa, Dakṣa ans Aṃśa, eventually folding in Sūrya and Mārtaṇḍa, growing up to twelve in number over time. There is, moreover, a common grouping of solar deities in the Vedic literature consisting of Sūrya, Savitri, Mitra, Viṣṇu, Pūṣan and Bhaga, often also including the Aśvins, Ādityas and Vivasvat (Srivastava 1972, 47).

We see a correspondence between these solar deities and different aspects of the Sun: Savitri, for example, represents the simulative aspect, or spiritual power of the Sun (Srivastava 1972, 66–80), most famously represented in the Gāyatrī hymn advancing "the belief that solar light is the symbol of ultimate knowledge and reality" (Srivastava 1972, 76); Mitra (meaning 'friend'), as the name suggests, represents the Sun's benevolent, supportive aspect (Srivastava 1972, 80–6); Pūṣan his propensity to grant prosperity (Srivastava 1972, 98–113). Vivasvat, is connected to fire sacrifice (Srivastava 1972, 113–16); and Viṣṇu, is variously associated with the swift motion and generative power of the Sun (Srivastava 1972, 86–98). The Aśvin twins tend to correspond to the healing power of the Sun, though they are also fairly obscure, their duality perhaps representing dark and light, or the twilight (Srivastava 1972, 122–40). The horse (*aśva*) is one of the prime symbols of the Sun well beyond the association with the Aśvins. The second very prominent symbol of the Sun would be as a bird.

The most common epithet of the Sun in the Vedic hymns is Sūrya (Srivastava 1972, 48–66). Sūrya is explicitly invoked as the great giver of light, dispeller of darkness bar none (Srivastava 1972, 52–3). It naturally follows that he is associated with sight, and witnessing:

> 1 MAY Sūrya guard us out of heaven, and Vāta from the firmament,
> And Agni from terrestrial spots.
> 2 Thou Savitar whose flame deserves one hundred libations, be thou pleased:
> From failing lightning keep us safe.

3 May Savitar the God, and may Parvata also give us sight;
May the Creator give us sight.
4 Give sight unto our eye, give thou our bodies sight that they may see:
May we survey, discern this world.
5 Thus, Sūrya, may we look on thee, on thee most lovely to behold,
See clearly with the eyes of men (Ṛg Veda X.158).

(Griffith 1896b)

Sūrya is also explicitly connected with healing. He is also not only related to Time as its instrument, being the maker of day and arbiter of hours, he is also equated with Time itself (Srivastava 1972, 65). Beyond his role as representing abstractions such as 'time' and 'healing', the Vedic literature anthropomorphizes Sūrya, he whose rays serve as his hands or as seven horses of his chariot drawn across the firmament. Sūrya is the son of Aditi, lover of Dawn, husband of Saraṇyū, father of Yama, and is even described as the priest of the gods (Srivastava 1972, 50–1).

In addition to the mythologization of the Sun, there are a number of references in the Vedic literature pertaining to worship of the Sun. For example, the Sun was worshipped at four junctures – sunrise, zenith, sunset and midnight – with Sūrya being explicitly connected to the rising Sun. While there are isolated associations of different deities corresponding to each juncture – for example, Vivasvat relating to the rising Sun, Sāvitṛ relating to the setting Sun – there is no ultimate distinction to be drawn. There is also reference in the Vedic literature to ritual aspects of Sun worship pertaining to marriage, initiation and ceremonies, (Srivastava 1972, 160–70).

Sūrya is construed as a spiritual force in the Vedic literature, described as the soul of all that moves and does not move (*sūrya ātmā jagatastasthusaśca*, RVI.115.I). This, of course, may well be a later development as it hints at the upaniṣadic world-view (Srivastava 1972, 58–64). Yet, to my mind, the hymn decidedly represents the ethos of Vedic religion:

1 THE brilliant presence of the Gods hath risen, the eye of Mitra, Varuṇa and Agni.
The soul of all that moveth not or moveth, the Sun hath filled the air and earth and heaven.
2 Like as a young man followeth a maiden, so doth the Sun the Dawn, refulgent Goddess:
Where pious men extend their generations, before the Auspicious One for happy fortune.
3 Auspicious are the Sun's Bay-coloured Horses, bright, changing hues, meet for our shouts of triumph.
Bearing our prayers, the sky's ridge have they mounted, and in a moment speed round earth and heaven.
4 This is the Godhead, this might of Sūrya: he hath withdrawn what spread o'er work unfinished.

When he hath loosed his Horses from their station, straight over all Night spreadeth out her garment.

5 In the sky's lap the Sun this form assumeth that Varuṇa and Mitra may behold it.
His Bay Steeds well maintain his power eternal, at one time bright and darksome at another.

6 This day, O Gods, while Sūrya is ascending, deliver us from trouble and dishonour.
This prayer of ours may Varuṇa grant, and Mitra, and Aditi and Sindhu, Earth and Heaven

(Ṛg Veda I.115) (Griffith 1896a)

In the Upaniṣadic literature, the Sun is explicitly construed as spiritual symbol of the self:

> Let a man meditate on the udgītha (Om) as he who sends warmth (the sun in the sky). When the sun rises it sings as Udgātri for the sake of all creatures. When it rises it destroys the fear of darkness. He who knows this, is able to destroy the fear of darkness (ignorance).
>
> (Chāndogya Upaniṣad 1.3) (Muller 1879b, 7)

The Sun is also worshipped as an instrument of spiritual purification:

> The all-conquering Kaushītaki adores the sun when rising … saying: "Thou art the deliverer, deliver me from sin." In the same manner he adores the sun when in the zenith, saying: "Thou art the highest deliverer, deliver me highly from sin." In the same manner he adores the sun when setting, saying: "Thou art the full deliverer, deliver me fully from sin." Thus he fully removes whatever sin he committed by day and by night. And in the same manner he who knows this, likewise adores the sun, and fully removes whatever sin he committed by day and by night.
>
> (Kauśītakī Upaniṣad 2.7) (Muller 1879a, 285)

### *1.2.2 The Sun in epic sources*

#### *1.2.2.1 The Mahābhārata*

While one may regard The *Mahābhārata* as a whole as an allegorical battle of dark and light as waged between the forces of (solar) Viṣṇu's avatāra, Kṛṣṇa, and their devious opponents, the marks of solar veneration in India's great epic – and the epic period more broadly[4] – are much more glaring than this. This is the first place we see mention of an explicit Saura sect. It is in fact one of the five most prominent sects within India's great epic, including which are Gaṇeśas, Śāktas, Śaivas, Vaiṣṇavas and Sauras. For example, we are told that there are 1,008 Sauras, steeped in Vedic learning, in attendance at the Pāṇḍava camp. The presence of a solar sectarian following may be further inferred from some of the proper names in the *Mahābhārata* such as Sūryadhvaja, Sūryadatta (Srivastava 1972, 181). Epic expressions of solar veneration are marked by the idiom of devotionalism and full-fledged anthropomorphism of the Sun, for example, Sūrya appearing in human form to conceive Karṇa with Kuntī.

Aside from – and perhaps because of – the Sun being his unwitting father, the Sun was an object of great devotion and veneration for Karṇa. We are told that he "worshipped the sun until his back was burned [during which time the steadfast Karṇa] sat muttering prayers" (MBh I.104.15) (van Buitenen 1973, I: 241). In an exchange between father and son where the Sun attempts to warn Karṇa of Indra's plot to deprive him of his protective armour, the Sun states:

> you are my devotee and I have to protect my devotees. And I know that this man here is devoted to me with the strongest devotion, strong-armed Karṇa. If devotion to me has arisen in you, then do as I say …
>
> (MBh III.285.6–7) (van Buitenen 1975, II: 782)

Likewise, Karṇa responds with: "thou knowest that to no other God am I as strongly devoted as to thee. Neither my wife, nor my sons, nor my own self, nor my friends are as close to my devotion as thou art" (MBh III.286.1–3) (van Buitenen 1975, II: 783). The story of Karṇa, along with the relationships between this solar thread and Mārkaṇḍeya, shall be discussed in Chapter 4 "Mapping Mārkaṇḍeya".

Yudhiṣṭhira himself worships the Sun at the outset of Book III, "The Book of The Forest" (MBh III.3), by reciting his 108 names. He does so to seek the Sun's blessing in feeding his entourage whole in exile. This exchange showcases not only the devotional idiom to seek a deity's blessing through ritualized laudation, it also showcases the beneficial aspect of the Sun, invoked to sustain the Pāṇḍava camp for thirteen years in forest exile.

Even King Saṃvarṇa, the ancestral patriarch of the Kuru dynasty, father of Kuru, worships the Sun:

> King Saṃvaraṇa, was wont to worship the Sun with offerings of guest gifts and garlands, with fasts and observances, and with manifold mortifications. Obediently and unselfishly and purely, the scion of the Pauravas worshiped the splendiferous Sun with great devotion as He rose.
>
> (MBh I.11.12–14)

It is in fact because of this devotions that he is given the Sun's daughter, Tapatī, in marriage.

> So, it came about that the Sun judged the grateful and law-minded Saṃvaraṇa on earth to be Tapatī equal in beauty. He then desired to give the maiden in marriage to that sublime King Saṃvaraṇa, O Kaurava, whose descent was glorious.
>
> (MBh I.11.12–15)

Beyond evidencing a full-fledged Saura cult, India's great epic riff on Karṇa's solar symbolism throughout, which, in the words of Adam Bowles, "provides a mythic underpinning to his rivalry with Arjuna, the son of the storm-god Indra, who is a rival to Sūrya in the earlier Vedic period of Indian mythology" (MBh VIII – Bowles Translation; 2006–2008, 45 n. 13). Indeed, Arjuna "had been created by the mighty Indra for power's sake, so that he might destroy the mighty Karṇa" (I.143.38; Bowles Translation; 2006–2008, 301). The MBh is also cognisant of the the relationship between Yama and the Sun we see in Vedic myth; Yama tells Arjuna: "Karṇa, who is a particle of my father, the God who sends heat to all the worlds, the might Karṇa, will be slain by you" (MBh III.42.20; Bowles Translation; 2006–2008, 304).

#### *1.2.2.2 The Rāmāyaṇa*

The Sun is the progenitor of the solar line of epic kings, and this is the illustrious ancestor of Rāma himself. Beyond this, there is a crucial point in the plot of the *Rāmāyaṇa* at which the Sun is worshipped. While absent from the Critical Edition, several manuscripts (particularly of the southern recension of the work) include a very popular sixty-four-verse Hindu hymn to the Sun, the Ādityahṛdaya, in Book VI of the *Vālmīki Rāmāyaṇa* (1–64). The Ādityahṛdaya enjoys a vibrant ritual life, intoned by Hindus to invoke the Sun. Sage Agastya teaches the hymn to Rāma on the battlefield during his engagement with Rāvaṇa so that Rāma – by propitiating the Sun – may gain the requisite power to defeat his foe once and for all, which he does upon learning the hymn. It should also be noted that the Sun is the mythological father of the vānara Sugrīva, whom Rāma helps install as the king of the monkey folk (by slaying Sugrīva's brother and rival Vālin), in exchange for Sugrīva's allegiance and aid in recovering Sītā.

### *1.2.3 The Sun in Purāṇic sources*

#### *1.2.3.1 The Mahā-Purāṇas*

Generally speaking, while the early Purāṇas continue in much the same vein as Vedic religiosity, the more popular name for the Sun is known as Āditya over Sūrya. In the myths of the *Mārkaṇḍeya Purāṇa* (102.14), we are told he is named Āditya not because he is the son of Aditi, but because he is born first in the universe. The Purāṇas give elaborate descriptions of the iconography and chariot of the Sun, along with Saura vratas and rites. Solar veneration takes on full-fledged devotional (*pūjā*) to Solar icons (*mūrtīs*) in the Purāṇas. There are a handful of moments where Purāṇic characters explicitly worship the Sun for their purposes: Yajñavalkya worships the Sun to get the text of the Yajus (236); Satrājuta worships the Sun to earn a special gem (237). The only other place the Sun is worshipped in the Mahāpurāṇas is by Brahmā, Aditi and Rājyavardhana in the MkP (discussed at length in Chapter 2). The benevolent function of the Sun proper to Vedic literature is retained in the Purāṇas. Yet, in the MkP, we see a destructive aspect of the Sun (mirroring the destructive aspect of the Goddess), which, to my knowledge, is absent elsewhere in the Purāṇas.

Srivastava notes that Sun worship on the ground of Indian soil from about third to twelfth century CE. Sun worship in some form or other is mentioned in Vāyu, Viṣṇu, Brāhmaṇḍa, Matsya, Mārkaṇḍeya, Bhaviṣya, Brahmā, Skanda, Varāha, Agni, Garuḍa, Viṣṇudharmottara, Bhaviṣyottara, Kālikā and Sāmba Purāṇas (Srivastava 1969, 230). The *Agni Purāṇa* (Chapters 51; 73; 99) and *Garuḍa Purāṇa* (Chapters 7, 16, 17, 39) deal with proper iconography and ritual worship of the Sun. Interestingly, Chapter 50 of the *Agni Purāṇa* describes the proper characteristics of Caṇḍī iconography. The *Matsya Purāṇa* also gives detailed instructions regarding construction of images, iconography of the nine planets and on vows (*vratas*) for the Sun (CCLXI.1–7; XCIV.1) (Srivastava 1969, 241). The *Vāyu Purāṇa* (CVIII.36) "states that in the Gayātīrtha there are installed four images of Sūrya which are expressions of the four different yugas and if they are seen, touched, and worshipped liberation of ancestors is guaranteed" (Srivastava 1969, 240). The *Viṣṇu Purāṇa* (2.8–10) offers descriptions of the Sun, his chariot, his horses and his nature, along with information pertaining to his path across the sky.

The only places where we see substantial discourse on Saura practices are in the *Sāmba Purāṇa*, and the *Bhaviṣya Purāṇa* which borrows therefrom. The *Bhaviṣya Purāṇa* (Chapters 47–215) functions as a compendium of Saura material, with extensive passages borrowed from the *Sāmba Purāṇa* (Rocher 1986, 152). In the words of Rocher:

> Although there are references to an Aditya° and a Surya° – the Saura° is decidedly Śaiva –, the two most important puranic texts connected with Surya and sun worship are the Sāmba and the Brāhmaparvan of the Bhaviṣya. References in these texts to Magas, sun worshiping brahmans of Śākadvīpa and to Sāmba bringing them from there to India, attracted the attention of scholars from an early date onward.
>
> (Rocher 1986, 115)

This is discussed in the following section.

### *1.2.3.2 Minor Saura texts*

There are relatively few surviving explicitly Saura Sanskrit texts. With respect to works which praise the Sun, Gonda makes mention in his Sanskrit Medieval Literature section of his edited series *A History of Indian Literature* only of Mayūra's early seventh-century *Sūrya-Śataka* (Gonda 1977, 251) and to a *Sūrya Gītā* in one lone sentence as follows: "The Surya-Gita must belong to the comparatively late works of this genre because it has undergone the influence of Rāmānuja's Viśiṣṭādvaita philosophy" (Gonda 1977, 276). The obscure *Sūrya Gītā* expounds Viśiṣṭādvaita philoosphy. There exists a *Saurasamhitā* among the six saṃhitās of the *Skanda Purāṇa*: Sanatkumāra, Sūta, Śaṅkarī or

Agastya, Vaiṣṇavī, Brāhmī, and Saura or Saurī (Rocher 1986, 234). While it is Śiva who is supreme in this work, the Saurasaṃhitā is not without adoration to Sūrya (Rocher 1986, 237). There also exists, among the thrity-one minor Upanishads associated with the Atharva Veda, a certain *Sūrya Upaniṣad* wherein Atharvangiras extols the virtues of the Sun. It identifies the ātman with Sūrya, the prime cause of the phenomenal world, the essence of Brahmin, at one with the gods of heaven. It also prescribes ritual utterance of mantric formula in honour of Sūrya, and lists the benefits of proposed recitation.

The *Sūrya Śaṭaka* was composed by Mayūra, a seventh-century Sanskrit poet who was allegedly the rival of the poet Baṇa (author of the Caṇḍī-Śataka). The work consists of 101 stanzas each "invoking the aid, protection or blessing of Sūrya, or of his rays, his horses, his chariot, his charioteer, or his disk" (83–4). Quackenbos notes that he is petitioned explicitly for protection in thirty stanzas, prosperity in fifteen stanzas, removal from misfortune in eleven, happiness in seven and the bestowal of welfare and satisfaction of requests in eleven stanzas; compare this to cessation of rebirth in only two stanzas (Quackenbos 1917, 84). Sūrya's rays (1–43), his horses (44–9), his charioteer, Aruṇa (50–61), his chariot (62–72), then the solar disk itself (73–80). The remainder of the poem touches on several themes, including comparison to Brahmā, Viṣṇu, Śiva (91–3), Sūrya's supremacy (94), and various mythological allusions (e.g. to the churning of the ocean myth). The Caṇḍī-Śataka and Sūrya-Śataka are fairly close in length (the Caṇḍī-Śataka being 102 verses whereas the Sūrya-Śataka is 101), both in the sragdharā meter (aside from the six śārdūlavikrīḍita verses of the Caṇḍī-Śataka), and share a similar poetic style, and common verbal forms. In his comparison between the two, Quackenbos notes that:

> as regards subject-matter, both poems deal with well-worn themes – the praise of deities Sūrya and Caṇḍī respectively – as both authors, Mayūra and Bāṇa, have embellished their productions with numerous allusions drawn from the vast and seemingly inexhaustible storehouse of Vedic, Epic and Puranic mythology.
>
> (Quackenbos 1917, 264)

Important for our purposes is that the poem betrays familiarity between hymns to Sūrya at MBh III.3.15–79; MkP 107–110; VP 2.8–10.

#### *1.2.3.3 Saura upa-Purāṇas*

There are four lost Saura upa-Purāṇas that we know of: 1) the *Sauradharma upa-Purāṇa* is a lost Saura text mentioned in the *Bhaviṣya Purāṇa*, dated around 800 CE, dealing with the prescribed duties of the Sauras (Hazra 1958, 347–9); 2) the *Sauradharmottara upa-Purāṇa* is yet another lost *Saura upa-Purāṇa* dealing with the Saura duties, which Hazra dates around 900 CE (Hazra 1958, 349); 3) the *Sūrya Purāṇa*, now lost, is probably an early work (Hazra 1958, 349), which, as Rocher states: "There are several indications to suggest the existence, at one time, of a *Sūrya Purāṇa*, a Saura upapurana different from the *Samba* and the *Saura* [Purāṇas]" (Rocher 1986, 238); and 4) the lost *Saura Purāṇa* is not to be confused with the *Āditya Purāṇa* as often is the case. While its narrator is Sūrya, it is a decidedly Śaiva work: it is Śiva's supremacy which is extolled therein, though the work at times associates Śiva with the Sun.

The *Āditya Purāṇa* is one of the earliest, most popular upa-Purāṇas, cited by Alberūnī as one of the Purāṇas he had come across. As Rocher mentions:

> The Aditya Purāṇa figures in al-Bīrūnī's list of eighteen puranas; it is one of the three puranas which he has actually seen, and he quotes a few verses from it in translation. The *Aditya Purāṇa* is also frequently quoted by the *nibandhakāras*, on a large variety of topics: death and ritual for the dead, impurity, marriage and duties of married life, donations, *vratas*, and festivals.
>
> (Rocher 1986, 134)

Hazra dates it at fifth century CE and places it most probably in North India (Hazra 1963, 492). It is distinct from the lost *Saura Purāṇa*. Despite its name, the *Āditya Purāṇa* is not a Saura Purāṇa per se: "it was a non-sectarian work dealing with the praise and worship of Sūrya, Viṣṇu, Śiva, Durgā and other deities" (Hazra 1963, 495) (for a detailed examination of the various themes pervading the purāṇa, see Hazra 1963, 495–501).

#### *1.2.3.4 The Sāmba Purāṇa*

The *Sāmba Purāṇa* is a work of eighty-four chapters, which tells the story of Kṛṣṇa's beautiful son, Sāmba, and his building of a Sun temple, at which he installs Magian priests to officiate. Sāmba is cursed with leprosy because of his dalliances with his father's wives, and so Nārada advises Sāmba to worship Sūrya for healing, which he does. Sūrya is pleased by Sāmba's worship and requests that Sāmba erect an image of him on the banks of the Candrabhāgā river. While bathing, Sāmba finds an image and establishes it in Mitravana, where he builds a temple to house it. In searching for priests for the temple, he again seeks the counsel of Nārada who sends him again to see the Sun. Sūrya counsels him to bring the Maga priests (brahmins from Śākadvīpa, which is perhaps Scythia) to serve as temple priests. Sāmba flies to Śākadvīpa on Garuḍa (whom he asks Vāsudeva's permission to borrow) and returns with eighteen Maga families

As mythologized in the *Sāmba Purāṇa*, the arrival of Magi Sun-priests into India is indisputable given the preponderance of evidence from a number of sources – epigraphy, foreign notices, Ptolemy (second century CE), Varāhamihira (sixth century CE) (Srivastava 1988, 144). The *Viṣṇu Purāṇa*, too, mentions Magas as brāhmaṇas of Śākadvīpa, that is, the magi of Persia (2.4.69–70). There is archaeological evidence that "the Magas entered into India for the first time in wake of the Achaemenian invasion of the 6th–5th century B.C" (Srivastava 1989, 151).

Srivastava innovatively argues that they arrived in three waves: the Achaemenid invasion (fifth–fourth century BCE); the Śaka-Kuṣāna period (first–second century CE); and finally as part of the reaction to the Islamic invasion of Afghanistan in fifth–sixth century CE, by which time they were folded into Indian society as brahmins proper (Srivastava 1989, 158). Varāha Mihira, the sixth-century author of the astronomical-astrological work *Bṛhad Saṃhitā*:

> makes it plain that in his day Sūrya was represented in his images in Persian fashion, and he lays down the rule for the installation and consecration of these images and their temples by Magians, using the very sloka which occurs in the [Bhaviṣya] Purana.
>
> (Farquhar 1920, 153)

Solar iconography from the Kushana to post-Gupta attests to a foreign influence (Pandey 1984, 204). However, while Pandey takes it as evidence that "an inscription at Govindpur in Gaya District dated the Śaka year 1059 (1137–38 A.D.) also supports the view that Magas were brought into the country by Samba" (Pandey 1984, 204), this evidences only that the *Sāmba Purāṇa* was a well-established text in that region at that time.

It is evident that this group of Sun-priests, and their practices enrich existing Indian Sun worship, evolutes of Vedic and Epic religiosity. Srivastava notes that the Sun cult is unique among religious systems in India insofar as it "came to be indistinguishably associated with a foreign priesthood" (Srivastava 1988, 109), namely, that of the Magian priests of Iran variously referred to as Maga, Bhojaka, Vācaka, Pūjaka, Sevaka, Śākadvīpīya Brāhmaṇa and Sūryadvija. There are several textual references of the arrival of Maga priests from the land of Śākadvīpa. Both the *Mahābhārata* and *Viṣṇu Purāṇa* consider Magas as one among the four castes of Śākadvīpa (Pandey 1984, 203). The Magian priesthood's most marked impact on Saura practice was on the introduction of solar iconography whereas the Sun was previously invoked in disk form (Srivastava 1989, 154). This strand of Sun worship was ultimately woven into the tapestry of orthodox Indian religion to the point of appearing in Sanskrit literature.

Among all Purāṇic works, it is only the *Sāmba Purāṇa* which deals principally with the Indian Saura cult we see first mentioned in the *Mahābhārata* (with Magian influence in addition). Hazra proposes it was composed some time between 500–800 CE, and Srivastava argues that it was composed in primarily two geographical locations: the Punjab and Orissa (Srivastava 2013, xii). It contains various Saura stories, ritual prescriptions and even fleshes out a description of Sūrya loka. In the words of Rocher: "This story of the origin of sun worship in Jambudvīpa is the principal theme of the purana; it is, of course, interrupted and followed by various stories, many of which are meant further to glorify Sūrya and his worship" (Rocher 1986, 217). Not only is all of the Saura material we see in the *Bhaviṣya Purāṇa* borrowed from the *Sāmba Purāṇa*, the *Skanda, Brahmā, Varāha, Agni* and *Garuḍa Purāṇas* all borrow their material from the *Sāmba Purāṇa* (Srivastava 1969, 246–7).

The *Sāmba Purāṇa* firmly establishes the sectarian supremacy of Sūrya, wherein he is praised as the highest among the gods, indeed the original, primordial source of divine power from whom the universe was manifest at creation, and into whom the universe is dissolved at the time of cosmic dissolution. Therefore, he is worthy of worship and devotion: Sūrya alone is to be worshipped for final release from the bondage of saṃsāra (Hazra 1958). The existence of the *Sāmba Purāṇa* evidences the historical presence of a thriving sectarian movement dedicated to solar veneration, marked by Magian influences, asserting the supremacy of the Sun. Hazra's conjecture about the historical forces behind the production of such a work are reasonable. He surmises that the existing Indian cult needed to legitimize the Magas as full-fledged brahmins to authorize the Magian influences on their solar veneration, probably because these influences had become too popular to be neglected. This is a reasonable accourt for why the DM should inhabit the MkP as well: clearly, fully born Goddess worship did not spring out of nowhere and appear in Brahmanical fold in the mouth of Mārkaṇḍeya. As Hazra concludes: "the Sāmba Purāṇa had to be written and chapters had to be inserted into the Bhaviṣya and other Purāṇic work" (Hazra 1955, 63). Hazra's is the only sustained study of the *Sāmba Purāṇa* (Hazra 1958, 32–108). Srivastava has produced the only critical edition and English translation of the *Sāmba Purāṇa* (Srivastava 2013), following up on the prompting of Hazra from forty years prior (Srivastava 2013, xvii). Hazra provides a detailed summary of the Purāṇa's contents (Hazra 1958, 36–57), as:

> preeminently the work of the Sauras [wherein] the Sun is called the highest deity and the Supreme Brahman. He is both the individual and supreme soul and is both one and many. While residing as kṣetrajña in the material body this Supreme Being, who is both personal and impersonal, remains formless and is not contaminated by actions or influenced by the objects of senses. When transcending the three guṇas he is called Puruṣa. It is he who is worshipped in different forms by gods and by me in the different stages of their life, and who pervades the universe and is its protector and regulator.
>
> (Hazra 1958, 56–7)

One would readily conjecture the SM derives inspiration from the materials in the *Sāmba Purāṇa*, perhaps sculpting that material to conform to the contours of the DM as a successful textual formula for establishing within the folds of Sanskritic Brahmanism a foothold of the burgeoning sectarian cult. Marrying the content (or at least inspiration) of the *Sāmba Purāṇa* and the form of the *Devī Māhātmya*, the ancient Indian Sun worship birth the SM, and in so doing, receives the same sanction from Mārkaṇḍeya as do their Śākta counterparts. Frankly, for all we know, it was the Śākta authors who were inspired by their Saura counterparts. All we can say with certainty is that these texts partake in an important sectarian symbiosis, and moreover – as is argued in this work – that

that symbiosis is part of a larger ideological ecosystem pervading the MkP, defined by the ethos of preservation as articulated in *pravṛtti* religion, celebrated in the work of kings, the Goddess and the Sun.

## 1.3 Synchronic strategy

First, this is a textual project. Rather than examining iconography, inscriptions, ritual practices, temple architecture and historical documents, I adopt as my data Sanskrit texts. Second, I specifically analyse Sanskrit *narrative* texts. Third, as is my prediction, I undertake *synchronic study* of the Sanskrit Saura and Śākta narratives I examine. Studies such as this correct the scholarly impulse to jump to diachronically dissecting Sanskrit narrative texts. Before embarking on an ancient city archaeological dig, should one not register and appreciate the city as it stands? Insofar as this is a synchronic study, I invoke the work of Umberto Eco in understanding the world within the text, a world designed to elicit interpretation (Eco 1994). The major fallacy in the study of Indian myth is that scholars seem to think this literary principle is nullified by multiple authorship over multiple historical junctures. This could not be further from the truth: the principle which Eco so masterfully maps (as the great semiotician and lover of literature that he was), is enriched, not nullified, by the presence of multiple authors as in the Purāṇas because each subsequent author has retained an *attentiveness to the essential themes of the text*. Such 'renovations' are misguidedly taken for 'intrusion'. The final redactions we have of the epics and Purāṇas constitute the most upgraded to the religious software powering Indian religion. And these upgrades were implemented in the face of tremendous thought and attention to the interplay between narrative form and content. The *Mahābhārata*, for example, is one of the most sophisticated, structured pieces of literature on the planet not *despite* the fact that it results from extensive diachronic redaction, but *because* that redaction was done with astute awareness to the world within the text.

Sanskrit narratives adopt a most potent hermeneutic device: narrative frames. Eco certainly has enough to say about interpreting stories, but what about diachronically produced stories within stories? I have some thoughts on the matter. Beyond mere musings, these thoughts make up the methodology I use to grapple with Sanskrit literature. The ensuing apparatus has been derived from extended exposure to Sanskrit narrative texts, with an eye to understanding the ways in which individual episodes relate to one another. It was abundantly clear to me that frame narratives are in no way haphazard. In trying to grapple with such texts temporally, we neglect to first grapple with them thematically. The following theoretical schema on how to read frame narratives was not hatched overnight, rather it arose piecemeal over much time as I floundered to find the means of expressing the specific relational patterns I began to perceive and especially in order to disambiguate the five different entities to which I interchangeably referred to as narrative "frame". This section articulates concepts and practices implicated in the reading of Sanskrit narrative text which I had long since internalized.

### *1.3.1 Framing the framing*

A narrative's (intrinsic) framing consists of what occurs at the very beginning of the episode coupled with what occurs at the very end of the episode, and there is great import to be derived from a narrative's framing (framing import). While the narrative elements which *extrinsically* frame an episode through association (i.e. its preceding and subsequent associates) do not generally work in tandem, the elements comprising its intrinsic framing *always* work in tandem. They comprise the frame proper, as one might frame a portrait. The intrinsic frame – in order to be a "frame" – is necessarily bifurcated into a front-end initial component (referred to herein as the frame's initial frame) and a back-end corollary of that component (referred to herein as the frame's terminal frame). It is the correspondence between the initial and terminal frame, which clasps any narrative tributary to the body of the larger narrative. Framing is not a strict science. While there is certainly an analytic dimension at play, interpreting frames remains an art and ultimately bucks the yolk of strict systemization. But the systematic efforts undergirding the seemingly chaotic surface of Sanskrit narratives certainly comprises a kind of engineering all of its own. It should strike us as meaningful that there are no loose threads regarding frame narratives: when a frame is opened – however briefly, however tangentially, however fancifully – it is *necessarily* closed. And this occurs on all levels of narrative throughout a multidimensional work. A frame is more than the mere edge of a portrait which holds it in place. Just as a physical frame serves to preserve, showcase, highlight and support a portrait, so too does a framing narrative relate to that which it frames. How one prefaces or concludes any given statement will surely impact the reception of that statement. The specific configuration of tales, subtales and narrative frames resulting from the process of assemblage will necessarily influence the manner in which one receives any of those individual tales, subtales or narrative frames independent of that configuration. While it functions in tandem with its terminal teammate, the vast majority of the heavy lifting with respect to thematic import and narrative contextualization is shouldered by the frame's initial element. A narrative entity's expositional import itself is positioned squarely in proximity of its initial framing.

The first type of import, *association import* might be derived from examining the manner in which a narrative element might be extrinsically "framed" by its preceding narrative associate and its subsequent narrative associate. For example, Chapter X of the *Bhagavad-Gītā* (BhG) has for its preceding narrative associate Chapter V, while Chapter Y serves as its subsequent narrative associate. These extrinsic associates are in oblique relationship since they do not extend the same storyline sequence. One might perceive purpose behind why Chapter X comes between these two. The same principle can (more obviously) apply to narrative entities which are sequentially associated. For example, the fact that the Pāṇḍavas engage Citraratha immediately after hearing the birth of Dṛṣyadyumna (its preceding narrative associate) and immediately before Draupadī's *svayamvara* (its subsequent narrative associate) would hold import for interpreting their encounter with the Gandharva king. Association import addresses implicit framing (the whole remaining three address explicit framing), hence it is the weakest of the four types of import, but it is not without utility.

The second type of import, *framing import*, refers to intrinsic framing of the episode as discussed above (to be disambiguated with association import, which draws upon more loose "framing" of extrinsic narrative entities). It takes its cue from the interplay between how a narrative entity commences (its initial frame), and how it concludes (its terminal frame). The next two types of import can be said to be specialized forms of framing import.

*Expositional import* comprises three essential elements, the first two of which are the expositor import (pronounced themes as manifesting the biography and career of the expositor), and the interlocutor import (pronounced themes as manifesting the biography and career of the expositor). Epithet import provides an avenue of further colouring, depending on the specific descriptor ascribed to the expositor or interlocutor. For example, I have drawn on the principle of epithet import to demonstrate the structurally meaningful deployment of the epithet Acyuta in the BhG (Balkaran 2020).

The third element of expositional import (in addition to interlocutor import and expositor import) is *prompting import*, that is, the series of questions, requests, declarations and summations exchanged between interlocutor and expositor in order to cue us as to the contours of the exposition. A narrative entity is often marked by an interlocutor prompting an expositor in its initial frame. This prompt, along with the series of prompts between it and the terminal prompt (the prompt marking the end of the exposition, which will often be the terminal frame of a narrative entity) will be collectively charted in the generation of the Exposition Guide. The expositional import can be quite influential since the expositor's reputation will precede the initial frame of exposition, and will invariably colour the discourse. To invoke, for a moment, a common modern 'purāṇa' (*Lord of the Rings*), an exposition – from its inception – would have a very different colouring if Lady Galadriel were the expositor as opposed to Aragorn. Further, it would matter significantly (with respect to the latter of these expositors) as to whether or not Aragorn had yet become King Aragorn: the general framing (the second import discussed above) will tell us the conditions under which the expositor speaks, and so is not limited to the expositional import. Suffice to say, much can be drawn into the narrative entity by means of its expositional import.

The fourth, final, and most powerful form of framing is *enframement import*. Part of the reason why this type of import is so sophisticated is because it draws from at least two thresholds of exposition (and therefore draws upon two sources of expositional import): an outer exposition pertaining to the narrative order governing the initial framing of the confluence (e.g. in the case of the Gītā, Sañjaya expositing for Dhṛtarāṣṭra), and an inner exposition pertaining to a subsequent narrative order through the installation of a new expositor (Kṛṣṇa, expositing for Arjuna), which, in large part, is the purpose of the interlacement itself. Enframing is a powerful trope because it grants that which is framed access to potentially multiple exposition imports based on the number of narrative orders implicated in the assemblage to that point. In the case of the teaching we find in the Gītā, one might derive expositor import not merely from Kṛṣṇa, but also (indirectly) from his mouthpiece Sañjaya: we might, for example, note that both of these expositors are charioteers. We can even choose to trace the discourse to another level of enframement in acknowledging that Sañjaya, too, has a mouthpiece: his words flow into a higher order of narrative, being relayed by Vaiśampāyana to Janamejaya: in this case, we might note that all the expositors of all three narrative orders enframing the Gītā sally forth in their exposition at the behest of royal interlocutors. Let us, for the sake of this exercise, confine our examination to the two primary thresholds of expiation outlined in the Enframement Guide below.

In addition to the exposition imports to be derived, one can (and should) derive tremendous import specifically from the *impetus* – the bridging narrative between these two expositional thresholds. In a sense, one can perceive the bridge narrative in the foreground of the enframement process, itself enframed by two expositional thresholds. The substance of the bridge, I call the impetus. The bridge narrative is specifically crafted in order to usher the audience across from the first narrative threshold to the second, preparing them to receive the content of the second, both holding *and* shifting their attention. Also, and most crucially, it serves as the impetus for the launching of the second exposition. The impetus manifests as the problem or issue which needs to be addressed, which paves the way for the ensuing narrative order to address that impetus. If the expositor import offers insight into *who* is speaking, and the interlocutor import offers insights into *whom* they address, the impetus (bridge narrative) tells us *why* they are speaking. This why will have multiple dimensions, beyond what is expressed in the prompt of the interlocutor. As will be shown, there will be multiple 'whys', but the impetus defines the ultimate 'why' guiding the exposition. While the prompting will tell us what the interlocutor desires to know, the impetus tells us why that knowledge is important. The prompt will indicate the question the exposition is answering, but the impetus provides us with the problem which needs to be addressed by that exposition, making clear to us what it hopes (and needs) to accomplish at that narrative juncture. The impetus (i.e. the bridge between interlocutor thresholds) will disclose the very purpose for establishing an additional order of exposition and installing within it an additional expositor. The tripartite import to be derived from the outer expositional import, the inner expositional import and the impetus import, is what collectively comprises the enframement import showcased in the Enframement Guide. Given that enframement is an aspect of interlacement (the other half being embedment), one could easily emphasize embedment, and with this draw up an embedment guide.

*Inception import* is the most all-encompassing of the avenues of import. It registers the significance to be derived from the very beginning (the inception) of any of the constituent elements of a narrative entity, in and of itself, without looking to a concluding corollary. One might look to the inception of a segment of speech, especially the first word or verse uttered, for example, Hiltebeitel notes of Kṛṣṇa in the *Mahābhārata* that "his words are authoritative and definitive, and his first word in the epic is '*dharma*'" (Hiltebeitel 2010, 119). One might look to the inception of an event, or action, inspecting the auspices under which it arises. One might also look to the inception of a character, be it their birth, their creation, their arrival or the inception of a relationship between character, for example, how they first meet and bond. To show how this might work: the BhG begins with "dharma-kṣetre kuru kṣetre", arguably, by virtue of what we are calling the "alpha-principle" (import derived from beginnings), it is used purposefully. It "frames" the Gītā insofar as the Gītā occurs along two planes: physically along the plane of Kuru; and metaphysically along the plane of dharma. If we narrow our field of observation, and we focus in on the very first term (within the first verse), again relying upon the alpha principle, we note the very first word is dharma: at its very inauguration, the Gītā tells us that it is firstly about acting along the plane of dharma, and secondly about acting along the plane of Kuru. Only at face value is the Gītā about the activity within the field of Kuru, and, might more aptly be described as activity within the field of dharma. In relying on the alpha principle (rather than the alpha–omega principle), we need not necessarily seek an omega corollary: we look to the first verse, without looking to the last verse; we look to the first term within that verse without looking to the last term within that verse. The omega corollary kicks in when we need to close off (frame) a narrative entity to make way for a new one. So, arguably, what is invoked in this verse can be said to implicitly be "closed off" by virtue of the conclusion of the entity as a whole.

These function as avenues of intelligible import precisely because the compositional mechanics exerted to construct these avenues were done for the sake of hermeneutic influence: acts of non-storyline-sequential assemblage ('unwieldy framing') have been undertaken in order to facilitate interpretation of the entity being assembled. This is not to say that one ought to restrict oneself to walking down the avenues to which these conventions point – one is free to interpret how one will. What I wish to accomplish in this work is to exhibit the extent to which enframement is a highly purposeful enterprise.

### *1.3.2 Two guiding principles*

Prior to commencing our methodological demonstration through analysis of the Gītā proper, I must first remark on what I call "guiding principles". This study notes the prevalence of two compositional principles within the assemblage of Sanskrit narrative entities, and suggests that they have been purposefully implemented for the sake of hermeneutic suggestion. The first of these is the *alpha–omega principle*, which is the inbuilt mutual correspondence between the initial and terminal element of any narrative entity, serving to thematically frame what lies between. The heavy lifting of framing is accomplished largely by the alpha element in the alpha–omega correspondence. The omega mostly serves to hearken to, or invoke, its correspondent alpha counterpart signal the close of one narrative segment, and paving the way for a subsequent alpha element to hold sway. This principle governs all four types of import, save for inception import.

The alpha element is the active ingredient in the framing duo, and therefore we can perceive an *alpha principle* as implicit within the alpha–omega principle described above. However, I will use the term alpha principle (as opposed to alpha–omega principle) to mean where I refer to import derived from a beginning, in the absence of an obvious backend corollary. The alpha–omega principle pertains to the four imports, since they all entail types of framing, where there is a beginning component, and an end component. However, it is the beginning of anything which is truly telling. Indeed, one can never really arrive for good at a terminal point, for it merely paves the way for subsequent beginning. This principle explicitly governs only inception import, though, of course, is implicated in all types of import since the initial aspect of any frame will hold much more sway on the impact of that frame.

My methodology is primarily empowered by these principles which are quite basic in its fundamental operation, and quite far reaching when applied to collected sub-narratives. Given any narrative unit, however large or small (be it a scene, an episode, a sub-narrative, a parvan, a kāṇḍa, an epic, a Purāṇa), thematic threads spun at the beginning of that unit (its alpha juncture), will necessarily be tied into the end of that unit (its correlate omega juncture). Those threads might be tied into the alpha juncture of the subsequent unit, or simply tied off. An alpha juncture may be what precedes an episode, in which case its omega correlate would be what follows that episode. Rather, an alpha juncture might be what occurs at the very beginning of an episode, and its omega correlate would be what concludes the episode. There will by definition exist a direct correlation between the number of alpha junctures and the number of omega junctures – else, we are not dealing with an alpha–omega scenario. However, as shall be made clear, this principle greatly predominates the placement of episodes alongside one another, and especially, the placement of episodes within one another. The very existence of a frame narrative is predicated upon the alpha–omega principle, for segments which constitute the frame serve as the alpha (that which commences) and the omega (that which concludes) whatever it is it is being framed. Given the statistical virtual impossibility that these should have occurred by chance, I must infer that this was one of the guiding principles of our narrative assemblers, as they crafted, revised, collected, and framed various narratives.

One might argue that these two junctures are where one's attention naturally alights. The most impactful and/or memorable junctures when engaging a temporal work of art (as opposed to still-standing works of art), are its beginning and its ending. These two points serve to define it. And, of course, the beginning of any enterprise is crucial. The narrative, event, or prompt which frames a tributary serves as our introduction to that tributary – our first impression if you will. Beginnings are important. We don't want to "get off on the wrong foot" or "wake up on the wrong side of the bed". We put tremendous energy into one's wedding day since it is the opening frame of a marriage. Or, the obvious, we celebrate a birth as the opening frame of a life of possibilities. I have yet in my travels to come across a crevice of South Asia which is unconcerned with the auspices under which events and people arise. Inception import is what has kept innumerable astrologers fed over the centuries. While I readily concede that the process wherein narratives are embedded within other narratives in South Asian literature is an art, and not a science, I assert that it is a much more formulaic practice than we might realize. Its mechanics (largely driven by the alpha principle) suggest the exertion of conscious effort in order to purposeful place narrative at junctures where their themes resonate with the themes of the greater work as manifesting at that juncture. This resonance mutually amplified by the themes of the subnarrative, and the larger narrative.

## Notes

1 For a terse summary of the voices resounding throughout the history of scholarship on the MkP (most notably, as featured in this section, that of Wilson, Pargiter, Winternitz, and Hazra), see Rocher 1986, 191–6.
2 For a comprehensive examination of Sun worship in India at every phase, see Srivastava 1972.
3 See Chapter 3, "The Vedic Tradition" (Srivastava 1972, 41–175).
4 See Chapter 4, "The Epic Stream" (Srivastava 1972, 177–202).

## Works cited in this chapter

Agrawala, Vasudeva Sharana. 1963. *Devī-Māhātmyam: The Glorification of the Great Goddess*. Varanasi: All-India Kashiraj Trust.

Bailey, Greg. 2005. "The Pravṛtti/Nivṛtti Chapters in the Mārkaṇḍeyapurāṇa". In *Epics, Khilas and Purāṇas. Continuities and Ruptures*, edited by P. Koskikallio, 495–516. Zagreb: Croatian Academy of Arts and Sciences.

Balkaran, Raj. 2019. *The Goddess and The King in Indian Myth: Ring Composition, Royal Power, and the Dharmic Double Helix*. London: Routledge.

Balkaran, Raj. 2020. "Arjuna and Acyuta: The Import of Epithets in the Bhagavad-Gītā". In *The Bhagavad-Gītā; A Critical Introduction*, edited by Ithamar Thedor. Delhi: Routledge.

Bowles, Adam. 2006. *Mahābhārata: Book 8: Karṇa*. Vol. 1. Clay Sanskrit Library. New York: New York University Press.

Bowles, Adam. 2008. *Mahābhārata: Book 8: Karṇa*. Vol. 2. Clay Sanskrit Library. New York: New York University Press.

Buitenen, J.A.B. van. 1973. *Mahābhārata: Book 1: The Book of the Beginning*. Vol. I. Chicago, IL: University of Chicago Press.

Buitenen, J.A.B. van. 1975. *Mahābhārata: Book 2: The Book of the Assembly Hall; Book 3: The Book of the Forest*. Vol. II. Chicago, IL: University of Chicago Press.

Desai, Nileshvari Y. 1968. *Ancient Indian Society, Religion, and Mythology as Depicted in the Mārkaṇḍeya-Purāṇa; a Critical Study*. Baroda: Faculty of Arts, M.S. University of Baroda.

Doniger, Wendy. 1996. "Saraṇyū/Saṃjñā: The Sun and The Shadow". In *Devī: Goddesses of India*, edited by John Stratton Hawley and Donna Marie Wulff, 154–72. Berkeley, CA: University of California Press.

Doniger, Wendy. 2014. "Saranyu/Samjna: The Sun and The Shadow". In *On Hinduism*. New York: Oxford University Press, 269–87.

Dutt, Manmatha Nath. 1896. *A Prose English Translation of Mārkaṇḍeya Purāṇa*. Calcutta: Elysium.

Eco, Umberto. 1994. *Six Walks in the Fictional Woods*. Cambridge, MA: Harvard University Press.

Farquhar, J.N. 1920. *An Outline of the Religious Literature of India*. London: H. Milford, Oxford University Press.

Gonda, Jan. 1977. *A History of Indian Literature. Volume II, Fasc. 1*. Wiesbaden: O. Harrassowitz.

Griffith, Ralph T., trans. 1895. "Atharva Veda: Book 19: Hymn 66: A Hymn to Agni as the Sun". In *Hymns of the Atharva Veda*. sacred-texts.com.

Griffith, Ralph T., trans. 1896a. "Rig-Veda Book 1: HYMN CXV. Sūrya". In *Rig Veda*. sacred-texts.com.

Griffith, Ralph T., trans. 1896b. "Rig-Veda Book 1: HYMN L. Sūrya". In *Rig Veda*. sacred-texts.com.

Hazra, R.C. 1955. "The Sāmba-Purāṇa, a Saura Work of Different Hands". *Annals of the Bhandarkar Oriental Research Institute* 36 (1.2).

Hazra, R.C. 1958. *Studies in the Upapurāṇas Vol. 1 (Saura and Vaiṣṇava Upapurāṇas)*. Calcutta: Sanskrit College.

Hazra, R.C. 1963. *Studies in the Upapurāṇas Vol. 2 (Śākta and Non-Sectarian Upapurāṇas)*. Calcutta: Sanskrit College.

Hazra, R.C. 1975. *Studies in the Purāṇic Records on Hindu Rites and Customs*. Delhi: Motilal Banarsidass.

Hiltebeitel, Alf. 2010. *Reading the Fifth Veda Studies on the Mahabharata: Essays*. Edited by Vishwa Adluri and Joydeep Bagchee. Leiden: Brill.

Muller, Max, trans. 1879a. "The Upanishads, Part 1 (SBE01): Kaushītaki-Upanishad: Adhyāya II". In *The Upanishads*. sacred-texts.com.

Muller, Max, trans. 1879b. "The Upanishads, Part 1 (SBE01): Khāndogya Upanishad: I, 3". In *The Upanishads*. sacred-texts.com.

Pandey, C.D. 1984. "The Magian Priests and Their Impact on Sun-Worship". *Purāṇa* 26 (2): 203–5.

Pargiter, F.E. 1904. *Mārkaṇḍeya Purāṇa*. Calcutta: Asiatic Society of Bengal.

Quackenbos, George Payn. 1917. *The Sanskrit Poems of Mayūra*. New York: Columbia University Press.

Rocher, Ludo. 1986. *The Purāṇas*, edited by Jan Gonda. Wiesbaden: Harrassowitz.

Srivastava, V.C. 1969. "The Purāṇic Records on the Sun-Worship". *Purāṇa* 11 (2): 229–72.

Srivastava, V.C. 1972. *Sun-Worship in Ancient India*. Allahabad: Indological Publications.

Srivastava, V.C. 1988. "Two Distinct Groups of Indian Sun-Priests: An Appraisal". *Purāṇa* 30 (2): 109–20.

Srivastava, V.C. 1989. "Indian Sun-Priests". *Purāṇa* 31 (2): 142–58.

Srivastava, V.C. 2013. *Sāmba Purāṇa: An Exhaustive Introduction, Sanskrit Text, English Translation, Notes and Index of Verses*. Delhi: Parimal Publications.

Winternitz, Moriz. 1972a. *A History of Indian Literature. Vol 1*. New Delhi: Oriental Books Repr. Corp.

Winternitz, Moriz. 1972b. *A History of Indian Literature. Vol 2*. New Delhi: Oriental Books Repr. Corp.

# 2 Mirrored *māhātmya*s

## Saura–Śākta symbiosis in the *Mārkaṇḍeya Purāṇa*

This chapter looks at myths of the Sun in the MkP, identifying a second *māhātmya* of the MkP, the SM, lauding the supremacy of the Sun in parallel fashion as the more famous *māhātmya* of the MkP, the DM, lauds the supremacy of the Goddess. It suggests that these *māhātmya*s constitute a sectarian symbiosis united under the common theme of *pravṛtti dharma*, exemplified in the work of kings.

### 2.1 The splendour of the Sun

In commencing its discourse on the 7th Manu (at the outset of Canto 77), the MkP informs us that the Sun and his wife Saṃjñā[1] (77.1–7) beget a famous and learned Manu, namely, the current Manu Vaivasvata, along with Yama and Yamunā. Saṃjñā, having endured the sharpness (*tejas*) of the Sun for some time (77.8) and unable to bear it further, decides to take refuge with her father (77.8–10). In order to do so, she fashions Chāyā (a reflection/shadow-form of herself) who, under her instruction, agrees to take her place no. The goddess Saṃjñā then goes to her father Tvaṣṭṛ's abode where she is respectfully received. Having remained there for some time, Tvaṣṭṛ advises her to return to her husband (15–21). Agreeing to his counsel, she salutes her father respectfully and secretly departs for the Northern Kurus, unbeknownst to him, still fearing the sharp splendour of the Sun. She practices austerities and changes herself into the form of a mare (77.22–23).

Meanwhile the Sun, unaware of the ruse, begets a second family with Chāyā, one reflecting the first family by consisting also of two sons and a daughter, Manu, Śanaiścara and Tapatī. Yama exhibits envy when the younger children are favoured (77.24–25) and raises his foot in anger against Chāyā, whom he believes at this point to be his own mother. Astonished at his appalling behaviour, Chāyā curses Yama that his foot would fall to earth that very day (77.26–30). Yama, terrified of the curse, complains to Sūrya who summons Chāyā, and apparently seeing through the ruse, asks after Saṃjñā (77.30–33). Though Chāyā answers that she is his wife, Saṃjñā, and the mother of his children (77.34), the Sun repeatedly questions her and eventually enraged by her silence on the matter, threatens to curse her (7.35). Although she promised to

DOI: 10.4324/9780429322020-3

hold to the false story, even to the point of bringing curses upon herself, the Sun's glare succeeds in breaking through Chāyā's pretence. She confesses the truth, at which point Sūrya goes to pay a visit to his father-in-law, Tvaṣṭṛ, in order to reclaim Saṃjñā (77.36). Once there, he is reverently received (77.37). Tvaṣṭṛ, upon being asked after his daughter, responds, "She came indeed here to my house, saying she had been verily sent by thee" (77.38). Upon hearing this, the Sun concentrates his mind in yogic meditation and inwardly sees his wife in the form of a mare, practising austerities in the Northern Kurus and is furthermore able to perceive the purpose of her penance, namely that her husband should acquire a gentle form, beautiful to behold (77.40). Upon becoming aware of this, the Sun immediately asks of his father-in-law that his sharp splendour be pared down, to which Viśvakarman of course reverently complies.

The following Canto (78) commences with the praise of the gods and divine seers (*devarṣayaḥ*) who had assembled for the monumental event: the paring down of the Sun's *tejas*. Interestingly, this event appears to be construed as an auspicious one. While, for example, the waning of the moon is considered inauspicious, this appears to be a different scenario wherein excess energy is reabsorbed by the universe to grant the Sun a more balanced, benign form. Immediately following the fourteen-verse praise, the Sun begins to shed his splendour (78.15), which not only comprises the earth, sky, and heaven (*svarga*) from the aspects of him which comprised the Ṛg, Yajur, and Sāma Veda respectively (78.16), but the "fifteen shreds of his splendour which were pared off by Tvaṣṭṛ" (78.17) were used to craft Śiva's trident (78.17) the discus of Viṣṇu's discus, "the Vasus, the very terrible weapon of Śankara", Agni's spear, Kubera's palki (78.18) "and all the fierce weapons of the others who are the gods' foes, and of the Yakṣas and Vidyādharas" (78.19). The Sun at this point therefore "bears only a sixteenth part … of his splendour [which] was pared off by Viśva-karmaṇ into fifteen [other] parts" (78.20). Having successfully shed himself of his extraneous sharpness (which was harnessed to craft the weapons of gods and demons alike), the Sun assumes the form of a stallion and journeys to the Northern Kurus where he encounters Saṃjñā in her equine guise (78.21). Upon seeing the stallion approach, Saṃjñā, fearful of an encounter with a strange male, engages him face to face so as to guard her hindquarters (78.22). As their noses met, two sons were born in Saṃjñā's mouth, namely, Nāsatya and Dasra, (78.23), better known as the Aśvin twins. At the end of the Sun's emission, Revanta was born (78.24). The Sun then reveals his "own peerless form, and she gazing upon his true form felt a keen joy" (78.25) whereupon the Sun "brought home this his loving wife Saṃjñā restored to her own shape" (78.26). The myth then recounts the posts appointed to the children of the Sun as follows (78.27–34):

> Her eldest son then became Vaivasvata Manu; and her second son Yama became the righteous-eyed judge because of the curse … And Yamunā became the river which flows from the recesses of Mount Kalinda. The Aśvins were made the gods' physicians by their high-souled father. And Revanta also was appointed king of the Guhyakas. Hear also from me the

Sūrya (the Sun)
+ his wife Saṃjñā
begets→ Vaivasvata, 7th (current) Manu
→ Yama, god of the dead
→ Yamī / Yamunā River

Sūrya
+ his wife Chāyā
begets→ Sāvarṇi, the 8th (next) Manu
→ Śanaiścara, the planet of karmic retribution
→ Tapatī / Narmadā River

equine-Sūrya
+ equine-Saṃjñā (while in equine form)
begets→ Nāsatya (first of the Aśvin twins, divine physician)
→ Daśra, (second of the Aśvin twins, divine physician)
→ Revanta

*Figure 2.1* The *Mārkaṇḍeya Purāṇa* solar family tree.

> places assigned to the Shadow-Saṃjñā's sons. The eldest son of the Shadow-Saṃjñā was equal to Manu the eldest-born; hence this son of the Sun obtained the title Sāvarṇika. He also shall be a Manu when Bali shall become Indra. He was appointed by his father as the planet Saturn among the planets. The third of them, the daughter named Tapatī.

The second telling of the sequence of events between Sūrya, Saṃjñā, Chāyā and the two sets of three children occupies Cantos 106–108, and remains essentially the same. Saṃjñā again retreats to her father's abode, who advises her to return to her husband, and she again adopts the guise of a mare and departs for the Northern Kurus to practice austerities (106.10–12). In this version, it is Viśvakarman's suggestion that the Sun be pared down, though he readily agrees. When he is being pared down, there is great chaos amid the heavens and the earth (106.39–47), and the gods again praise the Sun (106.48–65). Then Viśvakarman offers his own praise (107.1–10) while pairing down the Sun's glory to one-sixteenth of its original status, forging with the remaining fifteen-sixteenths Viṣṇu's discus, and "Śiva's trident, Kubera's palki, the rod of the lord of the dead, and the spear of the gods' general [along with] brilliant weapons of the other gods with the Sun's splendour for the quelling of their foes" (108.3–5). The remainder of the canto details the same sequence of events and the same allotment of posts as in the first telling. However, the laudation of the Sun does not end with this recapitulated material.

While the exchange between Sūrya and his wives occurs as a stand-alone segment in Cantos 77–78 to introduce the current Manu and to thus contextualize the DM (which serves to introduce the next Manu), it makes a reappearance (in Cantos 106–108) in a lengthy passage embellishing the virtues of the

Sun (Sūrya), casting him as a supreme primordial power even above the gods themselves. Remarkably, the MkP dedicates a nine-chapter episodic trilogy to lauding the majesty of the Sun, which I shall refer to here as the *Sūrya Mahātmya* (SM). For the purposes of the discussion at hand, I shall note the

*Table 2.1* Parallels between *Devī* and *Sūrya Māhātmyas*

| ***Sūrya Māhātmya*, MkP 101–110 [occurring within succession of kings discourse, MkP 101–136]** | | ***Devī Māhātmya*, MkP 81–93 [occurring within succession of Manus discourse, MkP 53–100]** | |
|---|---|---|---|
| *Canto* | *Content* | *Canto* | *Content* |
| **SM Introduction 101** | Sage Mārkaṇḍeya introduces the Sun; Krauṣṭuki asks to hear about his greatness in full (101.15–17). | **Introduction 81** | Sage Medhas introduces the Devī; Suratha asks to hear about her greatness in full (81.45–81.46). |
| **SM Episode I 102–103** | Describes the Sun's cosmic role at the dawn of creation: Brahmā hymns the Sun to save the universe from his overpowering lustre. Hymn 1 by Brahmā (103.5–12) | **DM Episode I 81** | Describes the Devī's cosmic role at the dawn of creation: Brahmā hymns the Devī to save the universe from her overpowering darkness. Hymn 1 by Brahmā (1.54–87) |
| **SM Episode II 104–105** | The gods are overtaken by the demons and Aditi hymns the Sun so that he is born to her and combats them and restores sovereignty to the gods.<br>Hymn 2 by Aditi (104.18–29) | **DM Episode II 82–84** | The gods are overtaken by Mahīṣa and his demon forces and their collective wrath manifest the Devī who combats the demons and restores sovereignty to the gods.<br>Weapons forged by Tejas (82.19.82.28)Hymn 2 by Indra and the devas (4.1–4.42) |
| **SM Episode III 106–108** | Sūrya–Saṃjñā–Chāyā story [recapitulation of Cantos 77–78].<br>Hymn 3 by Viśvakarman (107.2–10)<br>Weapons forged by Tejas (108.3–5) | | |
| **SM Epilogue 109–110** | Krauṣṭuki interjects to ask for more details (109.1–2)<br>Hymn 4 by the brāhmaṇas (110.62–74)<br>Phalaśruti 110.37–43.<br>The Sun reinstates King Rājyavardhana's earthy reign. | **DM Episode III DM Epilogue 85–92; 93** | The gods are again overtaken, this time by Śumbha-Niśumbha and they invoke the Goddess, who again restores their sovereignty.<br>Hymn 3 by the devas (5.7–5.36)<br>Suratha Interjects to ask for more details (89.1–2)<br>Hymn 4 by Agni and the devas (11.1–34)<br>Phalaśruti (12.1–12.29)<br>The Devī reinstates King Suratha's earthy reign. |

*Table 2.2* The structure of the *Sūrya Māhātmya*

| | *Canto* | *# of Verses* | *Name* | | |
|---|---|---|---|---|---|
| Intro | 98 | 27 | Vaṃśa Anukīrtana | Genealogies | Introduction to Sūrya |
| Ep.1 (37; Creation) | 99 | 22 | *Mārtaṇḍa Māhātmya* | The Majesty of The Sun | Universe as aspects of Sūrya |
| | 100 | 15 | *Āditya Stava* | Hymn to the Sun (5–12) | Brahmā praises Sun |
| Ep. 2 (65; Heaven) | 101 | 38 | *Divākara Stuti* | Praise of the Sun (18–29) | Aditi praises Sun to defeat demons |
| | 102 | 27 | Mārtaṇḍa Utpatti | The Birth of Mārtaṇḍa | Birth of Mārtaṇḍa; Victory |
| RECAP (105) Sūrya–Saṃjñā–Chāyā | 103 | 65 | Bhānu Tanu Lekhana | The paring down of the Sun's body | Sūrya–Saṃjñā–Chāyā |
| | 104 | 11 | *Sūrya Stava* | Hymn to the Sun (2–10) | Viśvakarman hymns Sun |
| | 105 | 29 | *Ravi Māhātmya Varṇa* | The Majesty of The Sun | Weapons made; equine reunion; |
| Ep. 3 (121; Earth) | 106 | 78 | *Bhānu Stava* | Praise of the Sun (62–74) | Brāhmaṇas praise Sun |
| | 107 | 43 | *Bhānu Māhātmya Varṇana* | The Majesty of the Sun | Sūrya blesses King Rājyavardhana |
| | | 355 | | | |

overarching parallels in formal and thematic features between the two *māhātmya*s, highlighted in chart form in Figure 2.1.

The similitude between these two glorifications demonstrates a conscious compositional cross-pollination at play among the assemblers of these *māhātmya*s. In my search to illumine the glories of the Goddess (Balkaran 2019), I have stumbled upon a second *māhātmya* finding a home in the MkP, one intimately connected to the first, much better known one. For the structure of the SM, see Figure 2.1.

### *2.1.1 Mārkaṇḍeya introduces the greatness of the Sun (MkP 101)*

The SM material begins with the beginning of the section of the MkP detailing royal dynasties (*vaṃśānucarita*), an integral component of the idealized five-part purāṇic pañcalakṣana archetype discussed at the outset of this chapter. To set the scene, Mārkaṇḍeya has just finished relaying to Krauṣṭuki subtales pertaining to of the fourteen Manu-epochs (formally, the *manvantara* section; another of the five-pronged metric of Purāṇa discussed above) at the end of the previous chapter. As is customary of the genre, Mārkaṇḍeya's exposition here is spurred on by an interrogative prompt on behalf of the eager pupil. Krauṣṭuki, therefore, commences the chapter thus: "Now that I've heard you chronicle the Manu intervals in detail, I wish to hear in full the genealogy of all the earthly kings, beginning from Brahmā. Do describe them in detail, Venerable Sir" (MkP 101.1–2). Mārkaṇḍeya's immediate response corresponds with the thrust of Krauṣṭuki's query, as follows:

> Hear, my son, of the origins of kings, of their exploits, starting with the Creator whose line is adorned with hundreds of noble kings, steadfast with the sacrifice, and victorious in war. Merely hearing of the exploits of these high-souled kings, a man is delivered from his sins!
>
> (MkP 101.3–5)

Mārkaṇḍeya continues in stating that the great god Brahmā Prajāpati, desirous of creating other beings, produces Dakṣa from his right thumb, and a wife for Dakṣa from his left thumb (MkP 101.9–10). The resplendent Aditi is born to Dakṣa, of whom Kaśyapa begets the divine Mārtaṇḍa, the Sun (MkP 101.11). Here, Mārkaṇḍeya's exposition takes a most fascinating turn as he proceeds to describe the Sun as conferrer of boons identical with *brahman* (brahmā svarūpaṁ), the beginning, middle and end of the universe, who occasions cosmic creation, preservation, and dissolution. The universe in fact emerges from the Sun, we are told, in whom everything exists. The Sun comprises the world, the gods, the demons, and humanity. He is the essence of everything, indeed the supreme eternal soul (*sarvātmā paramātmā sanātanaḥ*) (MkP 101.12–15). The Mārkaṇḍeya concludes his grand introduction to the greatness of the Sun by mentioning that the Sun had taken birth in the womb of Aditi, mother of the gods, after she had worshipped for this outcome (MkP 101.12–15). This tantalizing snippet into the grandeur of the Sun successfully seduces Krauṣṭuki into upgrading his previous prompt with one explicitly seeking insight into the Sun's greatness, as follows:

> Venerable Sir, I wish to hear of the true from of the Sun (svarūpaṁ vivasvataḥ) and why this primordial god became Kaśyapa's son. O best of sages, I wish to hear in full how the Sun was worshipped by Aditi and Kaśyapa, what words he spoke when propitiated, and about his prowess once he incarnated.
>
> (MkP 101.16–17)

Mārkaṇḍeya's description of the Sun is nothing short of monumental from its very outset. He starts off by describing the forms of the Sun as: clear, supreme knowledge (*vispaṣṭā paramā vidyā*); eternal, expansive effulgence (*jyotirbhā śāśvatī sphuṭā*); liberation (*kaivalya*); visible manifestation (*āvirbhū*); freedom of will (*prākāmya*); insight (*jñāna*); comprehension (*saṁvit*); intelligence (*bodha*); conception (*avagati*); memory (*smṛti*); and discernment (*vijñāna*) (MkP 101.18–19). He adds to this riveting introduction, "Hear, illustrious sir, while I relay at length what you asked, that is, how the Sun became manifest" (*raver āvirbhāvo yathābhavat*) (MkP 101.20). It is noteworthy that Mārkaṇḍeya's pledge to declare "how the Sun became manifest" here implies that the Sun already exists in unmanifest form, transcending the various manifestations discussed in the SM. This corroborates the initial equation of the Sun with brahman itself at the outset of the discourse.

Mārkaṇḍeya goes on to relay that in the beginning, the world was enveloped in darkness when into existence sprang an imperishable egg. The egg split open and within it stood Grandfather Brahmā, the lotus-born creator of worlds himself (MkP 101.21–22). Out of Brahmā's mouth issues forth the cosmic utterance "OṂ", then *bhūḥ*, *bhuvaḥ*, *svaḥ* – mystic utterances expressing the essence of the Sun itself, we are told. All seven of the vibrational dimensions, in fact, are aspects of the Sun, each more gross than the one before it: *bhūḥ*, *bhuvaḥ*, *svaḥ*, *manaḥ*, *janaḥ*, *tapaḥ* and *satyam*. These dimensions oscillate in and out of existence, mere manifestations of the utterance oṃ, itself the first and the last, the supreme, sublime, subtle imperishable body of brahman itself (MkP 101.23–27).

### *2.1.2 The Sun and creation (MkP 102–103)*

#### *2.1.2.1 Canto 102: the greatness of the Sun*

When the cosmic egg split open, the fourfold Vedas pour forth from the four-headed creator god, each from one of his four mouths. The Ṛg Veda first emerges from his anterior mouth, then the Yajur Veda from his right mouth, followed by the Sāma Veda from his posterior mouth, and, finally, the Atharva Veda springs forth from his left mouth (MkP 102.3–6). Mārkaṇḍeya further comments on the overall quality (*guṇa*) of each compilation (MkP 102.1–7). Each Vedic corpus retains its own effulgence as before, uniting that effulgence with the supreme primordial effulgence encompassing the original utterance *oṃ*. Thus, the darkness is dispelled and the universe became completely clear in all directions: upwards, downwards, outwards. The effulgence of the Vedic meter forms an orb and joins with that supreme cosmic effulgence. Emanating from Āditya, the Sun, it serves as the cause of the universe (MkP 102.8–14). After declaring the times of day auspicious for the recitation of each Vedic corpus (MkP 102.15–18), Mārkaṇḍeya explains that Brahmā is one with the Ṛg Veda hymns at creation, Viṣṇu is one with the Yajur Veda hymns at the time of preservation, and Rudra (Śiva) is one with the Sāma Veda hymns at the time of comic dissolution. Moreover, he declares that the Sun is one with all of the Vedas. The Sun abides in the Vedas, whose very self is Vedic knowledge, who himself is the supreme Cosmic Man (*puruṣa uttama*). Therefore, the Sun is the cause of creation, preservation, and destruction: taking on various qualities (*rajas*, *sattva*, etc.), he assumes the appellations Brahmā, Viṣṇu, and the other gods (MkP 102.19–22). Mārkaṇḍeya concludes:

> Now ever to be praised by the gods is he whose body is the Veda, *Yet* who has no body, who was in the beginning, who is embodied in all mortals; *Who is* the Light that is the refuge of the universe, who has righteousness that passes knowledge, Who is to be attained unto in the Vedanta, supreme beyond *things that are* sublime!
>
> (MkP 102.22) (Pargiter 1904, 556)

*2.1.2.2 Canto 103: Brahmā hymns the Sun*

Mārkaṇḍeya continues: When the cosmic egg was heated, engulfed by the Sun's effulgence, lotus-born Lord Brahmā, being desirous of creating, thinks to himself,

> My creation although accomplished will assuredly pass to destruction through the intense glory of the Sun … Breathing beings *will* be bereft of breath, and the waters will dry up through his glory, and without water there will be no creation of this universe.[2]
>
> (MkP 103.2–3)

Thus, ensconced in thought, Lord Brahmā, grandfather of the world, fixes his mind intently on the blessed Sun and composes the following hymn (MkP 103.1–4):

> Brahma spoke:
>
> 5 I pay reverence *to thee* of whom everything consists
> Here, and who consistest of everything;
> Whose body is the universe, *who art* the sublime Light
> Whereon religious devotees meditate;
>
> 6 Who art composed of the Ṛig hymns, who art the repository of the Yajus hymns,
> And who art the origin of the Saman hymns;
> whose power passes thought;
> Who consistest of the three *Vedas*;
> *who art* half a short syllable as touching grossness,
> Whose nature is sublime, who art worthy of the fullness of good qualities.
>
> 7 To thee, the cause of all,
> who art to be known as supremely worthy of praise,
> The supreme Light *that was* at the beginning,
> not in the form of fire;
> And *who art* gross by reason that thy spirit is in the gods
> – *to thee* I pay reverence,
> The shining one, who wast in the beginning,
> the sublimest beyond the sublime!
>
> 8 Thine is the primeval power,
> in that urged on thereby I achieve *this* creation,
> which is in the forms of water, earth, wind and fire,
> Which has those *elements*, the gods and other *beings* for its objects,
> *and* which is complete with the word "Om" and other *sounds* –
> Not at my own wish;
> and *that I effect* its continuance and dissolution in the self-same manner.

9 Thou verily art fire.
By reason of thy drying up of the water thou achievest
The creation of the earth and the primeval completion of the worlds.
Thou indeed, O lord, pervadest the very form of the sky.
Thou in five ways protectest all this world.

10. They who know the Supreme Soul sacrifice with sacrifices to thee,
Who hast the nature of Vishnu, who consistest of all sacrifices, O Sun!
And self-subdued *ascetics*, who curb their souls and thoughts, meditate
On *thee*, the lord of all, the supremest, while they desire final emancipation from existence for themselves.

11 Reverence to thee, whose form is divine;
To thee, whose form is sacrifice, be reverence;
*Yea* to thee who in thy very nature art the Supreme Spirit,
Who art meditated upon by religious devotees!

12 Contract thy glory, since the abundance of thy glory
Tends to obstruct creation, O lord, and I am ready to begin creation!

(MkP 103.5–12) (Pargiter 1904, 556–8)

Pleased by the Creator's excellent praise, the Sun contracts his colossal effulgence, retaining but a bit of it. Thus, the illustrious lotus-born Brahmā, succeeded in creating the world, and – just as with ages past – proceeds to create the gods, the demons, and other divine beings, along with mortals, cattle and other *animals*, trees, creepers and the hell realms (MkP 103.13–15).

### *2.1.3 The Sun and the heavens (MkP 104–105)*

#### *2.1.3.1 Canto 104 – Aditi hymns the Sun*

Having created the world, as with so many times before, Brahmā proceeds to properly divide the castes (*varṇas*), the life stages (*āśramas*), the seas, the mountains, and the islands. The blessed lotus-sprung god then fixed in form the abodes of the gods, demons (*daitya*), serpents (*uraga*; synonymous with *nāga*), and the other beings in accordance with the Vedas (MkP 104.1–2). Brahmā had a son, the famed Marīci, whose son was Kaśyapa, whose son in turn was called Kāśyapa (he born of Kaśyapa). Wedding Dakṣa's thirteen daughters, Kāśyapa begot many offspring, among them were the gods, the demons, and the serpents (MkP 104.3–4).

Mārkaṇḍeya proceeds to list the various classes of beings born of Kāśyapa to each of his thirteen wives (MkP 104.5–10). The most prominent of these for our purposes are the gods – the devas, born of Aditi – and the three classes of demonic beings – the daityas, dānavas and rākṣakas born of Diti, Danu and Khasā respectively. The gods were foremost among Kāśyapa's sons, made to rule the worlds and partake in the shares of sacrifice by Brahmā, foremost of those attune to divine knowing (MkP 104.11). The hostile Daityas, Dānavas, and Rākṣasas teamed up to wage a war to overthrow the Devas. After 1,000 celestial years, the devas were defeated, as their Daitya and Dānava stepbrothers ascended to power (MkP 104.12–14).

Aditi beheld her defeated sons, ousted by the Daityas and Dānavas from dominion over the three worlds, deprived of their share of the sacrifice. Overcome with grief, she exerted mighty effort to propitiate the Sun. Fasting and practising self-restraint, she wholly concentrated her mind and hymned the Sun, that divine orb of light stationed in the sky.

> Aditi spoke:
>
> 18 Reverence to thee who hast a sublime subtle golden body, O splendour of those who have splendour, O lord, O repository of splendours, O eternal one!
>
> 19 And the ardent form which thou hast who drawest up the waters for the benefit of the worlds, O lord of the *heavenly* cattle, to that I bow reverently!
>
> 20 The most ardent form which thou hast, who bearest the nectar that composes the moon to take it back during the space of eight months, to that I bow reverently!
>
> 21 The well-fattened form which *thou hast*, who verily dischargest all that same nectar to *produce* rain, to that thy cloud-form be reverence, O Sun!
>
> 22 And that light-giving form of thine, which tends to mature the whole kingdom
>
> O plants that are produced through the pouring forth of water, to that I bow reverently!
>
> 23 And that form of thine which, when there is excessive cold by reason of the pouring forth of snow and other *causes*, tends to nourish the crops of that *winter* season – to the passing over of that thy *form* be reverence!
>
> 24 And that form of thine, which is not very ardent and which is not very cold, *and* is mild in the season of spring, to that be reverence, O divine Sun, *yea* reverence!
>
> 25 And *thy* other *form*, which fattens both all the gods and the pitṛis, to that which causes the ripening of the crops be revenence!
>
> 26 That one form of thine which, being composed of nectar for the vivification of plants, is quaffed by the gods and pitṛis, to that, which is the soul of the moon, be reverence!

> 27 That form of thine which, consisting of the universe, is combined with Agni and Soma these two forms of the Sun, to that, the soul of which is the good qualities, be reverence!
>
> 28 That form of thine which, named the three-fold *Veda* by reason of the unity of the Ṛig, Yajus and Sama *Vedas*, gives heat to this universe, to that be reverence, O luminous one!
>
> 29 That thy form moreover, which transcends that *former one*, which is enunciated by uttering the word "Om", *and* which is subtle, endless *and* stainless, reverence be to that, the soul of which is Truth!
>
> (MkP 104.18–29) (Pargiter 1904, 560–1)

In this manner, self-restrained, abstaining from food, the goddess worshipped the Sun day and night (MkP 104.30). After some time, the blessed Sun made himself visible in the sky to the daughter of Dakṣa. She beheld a bundle of fiery light both upon the earth and in the sky, difficult to gaze upon due to its halo of flame. The goddess, emboldened, thus addresses the Sun:

> Be gracious to me, I cannot gaze upon you, O lord of beasts. I first beheld you, while fasting, standing in the sky, most arduous to gaze upon. And even now on earth, I behold in you a globe of fire, as brilliant, as burning as before. Be gracious! Permit me to behold your form, O Maker of Day. Lord, you who show compassion to you devotees: I am your devotee; save my sons! (MkP 104.31–34). You are our soul support: you create the universe; you toil to preserve it; the universe passed to dissolution within you as well. You are the sole refuge for the creatures of all the world! (MkP 104.35). You are Brahmā, you are Viṣṇu, you are Śiva! You are Indra, Kubera, Lord of Wealth, Yama, Lord of Ancestors, Varuṇa, Lord of waters, and Vāyu the wind! You are the Moon, Agni (Fire), the lord of the sky, earth, and oceans! What praise can I offer to you who are the essence and form of all? (MkP 104.36). You are the lord of the sacrifice: brāhmaṇas praise you with various hymns as they conduct their rituals day in and day out. They who concentrating on you with firmly controlled minds, established in the state of yoga, attain the most sublime states.
>
> (MkP 104.37)

> You warm, ripen, protect and consume the universe. You make manifest the universe again and again through your water-laden rays You alone create it as Lotus-Born (Brahmā), protect it as Acyutya (Viṣṇu), and destroy it at the end of the age as Rudra (Śiva).
>
> (MkP 104.38)

#### *2.1.3.2 Canto 105: the birth of Mārtaṇḍa*

Thereupon emerging from the bundle of his own effulgence the Sun revealed himself to Aditi, appearing like glowing copper. Aditi falls prostrate before the effulgent Sun, and, upon seeing this, he grants her a boon of her desiring. Lying yet prostrate with her head on the ground, pressing her knees into the earth, answers as follows (MkP 105.1–3):

> Be gracious, O god! The Daityas and the Dānavas have grown powerful, snatching the three worlds from my sons, and their shares in the sacrifice along with it. Therefore, Lord of Rays, show me your favour in this regard: dispatch a portion of your rays to descend as their brother to destroy their enemies. You remove the afflictions of suppliants, you who are known as the preserver of existence (sthiti-kartṛ). Be gracious, O Sun, and show compassion towards my sons so that they may again partake of the shares of the sacrifice and once again become rulers of the three worlds.
>
> (MkP 105.4–7)

Thereupon the blessed Sun, robber of the water, showed favour to the prostate Aditi, stating: “I will take birth in your womb, Aditi, with my thousand portions, and swiftly destroy the enemies of your sons!” The divine Sun vanished from her sight. Having gained her heart’s desire Aditi ceased her austerities (MkP 105.8–10).

Among the thousand rays of the Sun, the special ray called Suṣumna incarnated in the womb of the mother of the gods. With her mind composed, she undertook the arduous cāndrāyaṇa penance among other austerities. Purified, she successfully conceived, knowing her embryo to be divine. Kaśyapa, ignorant of her boon, asked her in anger: “Why do you destroy the embryo within you with your incessant fasting?” Aditi replies “The embryo within me has not been destroyed, you wrathful man! It is itself meant for the destruction of our enemies!” Angered at her husband’s words, she then at once gave birth to a child that blazed brilliantly before them. Seeing that the child shone like the rising Sun, Kaśyapa fell prostrate and reverently praised him with ancient Ṛg Vedic hymns. Being thus praised, the Sun revealed himself from out of the fetal egg, filling the sky with his lotus-hued lustre. Then a voice, deep as thunder, issued from the sky,

> Since you speak of this egg (aṇḍa) as destroyed (Māritam), your son shall be called Mārtaṇḍa (a name of the Sun), he shall wield the Sun’s power on earth to slay those demons who rob you of your shares of the sacrifice.
>
> (MkP 105.19–20)

On hearing these sky-born words, the gods assembled, delighted and the demons were disheartened. Indra, chief of the gods, then challenged the demons to battle.

The battle between the demons and the gods raged on, all regions made bright by the lustre ensuing from the clash of their weapons. As soon as Mārtaṇḍa gazed upon the demons, they were burnt to ashes. Thereat the gods attained unparalleled delight, hymning both Aditi and effulgent Mārtaṇḍa. With the gods’ station and sacrificial shares restored, Mārtaṇḍa exerted his own dominion. Assuming an effulgent form, he became a spherical ball of fire: displaying his lustre in all directions like petals on the kadamba flower, he expanded his rays over the heavens and the earth.

### *2.1.4 The Sun's family (MkP 106–108)*

#### *2.1.4.1 Canto 106: the paring down of the Sun*

Viśvakarman fell prostrate to propitiate the Sun Vivasvat before giving him his daughter, Saṃjñā, in marriage. Vivasvat begat the Manu Vaivasvata on Saṃjñā, described in detail before. Vivasvat, Lord of Rays, actually begot three children upon Saṃjñā, two sons and a daughter all told: Manu Vaivasvata, the eldest, presided over the śrāddhas, then were born the twins Yama and Yamī. Mārtaṇḍa, with his exceeding effulgence, scorched the three worlds, to the detriment of all thing, moving and unmoving (MkP 106.1–6). Unable to bear his overbearing form, Saṃjñā gazes at her own shadow and says: "Farewell, I am off to my father's abode! You must remain here to care for my two sons and beautiful daughter. You do not reveal any of this to the Sun" (MkP 106.7–8). Her Shadow replies: "Go where you wish, goddess. I will do as you bid, and keep your confidence, unto enduring curses, and seizing of my hair!" (MkP 106.9). Saṃjñā then went to her father's abode and having spent a fair bit of time there, her father advised her again and again to return to her husband. Rather, she turned herself into a mare and departed for the Northern Kurus, where, as a chaste wife, she practiced austerities, fasting.

Meanwhile, Chāyā remained faithful to Saṃjñā's orders, assuming her form to wait on the Sun. The Sun begat of Chāyā (thinking it was Saṃjñā), another two sons, and another daughter. The first of these was the Manu Sāvarṇi, and the second son became the planet Saturn. Their daughter, Tapatī was ultimately chosen in marriage to be the bride of Saṃvaraṇa, upon whom he begat the patriarch Kuru. Chāyā was more affectionate with the younger children, who were her own, and did not show the same affection to the older three. While Manu tolerated the inequity, Yama could not. Yama, out of anger and childishness – and also due to the pressures of fate – threatened Chāyā–Saṃjñā with his foot. Full of resentment, Chāyā–Saṃjñā cursed Yama proclaiming that the very foot with which he threatened his father's wife will fall off.

Agitated by the curse, Yama relayed the situation to his father the Sun. Though he takes responsibility for the childishness of his actions, he wonders aloud how a mother could possibly curse her son so, before beseeching the Sun to intercede and show him favour. The Sun proclaims that the curse must come to pass, especially the curse of a mother. Nevertheless, he devises a compromise whereby insects carrying minute particles of Yama's foot fall to the earth, therefore both saving Yama's foot while fulfilling Chāyā's curse.

The Sun then confronts Chāyā demanding to know why she favours the younger children. Moreover, he adds that a proper mother could curse not even worthless children, inferring, therefore, that she could not possibly be Saṃjñā, and that she must be someone put there in Saṃjñā's stead. Upon being confronted, Chāyā, true to her word, gives no response in order to honour her lady's request. The Sun resorts to intuitive insight to perceive the truth of the matter. Seeing that the Sun was about to lay a curse on her, Chāyā reveals the ruse trembling in fear. Angered, the Sun paid a visit to his father in law, and, seeing him about to burn him with his wrath, Viśvakarman explains:

> Permeated with surpassing glory is this thy form which is so hardly endurable; hence Saṃjña, unable to endure it, practices austerities in the forest in sooth. Thou shalt now see her, Sir, thy own wife, beautiful in her behaviour, practicing most arduous austerities in the forest on account of thy *too glorious* form. I remember Brahma's word: if it please thee, my lord, I *will* restrain thy beloved form, O lord of heaven.
>
> (MkP 106.36–38) (Pargiter 1904, 569)

The Sun again agrees to being pared down, and the gods praise his glory while this takes place.

### *2.1.4.2 Canto 107 – Viśvakarman hymns the Sun*

> 1 While the Sun was being pared down, the Praja-pati Viśva-karman then uttered this hymn, wherewith his hair stood erect with joy, to the Sun.
>
> 2 "To the Sun, who is compassionate for the welfare of those who fall prostrate *before him*, who is great of soul, who has seven equally swift horses, who has great glory, who awakens the beds of lotuses, who splits asunder the covering of the veil of darkness, be reverence!
>
> 3 To him who works merit through the superabundance of fire, who gives many objects of desire, who reclines amid beams of radiant fire, who brings welfare to all the world, be reverence!
>
> 4 To the Sun, who is without birth, the cause of the three worlds, the soul of created beings, the lord of the *heavenly* cattle, the bull, highest among those who are greatly compassionate, the home whence the eye originated, be reverence!
>
> 5 To the Sun, who is maintained by knowledge, *who is* the inmost soul, the foundation of the world, desirer of the world's welfare, the self-existent, the eye of all the worlds, highest among the gods, boundless in glory, be reverence!
>
> 6 *Thou*, for a moment the crest jewel of the day-spring mountain, the honoured messenger of the hosts of gods to the world, thou, whose body consists of a thousand wide-spreading rays of light, shinest on the world, driving away the darknesses.

7 By reason of *thy* intoxication from drinking up like spirituous liquor the darkness of the world, thy body has acquired a deep red *hue*, O Sun, so that thou shinest exceedingly with masses of light that calls the three worlds into life.

8–9 Mounting thy equally proportioned chariot that sways about gracefully and is widely pleasing, with horses that are ever unwearied", O adorable *god*, thou coursest the broad world for *our* good.

10 O Sun, thou purifier of the three worlds, protect me, who am devoted to thy parrot-hued steeds, *and who am* most pure through the dust of thy feet, *and who am* prostrate *before thee*, O thou who art kind to folk that bow *to thee!*

11 Thus to the Sun, who exists as the procreator of all the worlds, *who is* the sole cause of the glory that calls the three worlds into life, who exists as the lamp of all the worlds – to thee, O choicest of the thirty *gods*, I ever prostrate myself!"

(MkP 107.1–11) (Pargiter 1904, 572–4)

### *2.1.4.3 Canto 108 – the majesty of the Sun*

Having thus chanted the glories of the Sun, Viśvakarman successfully whittles away fifteenth/sixteenth of his glory, keeping only one-sixteenth intact in the disc of the Sun. The Sun's body therefore became beautiful to behold. With the *tejas* pared away was fashioned Viṣnu's discus, Śiva's trident, Kubera's palki, the rod of the lord of the dead and the spear of the general of the gods. He also made other brilliant weapons with the Sun's excess effulgence, weapons designed for the vanquishing of their foe. Shorn of his excessive splendour, Mārtaṇḍa was resplendent from limb to limb (MkP 108.1–6).

Concentrating his mind, the Sun saw that his wife had taken the form of a mare, made inconceivably beautiful by her penance and self-restraint. The Sun arrived at the Northern Kurus, and approached his wife, having donned equine garb. Seeing the equine-Sun approach, and, mistaking him for a strange male, she met him face to face, intent on guarding her rear. As their noses joined, the Sun's *tejas* passed through his nostrils into the mare, begetting two gods, the Aśvin twins, Nasatya and Dasra, best of physicians. These sons of Mārtaṇḍa in equine form were born in the mouth of the mare. A third god, Revanta, was born at the termination of the Sun's (seminal) flow, clad in armour, holding a sword and bow, and a quiver of arrows and a quiver (MkP 108.7–12). The Sun then revealed his form. Seeing his new, mild form, Saṃjñā rejoiced. The Sun, the robber of the waters, took his loving (*prītimatī*) wife Saṃjñā home, who, too, had assumed her true form (MkP 108.13–14).

The Sun's first-born son became Manu Vaivasvata. And his second born, Yama, having suffered through his curse, favoured virtue (*dharma*), and became therefore the king of virtue (*dharmarājā*). With an eye to righteousness, impartial to friend or foe, the Sun appointed him regent of the departed souls. Well-satisfied, the Sun made Yamunā a great river. The great Sun appoints the Aśvin twins physicians to the gods, and Revanta was appointed as Lord of the Guhyakas, conferring blessing on mankind when worshipped (MkP 108.20–23).

The son of Saṃjñā's Shadow, Sāvarṇi was granted great fame to become the eighth Manu in future. He presently performs arduous penance on the summit of Mount Meru. His brother, Śani, became the planet Saturn according to the Sun's command. And the Sun's youngest daughter became that best of rivers, the Yamunā, which purifies the world (MkP 108.24–26).

### *2.1.5 The Sun and the earth (MkP 109–110)*

#### *2.1.5.1 Canto 109: the citizens hymn the Sun*

Krauṣṭuki interjects:

> Venerable Sir, though you have already relayed at length the greatness (māhātmya) of the primeval Sun god (along with the birth of his exalted offspring), I wish to hear in even greater detail about the Sun's greatness (māhātmya), O best of sages. Please tell it to me.
>
> (MkP 109.1–2)

Mārkaṇḍeya responds: "Be it heard *then!* I tell thee of the majesty of the primeval god, Vivasvat, what he did formerly when worshipped by mankind" (MkP 109.3) (Pargiter 1904, 577).

Once there was a famous king, Dama's son, *named* Rājya-vardhana. That lord of the earth well protected his realm. Righteously ruled, the realm, increased day by day in population and prosperity. While Dama's son was king, his citizens joyfully thrived, without impediment, disease, danger from serpents, or drought. He perfomed grand sacrifices, and gave gifts to all who asked; he even enjoyed sensory delight without straying from the path of righteousness (MkP 109.4–8).

While righteously ruling his kingdom, properly protecting his people, 7,000 years passed away as if a single day. One day, his queen, the noble Māninī, began to weep. After being repeatedly questioned by Rājyavardhana as to the cause of her distress, she finally confessed she was weeping because she spotted a gray hair among the king's ample locks of hair. With a smile, he addresses his wife, along with the nobles and citizens gathered at the court, as follows:

> Do away with your grief, beautiful lady. Do not weep. All living beings experience birth, growth, and decline. O *lady* of finest countenance, I have studied the Vedas; I have offered thousands of sacrifices; I have given *alms* to the brahmans; I have begotten sons; I have enjoyed along your side pleasures hardly available to most mortals; I have protected the earth well; I have proven myself in battle; I have laughed with my beloved

> friends; I have sported in the midst of the woods. What else is there left for me to do that you should be frightened by my grey hairs, my lady? Let my hair become grey! Let wrinkles come, O beautiful one! Let my body pass into weakness! For, I have been successful, O Manini! Now that you've spotted a grey hair on my head, O lady, then I shall take leave for the forest. In childhood, one undertakes a child's activities; likewise, in youth and in manhood; likewise, yet, does one resort to the forest in old age. Such was the path of my fore-fathers, and so too will be my path. I see no reason for tears. Away with your grief. This grey hair gives me joy, so please do not weep.

The nobles and citizens in attendance showed reverence to the king, as they address him with conciliatory words. They lament his impending departure for the forest, and declare they will accompany him and that all sacred rites will come to a halt once he takes up residence in the forest. They beseech him to abandon thos course of action since it obstructs dharma (*dharmopadghāthāya*). Crucial for our purposes is to note that their concerns fall squarely within the parameters of *pravṛtti dharma*, spanning Vedic religious rituals and the institution of kingship. What they say at the conclusion of their appeal is the smoking ideological gun: the merit he would earn performing austerities in the forest for the remainder of his life would be worth only one sixteenth of the merit he has amassed safeguarding the world as a righteous king. Compare this ratio also to the fifteen-sixteenths of his power that the Sun gives to Viśvakarman to forge protective weapons for the gods. Yet, the unabashed prioritization of *pravṛtti dharma* on behalf of the citizenship, the king must preserve and personify both strands of dharma's double helix. He therefore replies in an ironically sagacious, detached manner explaining to his citizens that he has already fulfilled his worldly duty (protecting the earth, begetting children), and now it is his time to heed the message from Death (his gray hair), install his son as king, abandon worldly pleasures, and head to the forest (MkP 109.34–37).

In the hope of departing for the forest, the king consulted his court astrologers for an auspicious time to anoint his son as ruler of the kingdom. But, on hearing this sad news of the king's looming departure, they confess that are too upset to figure out the correct timing. Although they are skilled and versed with the scriptures, they confess, voices choked by tears, that their learning has evaporated upon hearing the grievous news. This might make for an ideal place for erudite exposition on the spiritual imperative to detach oneself from debilitating emotion (as with the distraught, disenfranchised merchant and king of the DM who do in fact receive such teachings), but the MkP has something else in mind, something much more world-affirming. The masses arrive from far and wide, and, quivering with emotion, implore their king to be gracious and continue protecting them as they have been protected in past. They explain that the world will sink should he renounce, and that they simply cannot bear the thought of a throne bereft of his royal presence (MkP 109.41–44). Brahmanas, nobles, ministers all appeal to the king, again and again, but he remains determined to take up residence in the force, stating that Death would have it no other way. His ministers, dependants, citizens, brahmans and aged men assembled together and take counsel, thinking on what must be done. Devoutly attached to that most righteous king, they resolve to propitiate the Sun with austerities, and beseech him for the life of the king (MkP 109.45–49).

Firm in their resolution, they resort to various means of worshipping the Sun: some make arghya offerings; others recite Ṛig, Yajus and Saman hymns; abstaining from food, lying down on river sandbanks, weary with austerities; some performed fire sacrifices, reciting hymns; others stared directly at the orb of the Sun (MkP 109.50–54). As they strive to worship the Sun, a gandharva named Sudāman comes by and advised them that the Sun will become pleased to grant their desires should they worship him in a forest named Guruviśālā, frequented by the Siddhas, in the very mountainous Kāmarūpa Mountains. And so, they go there (MkP 109.55–56). Upon entering the forest, the worshippers find a gorgeous sacred shrine to the Sun there. Tirelessly fasting, they worshipped there with flowers, sandal paste, incense, fragrances, food, flame, recitations and sacrificial oblations; with composed minds, they praised the Sun, worshipping him all the while (MkP 109.59–61). They offer this hymn to the Sun:

> The brahmans spoke:
>
> 62 Let us approach the Sun as our refuge, the god who in splendor surpasses gods, Danavas and Yakshas, the planets, and the heavenly bodies;
>
> 63 the lord of gods, who dwelling also in the sky makes everything around brilliant, and penetrates the earth and the atmosphere with bis rays;
>
> 64 even him who has the names Aditya, Bhaskara, Bhanu, Savitṛi, Divakara, Pushan and Aryaman, Svar-bbanu;
>
> 65 him who has flaming rays, who is the fire which shall destroy the universe at the end of the four-ages, difficult to be gazed at, who persists to the end of the final dissolution; the lord of yogins, and the never-ending one; who is red, yellow, white and black;
>
> 66 him who dwells in the oblation made to Fire by ṛishis, and among the gods of sacrifice; imperishable, sublime, secret, who is the supreme gate to final emancipation from existence;
>
> 67 and who traverses the sky with hymns in the form of horses which are yoked together at his rising and setting; who is always intent on circumambulating Meru reverently.
>
> 68 And we have sought unto the light-giver, who is not true and yet true, who is a sacred multiform place of pilgrimage, who is the permanence of the universe, and is beyond thought;
>
> 69 him who is Brahma, who is Siva, who is Vishṇu, who is Praja-pati; who is the wind, the atmosphere and water, the earth and its mountains and oceans;

> 70 who is the planets, the constellations, the moon and other heavenly bodies, trees bearing blossom and fruit, other trees and herbs; who sets in motion righteousness and unrighteousness,' among created beings, those which are manifest and those which are not manifest.
>
> 71 Brahma's body, and Śiva's, and Vishnu's is the body, of thee, the Sun, whose special nature is three-fold indeed.
>
> 72 May the Sun be gracious! May the Sun, of whom, as lord without beginning, all this world composes the body, and who is the the life of the worlds – may he be gracious to us!
>
> 73 May the Sun, whose first form is luminous and can hardly be gazed upon because of its circle of splendour, and whose second form is the gentle lunar orb – may he be gracious to us!
>
> 74 And may the Sun, from those two forms of whom this universe has been fashioned consisting of Agni and Soma – may he, the god, be gracious to us!"
>
> (MkP 109 62–74) (Pargiter 1904, 581–2)

Once they worshipped him in full faith for three long months, the blessed Sun is pleased, and descends to display himself before them, in all his effulgence. The brāhmaṇas trembled with joy, and, bowing down in devotion, prostrate before the Sun, declaring: "we bow to you, O thousand-rayed Sun! Be gracious, o you who are the cause of everything; who are invoked for protection from harm; who are the site of all sacrifices; who are meditated upon by the yogis" (MkP 109.75–78).

### *2.1.5.2 Canto 110. King Rājyavardhana hymns the Sun*

Pleased by their worship, the Sun offers them a boon of their choosing, to which they requested that their king (Rājyavardhana) live 10,000 years, in good health, vast wealth, perpetual in his youth, and victorious over his enemies. The Sun grants their boon, and they joyfully reported what happened to their king (MkP 110.1–6).

Queen Māninī rejoices at the news, though the king ponders it awhile in silence. Māninī turns to her husband and joyfully exclaims, "How fortunate is this! May you prosper, my king, with long life!" But the king makes no reply, his mind numb with thought. She again addresses him, but he is lost in thought, his head cast down. She asks why he is not happy at this most fortunate time, given, after all, that he is to live free from sickness, in enduring youth for 10,000 years (MkP 110.7–12). The king scoffs at her congratulatory address on the bass that he has actually been granted 1,000 afflictions being made to live on for 10,000 years, forced to watch as calamity befalls everyone around him. He explains that he will be made to witness the deaths of sons, grandsons, great-grandsons and indeed all known relations, servants and friends. There will be no end to his grief; indeed, he will have to watch die the very same men undertaking penance for his longevity (MkP 110.13–18).

The SM authors here undertake an incredible manoeuvre, appropriating the ethos of 'all is suffering' innate to *nivṛtti* for the purposes of *pravṛtti*. The Sun departs for the mountains to undertake austerities and worship the Sun in search of a remarkable boon.

> Since, through his grace, I will live in enduring youth free from sickness for ten thousand years, I will continue ruling the kingdom tasting enjoyments with delight if the illustrious Sun grant us this boon: that all *my* people, *my* servants, you, my sons, grandsons and great-grandsons, and *my* friends *shall also* live ten thousand years! If the Sun does not grant this, Māninī, I will undertake austerities, abstaining from food until I perish.
>
> (MkP 110.21–26)

The Queen approves and even accompanies him to the mountaintop. They both enter the same Sun temple where the brāhmaṇas earned their boon, and ardently worship the Sun. They become emaciated through their fasting, practising severe austerities, enduring cold, wind and the Sun's own heat. After over a year of such austerities, the Sun is pleased and grants them the boon they seek, for the welfare of dependants, subjects, citizens and sons (MkP 110.27–31).

Upon gaining the boon, the king returnes to his city to rule his kingdom with joy, righteously protecting his people. He performs sacrifices, and performs charity day and night. Righteous and wise, he enjoys life in Māninī's company at the royal court, rejoicing with his sons, grandsons and descendents, along with his servants and citizens for 10,000 years, remaining youthful all the while. This tale celebrates the colossal power wielded by devout worship of the Sun, whereby King Rājyavardhana gains long-lived prosperity for his people and himself (MkP 110.32–36). Here ends the SM proper: the remaining verses of the Canto are dedicated to Mārkaṇḍeya extolling to his audience the merits of reciting the SM (MkP 110.37–43). Moreover, Mārkaṇḍeya commences the following Canto capping his exposition of the supremacy of the Sun, stating "such is the power of the divine Sun, without beginning or end, concerning whose majesty, you had asked. He is the Supreme Soul of the yogis who deeply contemplate on the state of yoga. He is the kṣetra-jña among those Samkhya seekers, and the lord of sacrifices among those who sacrifice. Brahmā, Viṣnu and Śiva support his supremacy" (MkP 111.1–3). Mārkaṇḍeya makes it clear he is moving on to other topics, but not without auspiciously concluding his monumental homage to the Sun.

### *2.1.6 The Goddess, the Sun and the story of Sāmba*

As outlined in Chapter 1, *the* quintessential Saura text is the *Sāmba Purāṇa*, most probably a source of inspiration for the authors of the SM. The story of Kṛṣṇa's son Sāmba is perhaps one of the best examples of the extent to which a character's story (at least in the world of Indian myth) goes far beyond any one textual account of that story. Rather than residing in a single text, the story transcends its individual iterations, each of which serve as snippets of a larger saga, like multiple peepholes towards a drama too vast to view from a single vantage point. While it is opaque as to why the Saura authors of ancient India would elect Kṛṣṇa's son as their narrative hero, particularly in light of the lunar associations of Kṛṣṇa, there is a tantalizing Śākta thread to Sāmba's tale, which is significant for this study in light of the Saura–Śākta ideological symbiosis it proposes.

The MBh relays the story of Sāmba's birth in the Anuśāsanaparvan during a decidedly Śaiva patch of text (13.14–16), one in fact culminating in the sahasranāmastotra praising Śiva (13.17). Kṛṣṇa performs great tapas to Śiva in Upamanyu's Himalayan hermitage in order to obtain a son. He goes there at the behest of his wife, Jāmbavatī, whose longing for a son was instigated by her co-wife Rukmiṇī giving Kṛṣṇa several sons. Pleased by Kṛṣṇa's tapas, Śiva appears. But he does not appear alone. Śiva appears before Kṛṣṇa alongside his feminine consort: there

> stood the Lord in his full glory of heat, energy and beauty together with the Goddess, his blazing wife. There the Holy One, the Great Lord, shone together with the Goddess like the sun united with the moon in the midst of a cloud.
>
> (von Simson 2007, 236) (13.15.8–9)

Śiva and the Goddess together appear to grant Kṛṣṇa's boon. It is in fact the Goddess who announces that her husband has granted him a son who will be known as Sāmba (13.16.5). Why would this be? According to von Simson (von Simson 2007), this "whole arrangement is apparently meant to give a hint as to the name's meaning: 'Sāmba' can be understood as a *bahuvrīhi* compound derived from *sa* + *ambā*, meaning '(Lord Śiva) accompanied by the Mother (i.e. his consort Umā)' " (von Simson 2007, 236). The Śiva Purāṇa's account of the story of Sāmba in fact makes this connection even more explicitly, stating that it was 'Śiva Sāmba', who appeared at the end of the rainy season to grant Kṛṣṇa a son subsequently named Sāmba (von Simson 2007, 236).

Aside from the boon of his birth, the *Mahābhārata* includes only one additional episode of this otherwise invisible character. Sāmba plays a key role in bringing about the fulfillment of Kuntī's curse, that is, the destruction of Kṛṣṇa's entire clan (the Vṛṣṇis). The story runs as follows. The sages Viśvāmitra, Kaṇva and Nārada visit Dvārakā, home of the Vṛṣṇis. During their visit, some young men decide to play a prank: they disguise Kṛṣṇa's son Sāmba as a woman and present him as the pregnant wife of one of the other men, Babhru. They have the audacity to ask the sages after the nature of Sāmba's unborn child. In response, they receive a curse, that is, that Sāmba will birth an iron club, which will lead to the destruction of the Vṛṣṇis (MBh 16.2.4–9).

Georg von Simson examines Sāmba's association with lunar mythology. Sāmba can also be considered as related to Soma (the moon, and Sa Umā), again invoking the interplay of Śiva "with the Goddess". Sāmba, the son of the lunar lord Kṛṣṇa, himself represents Sun conjoined the Moon, or a time of New Moon. His birth was the result of a blessing of Lord Śiva who appeared alongside the Goddess (sā+ambā=sāmba). Moreover, Sāmba loses his lustre (to leprosy) and regains it from the Sun in the *Sāmba Purāṇa*, like the moon passing from newness to fullness during its waxing cycle. According to von Simson:

> All this confirms our hypothesis that Sāmba represents the conjunction of sun and moon at the new-moon period. This is the point when the sun has withdrawn its splendour (light) from the moon, or, in terms of the myth, Sāmba is struck by leprosy. Correspondingly, the sun is about to start casting its splendour upon the moon again, meaning that Sāmba has to win the sun god's favour to get rid of the disease.
>
> (von Simson 2007, 245)

That the quintessential *Saura Purāṇa* revolves around the story of Sāmba can by no means be insignificant. There are no shortage of solar stories in Vedic and epic lore from which they could have drawn. The fact that they chose the product of Śiva "accompanied by the Goddess" (Sāmba) as their mythological calling card seems to add credence to an interplay between Goddess and Sun in ancient times. However, circumstantial the evidence is here connecting Śākta and Saura traditions through the story of Sāmba, one cannot dismiss the glaring parallels in the two *māhātmyas* of the MkP, discussed below.

## 2.2 Saura–Śākta symbiosis

There are a number of intriguing parallels between Mārkaṇḍeya's Saura *māhātmya* and its Śākta counterpart. With respect to form, the glorification of the Goddess assembled into the MkP's *manvantara* section occupies precisely one fourth of its allotted cantos (see Table 2.3).[3]

*Table 2.3* The Manu-intervals (*manvantaras*) of the *Mārkaṇḍeya Purāṇa*

| *Canto* | *MV Subsection* | *Manu* |
|---|---|---|
| 53 | 1st MV | Svāyambhuva |
| 54–60 | Geography | NA |
| 61–68 | 2nd MV | Svārociṣa |
| 69–73 | 3rd MV | Auttama |
| 74 | 4th MV | Tāmasa |
| 75 | 5th MV | Raivata |
| 76 | 6th MV | Cākṣuṣa |
| 77–79 | 7th MV | Vaivasvata |

*continued*

*Table 2.3* continued

| *Canto* | *MV Subsection* | *Manu* |
|---|---|---|
| 80 | 8th MV | Sāvarṇi (Sūrya) |
| 81–93 | *Devī Māhātmya* | NA |
| 94 (4–10) | 9th MV | Sāvarṇi (Dakṣa) |
| 94 (11–16) | 10th MV | Sāvarṇi (Brahmā) |
| 94 (17–21) | 11th MV | Sāvarṇi (Dharma) |
| 94 (22–31) | 12th MV | Sāvarṇi (Rudra) |
| 95–98 | 13th MV | Raucya |
| 99–100 | 14th MV | Bhautya |

*Table 2.4* The royal dynasties (*vaṃśānucarita*) of the *Mārkaṇḍeya Purāṇa*

| *Canto* | *V Subsection* | *King* |
|---|---|---|
| 101.1–8 | V | INTRO |
| 101.9–110 | SM | NA → Rājyavardhana |
| 11–136 | V | Several |

This makes for an intriguing parallel: the glorification of the Sun 'interrupts' the MkP's genealogy section (directly following the *manvantara* section), also occupying precisely one fourth of *its* respective chapters (see Table 2.4).[4]

The Purāṇas claim that their genre is distinguished by "five marks" (*pañcalakṣaṇas*) as indicated by the fifth-century Sanskrit lexicon, *Amarakośa*. While the *Amarakośa* does not specifically indicate what these five distinguishing features are, several Purāṇas detail the "five marks" to be: *sarga* (creation or evolution of the universe), *pratisarga* (re-creation of the universe after its periodic dissolution), *vaṃśa* (genealogies of gods, patriarchs, sages, and kings), *manvantara* ("Manu-intervals" – cosmic cycles – each of which is presided over by a Manu, a primordial patriarch), and *vaṃśānucarita* (accounts of royal dynasties) (Coburn 1985, 21).

The MkP provides an account of Manu-intervals (*manvantaras*) – intervals of cosmic time over which a primordial patriarch, a Manu, rules supreme. There are fourteen Manu-intervals of each cosmic cycle (*kalpa*), and we are currently in the reign of the seventh Manu, Vaivasvata. Each *manvantara* takes the name of its presiding Manu, thus the current age is known as the *vaivasvata-manvantara,* the age of the primordial patriarch, Vaivasvata. Sāvarṇi is destined to be the future Manu of the next age of this cycle of creation. The tales of the Goddess are therefore part of the story of Sāvarṇi, who is destined to be the future Manu of the next age of this cycle of creation.

Furthermore, each *māhātmya* contains four hymns to its respective deity, followed by a *phalaśruti* section occurring beyond the fourth and final hymn in each case. While the fact that each *māhātmya* is spurred on by the intrigue of a questioner is ubiquitous for its genre (in the case of the DM, King Suratha questions Sage Medhas, while in the case of the SM, Krauṣṭuki questions Sage Mārkaṇḍeya), what is noteworthy is the fact that each interlocutor interjects to request further details, which succeeds in calling forth the final episode in each case. In the case of the SM, Krauṣṭuki interjects to ask for more details as follows:

> Adorable Sir! Thou has well declared the birth of the Sun's offspring, the majesty of the primeval god and his nature at very full length. Nevertheless I desire, O best of munis, to hear more about the Sun's majesty comprehensively; deign therefore with favour to tell me of it.
>
> (MkP 109.1) (Pargiter 1904, 577)

Mārkaṇḍeya responds: "Be it heard then! I tell thee of the majesty of the primeval god, Vivasvat, what he did formerly when worshipped by mankind" (MkP 109.3) (Pargiter 1904, 577). Similarly, in the DM, Suratha interjects (89.1–2):

> It is simply wonderful that you, O blessed one, have told me this Māhātmya of the Goddess's activity connected with the slaying of Raktabīja. I want to hear more, about what Śumbha and the outraged Niśumbha did when Raktabīja was killed.
>
> (Coburn 1991, 68)

In the case of Krauṣṭuki's interjection, it occurs at a natural break in the narrative, where not only has an entire episode been completed, but one could understand why Krauṣṭuki would get the impression that Mārkaṇḍeya was done with glorifying the Sun since he finishes the last episode with a mini-phalaśruti as follows: "This story of the majesty of the primeval god, the high-souled Mārtaṇḍa, when listened to, quells the sin that has been committed by day or night" (MkP 108.29) (Pargiter 1904, 576). In the case of Suratha's interjection, however, Medhas is in the middle of the greater episode of the tyranny of Śumbha and Niśumbha, having only completed a sub-episode of the slaying of Raktabīja. There is no indication that Medhas would not have gone on anyhow, and I have therefore long been puzzled by the presence of the seemingly entirely superfluous interjection. It must serve some purpose in advancing the narrative, because the speaker is already in medias res of his narrative, so it makes little sense that he would be interrupted to continue it. I would like to suggest that while Suratha's interjection serves no particular purpose with respect to the narrative unfolding of the DM, it does serves a purpose with respect to mirroring the form of the SM. Regardless of this potential causal relationship, these interjections occur between the third and fourth hymn of their respective *māhātmya*.

Even more so than their formal features, the content of each of these *māhātmya*s bespeaks of an intended parity between Sun and Goddess. First, there is a movement among the episodes – descending from the cosmic sphere at the time of creation, to the heavenly sphere, to the terrestrial sphere – which is mirrored in each. The first portion of each *māhātmya* establishes the cosmic supremacy of its respective deity insofar as Brahmā himself praises each deity as a self-existent supreme cosmic principle, invoking them for the sake of preserving the universe. This is followed in each text by its deity being called upon to save the gods of heaven. In the SM, we are told that since the gods (devas) "were vanquished for a thousand divine years, and the powerful daityas and dānavas were victorious" (MkP 104.14) (Pargiter 1904, 560), that Aditi, the mother of the gods, "seeing her sons cast out and robbed of the three worlds by the Daityas and Danavas … and deprived of their shares of sacrifices, was exceedingly afflicted with grief, and made the utmost efforts to propitiate the Sun" (MkP 104.15) (Pargiter 1904, 560). She earns a boon by hymning the Sun, and asks that he be born in her womb so as to aid his then would-be brothers, the gods, in gaining victory. As with the DM, it is necessary to contextualize this second episode (where the Sun takes birth in Aditi's womb at her behest) with the first episode so that we properly understand that the Sun here is being manifested, not created. But this clarity would be obscured were it not to follow episode one which unambiguously establishes the Sun a status beyond birth and death. The same is true in Episode II of the DM where one would think that the goddess was actually being "created" by the gods (since she emerges from the fire of their wrath), rather than merely manifesting therefrom. Both texts include this "heavenly throne" episode (in the DM, the Devī again saves the gods from perilous demons, and in the SM, we hear of the episode of the solar family as occurring in 78 and 79), before concluding by reestablishing the reign of an earthly king – Rājyavardhana in the SM and Sauratha in the DM.

That Goddess and Sun readily stand to represent preservation is fairly intuitive, and has been specifically argued herein. What is most crucial for our purposes is that their commitment to preservation is expressed not only in their personal acts of cosmic protection and governance, but in their consecration of kings, earthly emblems of preservation. As such, both DM and SM conclude with coronations: both moved by the steadfast austerities of their respective devotees, the Goddess restores the sovereignty of King Suratha in the DM, and the Sun restores the reign of King Rājyavardhana[5] in the SM. The latter of these kings deserves special attention at this juncture, for his plight (and the boon counteracting that plight) is most unusual, and most telling indeed. After reigning prosperously, and protecting the earth for 7,000 years, King Rājyavardhana's Queen, Mānini, finds a grey hair upon his head (which in classical Indian treatises signals that a householder should retreat to the forest to commence his forest-hermit stage of life) and she therefore greatly laments. The king stoically reminds her that they have been quite prosperous and pious, and that death is inevitable, and she should not weep. The citizens, too, protest at their pending loss of a king (though Rājyavardhana has an heir who he would happily install). The entire citizenry take to propitiating the Sun in order that King Rājyavardhana may have an increased life span and after three months of their collective penance, the Sun appears and grants them a boon, to which they ask, "if thou art pleased with our faith, then let our king live ten thousand years, free from sickness, victorious over his enemies, rich in his treasury, and with firmly-enduring youth! May Rājyavardhana live ten thousand years!" (MkP 110.3–4) (Pargiter 1904, 583–4). The Sun of course grants the boon and then it is the king's turn to lament that he should greatly outlive all of his loved ones, and generations of his descendants, and suffer bitterly for it. Rājyavardhana then resolves to journey to the mountains and practice austerities to earn from the Sun the boon that the entire kingdom should also live 10,000 years. After over a year of penance, the Sun grants the king's wish, and he lives happily ever after for 10,000 years.

This episode pays no attention to the fact that all invoked would theoretically end up in exactly the same turmoil in 10,000 years as they did at the beginning. It is so intent on celebrating life, that it glosses over the inevitability of death. It is an unabashed homage to *pravṛtti*, eclipsing the wisdom of *nivṛtti* religion. To touch upon a real-life correlate, when one decides to acquire a pet, one knows within them that the pet is not immortal, and that in all probability, will predecease its owner. Yet, one finds it worthwhile to indulge the desire to enjoy whatever time might be allotted with the pet, irrespective of the price one incurs through suffering the inevitable loss of that pet. Likewise, the austerities of king and citizenry alike are worth the temporary respite from the clutches of death. It is a tributary which sings with abandon the praises of preservation, and the enjoyment of life in this world, as represented by the preservation of king, kingdom, and citizenry. Rājyavardhana literally translates to "Increased Sovereignty",[6] a sovereignty to be increased by 10,000 years to be exact. But his tale not only serves to augment the length of one of the kings in the solar dynasty, but also serves to increase the appreciation of *pravṛttic* esteem for all things worldly, hoisting it, in this case, to a status more coveted than life everlasting a la *nivṛttic* liberation. Thus, the Rājyavardhana episode adorns the SM as its terminal frame, which itself (along with the DM) serves to celebrate (necessarily temporary) preservation, rather than transcendence of this realm, and befits the discourse of Mārkaṇḍeya, the only known embodied being to be preserved in flesh within this realm across the cosmic cycles of creation and destruction.

The association between these two *māhātmya*s of the MkP is undeniable, and attests to an affinity between the ways in which they portray their objects of laudation. Goddess and Sun are united insofar as their respective grandeurs serve as fonts of universal preservation, but in excess, their might becomes dangerous to the point of imperilling the world that they create. Like the Indian king, the Sun is life-giving and supportive, but so overpowering, that one can barely withstand the direct sight of it. Thus, though "this universe became most stainless then through the sudden destruction of darkness" (MkP 102.12) (Pargiter 1904, 555) because of the fire of the Sun, it is that same light which causes Brahmā to think to himself, while creating the universe, "My creation although accomplished will assuredly pass to destruction through the intense glory of the Sun" (MkP 103.12) (Pargiter 1904, 556), and so resolves to hymn the Sun, in the final verse of which he requests: "Contract thy glory, since the abundance of thy glory tends to obstruct creation, O lord, and I am ready to begin creation!" (MkP 103.12) (Pargiter 1904, 558). Sūrya's excessive power in the form of his *tejas* needs to be subdued at the behest of Brahmā, Aditi, and Viśvakarman. But this excessive *tejas*, upon being pared down, is harnessed for the welfare of the universe in the crafting of divine weaponry.[7] By Mastsunami's count, this solar story occurs at a staggering sixteen Purāṇic junctures alone (Matsunami 1977, 218–19),[8] not counting the *Mahābhārata* and later literature. What he says of the MkP is most telling:

> the Mārkaṇḍeya Purāṇa has the peculiarity of introducing in the middle of this legend lauds in praise of the Sun, an addition that seems to be based on devotion. The beginning of the legend seems to be lost in this Purāṇa, and generally there are many lacunae if compared with the other Purāṇas.
> (Matsunami 1977, 222)

In examining "the myth" out of context, he loses sight of the brilliant manner in which the MkP harnesses this solar story.

Let us unpack the concept of "*tejas*", which is crucial not only to the narrative unfolding of the myth but to the essence, and ironically, to the inimicality of the Sun. Deriving from the verbal root *tij* – to "be or become sharp" (Monier-Williams *et al*. 2008) – the sharpness (*tejas*) of the Sun carries with it, in Sanskrit, similar connotations as in English, namely, sharpness of visual appearance, along with sharpness of personality. As such, it may mean "splendor", "fiery energy", along with "impatience, fierceness, energetic opposition" (Monier-Williams *et al*. 2008). Similarly, the adjective *tīkṣṇa*, derived from the same verbal root, may mean, for example, sharp, hot, or vehement. Regarding its laudatory dimension, *tejas* (of which the Sun has plenty) may also connote "spiritual or moral or magical power or influence, majesty, dignity, glory, authority" (Monier-Williams *et al*. 2008). While the Sun-god, Sūrya, has several epithets even in Purāṇic times (e.g. Āditya, Bhāskara, Bhānu, Savitṛ, Divakara, Pūshan and Aryamān, Svarbhānu are listed at MkP 109.64), this myth is tied specifically to the Sun's identity as Vivasvat. Both his first son and our age (named after that Manu) are known as Vaivasvata, "of Vivasvat". Hence, we are currently residing in the Vaivasvata Manvantara, The Manu-Epoch of Vivasvat. It might be worthwhile then, to come to know the meaning of Vivasvat. According to Monier-Williams, Vivasvat specifically translates in general as "shining forth, diffusing light", and in specific reference to the epithet of the Sun, as "The Brilliant One". It should come as no surprise that this myth is concerned with the lustre and thus illustriousness, of the Sun.

This notion of *tejas* is also directly tied to classical Indian discourse of kingship, therefore solidifying the association between solar and sovereign. According to Manu "like the sun among the gods in the celestial regions which destroys darkness by its *tejas* (brilliance-and-energy), the king (among men) eradicates sin from the earth." Manu further states that "nobody on earth is able even to gaze at him" (Gonda 1969, 25). Further still, "like the sun he possesses *tejas*, the supranormal principle of might, which enables him to perform great exploits" (Gonda 1969, 26). In episode II of the DM, the Goddess is said to derive from the *tejas* of the assembly of gods which is clearly mirrored by Manu's mythic account of the birthing of the primordial king; again born of the *tejas* of the gods. During this encounter, when all of the gods were bequeathing the Goddess with their weaponry, we are told that "the sun put his own rays into all the pores of her skin" (DM 2.23; see Coburn 1991, 41), which presumably would accord her with a lustre comparable to his own, one which is powerful and captivating, but dangerous to engage head-on. That the Goddess is associated with the kingly notion of *tejas* is hardly surprising given her role firstly as universal sovereign, and second, as one who safeguards and consecrates the office of the king in both heavenly and terrestrial realms. The DM casts the Goddess as sovereignty incarnate; that supreme power of preservation which gods and rulers borrow for the sake of protecting and supporting the cosmos and this world.[9]

The destructive imagery of the Sun is echoed in the story of the Sun's charioteer, Aruṇa, relayed in the *Mahābhārata*. The *Mahābhārata* narrates the tale of the co-wives of Kaśyapa, the daughters of Brahmā Kadrū and Vinatā. Having both been granted boons by Kaśyapa, Kadrū those 1,000 serpent sons whole Vinatā chose two sons, each possessing the strength of Kadrū's sons. Kadrū laid 1,000 eggs, while Vinatā laid two, each tended for 500 years at which point Kadrū's sons came forth. Envious and impatient, Vinatā prematurely cracked open one of her eggs in which she found a son, Aruṇa, whose upper body was formed, and lower body yet unformed. The son then cursed Vinatā to be enslaved to Kadrū for another 500 years, to be freed by the offspring of the second egg, Garuḍa, who would be invincible unless she prematurely terminates his gestation as well. Upon cursing Vinatā, Aruṇa then flies up to the heavens to serve as Sūrya's charioteer, himself the red dawn personified (MBh 1.14). Garuḍa emerges from his shell "ablaze like a kindled mass of fire" growing in power so as to terrify the gods with his fiery presence that the gods mistake him for fire itself. One line of the gods' subsequent praise of Garuḍa reads: "Just as the wrathful sun may burn the creatures./Thus dost thou devour them like the fire of sacrifice" (MBh I.20.12) (van Buitenen 1973, I: 78). And when he had been praised by the Gods and the hosts of seers, he withdrew his heat.

Twice during the DM, the imagery of the Sun is invoked to represent weaponry. During Episode II's climactic battle between the Devī and Mahīṣa, the great demon hurls a flaming weapon at the Goddess "as if it were the disc of the sun with shimmerings from the sky" (DM 3.8; see Coburn 1991, 45). Similarly, while Kālī (shortly after her first appearance in the text) engages the demons Caṇḍa and Muṇḍa, they launch a fury of arrows which "resembled a multitude of suns entering into the middle of [the] black cloud" of her gaping mouth (DM 7.17) (Coburn 1991, 62). We also hear of fire-clad weaponry, reminiscent of the Sun: "the spear that was released by Śumbha as he approached, terrible with its flames, Coming on like a great fire mass, that spear she hurled down with her firebrand." (DM 9.23) It is noteworthy that in all three of these instances, the weapons being launched are on behalf of the demonic forces, underscoring not only their power, but also their danger. These weapons represent the disruption of the cosmic order, which the Sun in its benign form ironically, is understood to uphold. It is telling that in his exploration of the epithet Caṇḍī as the angry, terrible or passionate one, the great DM commentator Bhāskararāya "notes how such language is conventionally used to talk about that which overwhelms, such as the terrible summer sun" (Coburn 1991, 134). This is also reminiscent of the fiery imagery of Durgā we see in Taittirīya Āraṇyaka 10 (duplicated in Ṛg Vedic Khila, Rātrī Sūkta 4.2.13) as follows:

> In her who has the color of Agni,
> flaming with ascetic power (tapas),
> the offspring of Virocana (vairocani)
> who delights in the fruits of one's actions.
> In the goddess Durgā do I take refuge;
> O one of great speed, (well) do you navigate.
> Hail (to you)!
>
> (Coburn 1985, 119)

In the climactic portion of Episode III, when the Goddess succeeds in defeating the great demon Śumbha, the text tells us that "The flaming clouds of portent that formerly had gathered became tranquil, And rivers once again flowed within their banks" (DM 10.24; see Coburn 1991, 73). The death of demonic discord (as personified by the tyrannical asura) coincides with the restoration of harmony, a time when the "whole universe became soothed, regaining its natural condition once more, and the sky became spotless" (DM 10.25; see Coburn 1991, 73). This moment of cosmic relief occasioned the joyous outpourings of song and dance on behalf of the celestial beings. Then "favorable winds began to blow, and the sun shone brilliantly [and] the sacred fires blazed peacefully" (DM 10.27–28) (Coburn 1991, 73). While the destructive imagery of fire is invoked by the flaming clouds of portent, once balance was restored, the sky became spotless, and the Sun – here used as the symbol of preservation and order – shone brightly. The restoration of balance represented by the shining Sun is mirrored in the line immediately following it, by the peacefully blazing ritual fires.

With respect to the relationship between *tejas* and the Goddess herself, we encounter an inversion in the DM: while the Sun's *tejas* creates weapons for the gods, it is the gods' *tejas* which creates weapons for the Goddess in the DM. The inverted motif of excessive *tejas* is also used in the manifestation of the Devī herself. At the beginning of Episode II, the host of gods, cast out of heaven by Mahīṣa and his demon hordes, complain to Viṣṇu and Śiva from whose anger-knitted brows great *tejas* emerges. This *tejas*, combined with that emitted from the bodies of all of the gods, coalesces to form the luminous form of the Devī herself. The momentous passage reads:

> And from the bodies of the other gods, Indra and the others,
> Came forth a great fiery splendor, and it became unified in one place.

> An exceedingly fiery mass like a flaming mountain
> did the gods see there, filling the firmament with flames.
> That peerless splendor, born from the bodies of all the gods.
> Unified and pervading the triple world with its lustre, became a woman.
> (DM 2.10–12) (Coburn 1991, 40)

And this inversion points to a greater inversion implicated in how the Sun and Goddess themselves are construed.

These glorifications not only run parallel to each other, but also serve as composite tales of the interplay and potency of shadow and light. These *māhātmya*s are the inverse of each other in much the same way that Chāyā is the inverse of Saṃjñā, or as Twilight is the inverse of Dawn. While, in the inaugural episode of the *Sūrya Māhātmya*, the universe is imperiled by the Sun's unbearable brilliance, in the case of the DM, it is imperiled by the Goddess' darkness of sleep over the eyes of Viṣṇu. And while the wrath of the Sun is expressed through his overbearing fire, the excessive power of the Devī is personified in her wrathful, destructive, shadow-ego, Kālī, the Dark One herself. In both cases, the powerful aspects of these deities which threaten the universe, and Brahmā must subdue at the dawn of creation (splendour for the Sun and darkness for the Goddess), menacingly rise up in subsequent episodes in their *māhātmya*s. The artistry of vision on behalf of the authors of the DM is exhibited in their ability to articulate the paradoxical totality of the Goddess, who, unlike the Sun, requires not consorts to express her powers of illumination and occlusion alike, and requires no separate agency to neutralize her volatile aspect; Kālī is always neatly folded back into the contained persona of Durgā throughout the DM. It is the Sun's sharp brilliance, which causes Saṃjñā to leave, casting her shadow behind her – a shadow which cannot exist without the light of the Sun. The mythology of Sūrya is so crucial to the text that the frame narrative of the king in the forest is itself framed by this story of Sūrya; every single manuscript of the DM, including the ones which circulate independently of their Purāṇic contexts, refer to Sūrya in their very first[10] and very last verses.[11] Recall that the opening verse refers to how Sāvarṇi was blessed to become sovereign of an age by the power of Mahāmāyā (the 'great illusion'), which may be understood to correlate to his birthmother, Chāyā ('shadow'), as both of these manifestations representing the Goddess' aspect of occlusion. But insofar as the Goddess is supreme, she also can be said to present Sāvarṇi's sovereign progenitor, Sūrya, reconfigured in the MkP to represent the sole universal power. She thus exalts King Suratha in the closing frame of the DM to the rank of Manu through a future birthing, through the pair of opposites which She paradoxically embodies: darkness and light, fire and shadow.

The Goddess of the DM represents profound ambivalences, and yet ambivalence, by nature, encompasses a greater scope than uniformity possibly can. For any given attribute, an opposite may be conceived. To express totality is to express paradox of combined opposites as only narrative can. Omni-benevolence and omni-malevolence are individually limited concepts. To be all powerful, one must be able to be both of these, and even beyond both of these. Insofar as the project of DM and SM alike are to represent the totality of the powers that be in a single personality of godhead, they must equip that personality with expressions of the dual aspects of the universe, good and evil, shadow and light. Hence the Sun's two śaktis (each equally as aspects of his own nature), and the Goddess' dual nature: if she is the Mahādevī, she must also be Mahāsurī. Her greatness would be curtailed if described as one and not the other. Saṃjñā and Chāyā are one, though viewed from different perspectives. Furthermore, while the Sun requires two consorts to represent this profound ambivalence, the Goddess does not. The female consort represents the power which is possessed by the male god. Yet, to be equated with the total sum of all power is to be necessarily distanced from possessors of power. For both the possessor and the power he possesses is limited. No matter how large a vessel, it may only contain the ocean of power in limited capacity. That ocean will manifest in a form sufficiently powerful to surpass the strength of any given possessor of power. Therefore, the Goddess of the DM is not only the mother of power insofar as she is all-powerful, but insofar as she constitutes power itself. She is one and the same as the universal field of power from which all beings, benevolent and malevolent alike, draw for their respective purposes.

The SM teaches that the sole universal principle, though eternal and the source of all life, fathers not only humankind, but also fathers death. Though the nature of the Sun is fundamentally a supporting, luminous one, in order for his supremacy to be expressed, he must also be the creator of both shadow and death. Likewise, the Goddess of the DM is described both as the Great Goddess and the Great Demoness, as the power of confusion and clarity, bondage and liberation alike. In light of this parity between Goddess and Sun, the MkP can render the essential nature of the Goddess as a dark one no more than it can do so for the Sun. The stories of both deities entail the interplay between darkness and light, but it is abundantly clear the figures central to each of these myths are overarchingly celebrated as keepers of order, as sources of light. Let us therefore be reminded that the third set of twins to be birthed in the solar saga are the divine aśvins, appointed as celestial physicians. The Sun, ultimately concerned with the preservation of mortal beings, also fathers medicine, along with death. Furthermore, both myth cycles are explicitly tied to earthly sovereignty insofar as the DM concludes with the restoration of the earthly sovereignty of King Suratha, and so too, at the end of the *Sūrya Māhātmya*, we hear of King Rājyavardhana's kingdom restored by the grace of the Sun. While Goddess, King and Sun all possess fierce, dangerous, foreboding aspects, their central purpose is the work of preserving the welfare of gods and humans alike. And what better place to house such tales than in a compendium like the MkP, which remind us at its very inception that the purpose of Viṣṇu taking on human form is so that he may engage in the compassionate work of preservation.

*Table 2.5 Sūrya Māhātmya* episode chart

| | | | | | | |
|---|---|---|---|---|---|---|
| Intro | 98 | 101 | 27 | Vaṃśa Anukīrtana | Genealogies | Introduction to Sūrya |
| Ep. 1: Creation (37 verses) | 99 | 102 | 22 | *Mārtaṇḍa Māhātmya* | The Majesty of the Sun | Universe as aspects of Sūrya |
| | 100 | 103 | 15 | Āditya Stava | Hymn to the Sun (5–12) | Brahmā praises Sūrya |
| Ep. 2: Heaven (65 verses) | 101 | 104 | 38 | Divākara Stuti | Praise of the Sun (18–29) | Aditi praises Sun to defeat demons |
| | 102 | 105 | 27 | Mārtaṇḍa Utpatti | The Birth of Mārtaṇḍa | Birth of Mārtaṇḍa; Victory |
| RECAP: Family (105 verses) | 103 | 106 | 65 | Bhānu Tanu Lekhana | The paring down of the Sun's body | Sūrya–Saṃjñā–Chāyā |
| | 104 | 107 | 11 | Sūrya Stava | Hymn to the Sun (2–11) | Viśvakarman hymns Sun |
| | 105 | 108 | 29 | *Ravi Māhātmya Varṇa* | The Majesty of The Sun | Weapons made; equine reunion; |
| Ep. 3: Earth (121 verse) | 106 | 109 | 78 | Bhānu Stava | Praise of the Sun (62–74) | Brāhmaṇas praise Sūrya |
| | 107 | 110 | 43 | *Bhānu Māhātmya Varṇana* | The Majesty of the Sun | Sūrya blesses King Rājyavardhana |
| | | | 355 | | | |
| FAMILY (77 verses) | 74 | 77 | 42 | | Hymn (2–14) | |
| | 75 | 78 | 35 | | | |

## Notes

1 Saṃjñā is the daughter of Tvaṣṭṛ, also known as Viśvakarman, the divine architect-tinkerer figure who roughly correlates to Hephaestus of the Grecian mythological heavens.

2 The Harivaṃśa also tells this story (Brodbeck 2019, 25–8) with this following twist:

> Because of his innate fiery energy, Mārtaṇḍa Āditya's body had in act been born with its limbs burned right off, and it really didn't look too good. Kashyapa, who didn't know what had happened, said out of affection: "This child can't be dead (mṛta) while he's still in the egg (aṇḍa)." That's why Kashyapa's son is called Mārtaṇḍa Dead-Egg. But Kashyapa's son Vivasvat always had an extraordinary quanity of fiery energy, my boy, and he used it to roast the three worlds (8.3–5).
>
> (Brodbeck 2019, 25)

A couple key differences in this telling are its Tvaṣṭṛī who recommends the Sun is pared down (8.31), and that he uses the excess energy to craft Viṣṇu's discus (8.45).

3 See Pargiter 1904. The Manu section occupies forty-eight chapters (Chapters 53–100) of which twelve (Chapters 81–92) are dedicated to relaying the glorious exploits of the Goddess, while Canto 93 tells us of the fate of Suratha, see Appendix 5.3.

4 See Pargiter 1904. The genealogies section occupies thirty-six chapters (Chapters 101–136) of which nine (Chapters 102–110) are dedicated to glorifying the Sun proper, while Chapter 101 introduces the genealogies. For the hymn-cantos in isolation, see Appendix 5.3.

5 Rājyavardhana is actually the son of Dama, whose exploits conclude the genealogy section. It is, therefore, Rājyavardhana's, and not Dama's, exploits who comprise the tail end of the exploits of solar kings to be found in the MkP. And yet, the exploits of Rājyavardhana are not found where one would expect (immediately following those

of his father Dama), but rather, were assembled as the terminal frame of the SM, serving to showcase Sūrya's role in the expanse of the sovereignty of the solar line of kings, and the affirmation of longevity and life on earth. This is dually useful insofar as it allows the discourse to end with the exploits of Dama, which make for an excellent terminal frame of the MkP as a whole.

6 Rājya can also mean the actual kingdom, and so this epithet can also mean increased kingdom. This connotation is supported by the Vāyu Purāṇa, wherein, as Pargiter notes, "Rajya-vardhana is called Rāṣṭhra-vardhana" (Pargiter 1904, 577), and rāṣṭra refers more the physical realm under the sway of sovereignty rather than sovereignty itself. The name Rājya-vardhana can also be taken as a *bahuvrīhi* compound meaning "He whose kingdom prospers."

7 As Desai writes:

> from the pared off lustre, Tvaṣṭṛ made the weapons of gods, *e.g.* he made Śiva's trident, Viṣṇu's discus, Vasus śaṅkus, Agni's spear, Kubera's palanquin, Yama's rod and Kārtikeya's spear. He also made brilliant weapons of other gods, Yakṣas, Vidyādharas etc.
>
> (Desai 1968, 163)

8 These are: *Brahmā Purāṇa* VI.1–52; *Brahmāṇḍa Purāṇa* II.59.33.84; *Vāyu Purāṇa* LXXXIV.32–84; *Mārkaṇḍeya Purāṇa* CIII.3–CV.46; *Bhaviṣya Purāṇa* I.79.17–81; *Matsya Purāṇa* XI.1–39; *Padma Purāṇa* V.8.35–74; I.8.36–75; *Kūrma Purāṇa* I.20.1–4; *Liṅga Purāṇa* LXV.2–16; *Viṣṇu Purāṇa* III.2.2–13; *Bhāgavata Purāṇa* IX.1.10–11; *Varāha Purāṇa* XX.5–19; *Agni Purāṇa* CLXXIII.2–4; *Gaurḍa Purāṇa* CXXXVIII.2–3; *Harivaṃśa* I.9.1–64; *Śiva Purāṇa* (upapurāṇa) V.35.1–41.

9 The association between Goddess and king is explored in detail in section titled "The Safeguard of Sovereignty".

10 "Sāvarṇi, the son of the Sun, will become Lord of the next Age./Hear as I relay his rise at length,/How by the grace of Mahāmāyā that illustrious son of the Sun,/Became Lord of an Age" (DM 1.1–2) (Balkaran 2020).

11 "Thus receiving a boon from the Goddess, Suratha, best of rulers,/Will receive another birth from the Sun, and/will become Sāvarṇi, Manu of the next Age" (DM 13.18) (Balkaran 2020).

## Works cited in this chapter

Balkaran, Raj. 2019. *The Goddess and The King in Indian Myth: Ring Composition, Royal Power, and the Dharmic Double Helix*. London: Routledge.

Balkaran, Raj. 2020. "A Tale of Two Boons: The Goddess and the Dharmic Double Helix". In *The Purāṇa Reader*, edited by Deven Patel and Dheepa Sundaram. San Diego: Cognella Academic Publishing.

Brodbeck, Simon. 2019. *Krishna's Lineage: The Harivamsha of Vyāsa's Mahābhārata*. New York: Oxford University Press.

Buitenen, J.A.B. van. 1973. *Mahābhārata: Book 1: The Book of the Beginning*. Vol. I. Chicago, IL: University of Chicago Press.

Coburn, Thomas B. 1985. *Devī Māhātmya: The Crystallization of the Goddess Tradition*. Columbia, MO: South Asia Books.

Coburn, Thomas B. 1991. *Encountering the Goddess: A Translation of the Devī-Māhātmya and a Study of Its Interpretation*. Albany, NY: State University of New York Press.

Desai, Nileshvari Y. 1968. *Ancient Indian Society, Religion, and Mythology as Depicted in the Mārkaṇḍeya-Purāṇa; a Critical Study*. Baroda: Faculty of Arts, M.S. University of Baroda.

Gonda, Jan. 1969. *Ancient Indian Kingship from the Religious Point of View*. Leiden: Brill.

Matsunami. 1977. "A Preliminary Essay in Systematic Arrangement of the Purāṇas – with Special Reference to the Legend of Yama's Birth". *Purāṇa* 29 (1): 214–32.

Monier-Williams, Ernst Leumann, Carl Cappeller, and Īśvaracandra. 2008. "Monier Williams Sanskrit-English Dictionary (2008 Revision)".

Pargiter, F.E. 1904. *Mārkaṇḍeya Purāṇa*. Calcutta: Asiatic Society of Bengal.

Simson, Georg von. 2007. "Kṛṣṇa's Son Sāmba: Faked Gender and Other Ambiguities on the Background of Lunar and Solar Myth". In *Gender and Narrative in the Mahābhārata*, edited by Simon Brodbeck and Brian Black. London: Routledge.

# 3 The story of Saṃjñā

## Mother of Manu, threshold of tradition

This chapter analyses the very important Vedic story of Saṃjñā. In addition to being the wife of the Sun, she mothers the very same Manu whose backstory the DM supplies. It first debunks the pervasive scholarly interpretation of this myth as a tale of 'the wicked stepmother' (Balkaran 2019) before arguing that this solar myth sits at the cusp of the Goddess narrative because it brilliantly encodes the astronomical alignment at which the Durgā Pūjā occurs (Balkaran 2018). This chapter not only deepens our discussion on the Saura–Śākta symbiosis occurring within the MkP, but also substantiates the existence of an ideological ecosystem within the MkP fuelling that symbiosis.

### 3.1 Debunking Doniger

The story of Saṃjñā that we find in the *Mārkaṇḍeya Purāṇa* (MkP) is as significant as it is mesmerizing, especially in light of its role as the backstory for the *Devī Māhātmya* (DM), immediately following it in the MkP. It indeed "stands at the threshold of another tradition, the beginning of the incorporation of the worship of the Goddess into Sanskrit texts" (Doniger 1999, 55). Wendy Doniger, the most prolific voice in expounding this myth, further remarks that:

> since the Markandeya Purana tells the tale of Samjna not once but twice and regards her as the mother of the Manu who rules in our age, the whole *Devī Māhātmya* is, in a sense, a footnote to the story of the shadow of Saranyu.
>
> (Doniger 1999, 55)[1]

However, the fact that the Saṃjñā myth is told twice is not necessarily indicative of its double importance (as compared to the DM), but rather, of its framing function of the DM: it is told immediately before and after the DM, serving to thematically contextualize the exploits of the Goddess. From the perspective of the DM – which glorifies the great goddess whose might surpasses even the creator's, and whose grace is responsible for installing the next Manu – it is the story of Saṃjñā which ornaments, and echoes, the Goddess' grandeur. But why would this be? What is it about the story of Saṃjñā that warrants its use as a foyer into the grandeur of the Great Goddess? How does the story of Saṃjñā – entailing an

DOI: 10.4324/9780429322020-4

exchange between Sūrya, the Sun, and his wives Saṃjñā and Chāyā – orient us in broaching the Goddess of the DM?

### *3.1.1 Structuralist sleight of hand*

Frame narratives function as guides to interpretation. A frame of course cannot function as a strict, dogmatic failsafe against dynamic, ongoing mythic exegesis, or else the fluidity of the Purāṇic genre freezes into cultural obsoleteness. They are more like irrigational guides, designed to channel the narrative flow into fertile grounds for embellishment and interpretation. While much might be gained by plucking a given myth out if its narrative context so as to compare it to myths of similar content, affording purvey of the structural functions of elements of the myth, much too is lost in the process. Furthermore, this approach implicitly holds subsequent articulations accountable to earlier versions (consciously or unconsciously), operating under the premise that earlier articulations are 'more authentic' in some way or another. Of course both diachronic and synchronic methodologies constitute viable means of gaining insight into the 'meaning' of a given narrative. However, I contend that if one is interested in grappling with a specific articulation of a narrative, one needs to commence with fully unpacking it within the narrative content proper to its articulation before (rather than instead of) proceeding to compare it to others of its kind. An individual mythic articulation need not be held accountable to its previous or subsequent incarnations. Yet when we compare mythic articulations from different historical horizons (which to be sure is a useful and important exercise), the process itself often constitutes a 'sleight of hand' of sorts, causing us to perceive contortions and occlusions which are very much functions of our methodological lens and not necessarily proper to their articulations themselves.

Wendy Doniger addresses the story of Saṃjñā at seven junctures throughout her work, in publications spanning forty years (Doniger 1976; 1980, 174–85; 1996; 1999; 2000; 2004, 60–70; Doniger O'Flaherty 1973, 276–92). She does so largely through the lens of earlier Vedic articulations of the myth and thus against the grain of the mythology of the Sun found in the MkP. In her 1976 publication, *The Origins of Evil in Hindu Mythology*, Wendy Doniger writes that "an important Vedic myth of two mothers is the story of Saṃjñā, the wife of the sun" (Doniger 1980, 349). It is important for our purposes to unpack her methodological approach. While she uses a modified structuralist technique in her first publication (Doniger O'Flaherty, 1973), Doniger writes that:

> the problem of evil does not easily lend itself to a structuralist approach, perhaps because so many of its jagged facets prove stubbornly irreducible … I have therefore used any tool that would do the job – a bit of philology, a measure of theology, lashings of comparative religion, a soupcon of anthropology, even a dash of psychoanalysis.
>
> (Doniger 1976, 9)

Despite this announcement, it appears that structuralism pervades the methodological milieu of this work nevertheless. Articulations of the Saṃjñā story (and its Vedic correlates pertaining to the goddess Saraṇyū, whom Doniger equates with Saṃjñā) appear at several junctures of Indian lore, ranging from Vedas to the Upaniṣads to, of course, the Purāṇas.[2] One might question the ability of any given author to translate and render thirteen mythic junctures ranging across two millennia of cultural and textual history in one fell swoop – but, graced by the powers of structuralist analysis, Doniger does just that. She presents "the" myth as follows:

> Saṃjñā gave birth to twins, Yama and Yamī, and then left her husband, creating as a substitute in her place an identical goddess called Chāyā ("dark shadow"). Her husband discovered the deception only when Chāyā mistreated her stepson, Yama; Yama tried to kick Chāyā and was cursed by her to lose his leg, a curse which his father later modified so that Yama fell to the underworld, the first mortal to die and king of all subsequent dead people. Vivasvat pursued Saṃjñā, who had taken the form of a mare, and in the form of a stallion (whose seed she drank) he begat the twin Aśvins upon her.
>
> (Doniger 1976, 349)

She then proceeds to offer analysis of her translation under the section heading, "The Good and Evil Mother" as follows:

> The oppositional pairs of the good and bad mother, the bright image (saṃjñā) and dark shadow, are linked with the motif of the fertile solar stallion pursuing the erotic, destructive mare. The sun himself is said to have been rejected and pushed from the breast by his mother, Aditi, or to have been threatened by her asceticism while still in her womb, becoming mortal because of this [n. 143 reads RV10.72.8–9] … Chāyā's hatred of her stepson results in a curse that makes Yama into the king of the dead. Thus the wicked, false mother is the source of the greatest of all evils, the kingdom of the dead.
>
> (Doniger 1976, 349)

In the first section of her analysis above, Doniger draws upon a binary pair of opposites – the good and the bad mother – in order to explain how Saṃjñā and Chāyā relate to each other and their purpose in the myth as a whole: the ill-treatment of Yama. She furthermore links this binary with a second pair of opposites, namely the fertile solar stallion and the erotic destructive mare. These theoretical tropes curtail the individual articulations of this tale in ways that can be (as is the case in the MkP's telling) contrary to *what we actually see in the text*. It is, for example, mystifying how one could perceive, based upon the MkP account, an "erotic, destructive mare" when we are explicitly told that Saṃjñā in her equine form performed austerities and fasted "like a chaste wife" (106.12), and that her efforts were geared towards pacification of her destructive husband. It is in fact Saṃjñā's steadfast celibate austerity which spiritually empowers her to reckon with her husband's overbearing *tejas*. Doniger nevertheless asserts elsewhere that sexual insatiability "is the telltale characteristic of the mare in Hindu mythology" (Doniger 1999, 48), and that this insatiability serves as an essential clue to Saṃjñā's "flight from marriage and motherhood" (Doniger 1999, 48). If Saṃjñā cared not for motherhood, it is doubtful that she would bother to craft a double and especially doubtful that she would instruct it to care for her children in her absence. Likewise, if she cared not for marriage, it is doubtful she would undertake austerities to ameliorate her husband's form. She flees from the Sun's excessive sharpness; once this is quelled, she gladly returns to both marriage and motherhood.

Reading the myths of the MkP through the lens of their "older, original" correlates is misguided, for, understandably in doing so, one might quite sensibly argue that:

> the fact the Saraṇyū myth is a hierogamy between a mortal and an immortal accounts for both Saraṇyū's desertion of her husband and her "trimming" of him: either the sun is impotent and abandoned by the goddess or he is too powerful and is therefore castrated, a no-win situation if ever there was one.
> (Doniger 1980, 183)

Similarly, as Robert Goldman points out, "the sun, of course, is the mortal par excellence in the Veda" (Goldman 1969, 278), and furthermore that he is "a progenitor of mortals. In the Rgveda, itself, he is said to be the father both of Manu (VIII. 52.1) and Yama (X. 14.1)" (Goldman 1969, 279). However, the Sun is *certainly* no mortal in the MkP. Therefore, while the myth of Saraṇyū and her husband in the Ṛg Veda may very well be one wherein "the male is a mortal while the female is immortal" (Goldman 1969, 275), this simply cannot be said to be true of the myth of Saṃjñā and her husband in the MkP. Not only is the Sun said to be immortal, he is described as the prime being among immortals, lauded variously as "the supreme light that was at the beginning" (103.7), "the eternal one" (104.19), "without birth" (107.4), "self-existent" (107.5), "lord without beginning" (109.72). Therefore, the mythology of Saṃjñā and Sūrya in the MkP is not a hierogamy between a mortal and an immortal, so this cannot possibly account for Saṃjñā's flight, or for the pairing down of Sūrya. Nor does it appear sensible to attribute Saṃjñā's flight in the MkP to either a distaste for motherhood or an insatiable sexual appetite. Saṃjñā in equine form is portrayed as neither destructive nor erotic; on the contrary, she maintains ascetic chastity in order to quell the destructive tendencies of an overbearing husband.

Let us now turn to the second section of the above analysis, regarding Chāyā's alleged hatred for her stepson, causing her to curse Yama and become "the source of the greatest of all evils, the kingdom of the dead" (Doniger 1976, 349). Neither account in the MkP correlates Chāyā's curse (that Yama's foot should fall off) with his status as the lord of the departed: the first account tells us that "because he is righteous of eye, impartial to friend and foe, therefore the dispeller of darkness appointed him over the southern region" (78.29) (Pargiter 1904, 506), while the second account tells us that the Sun "appointed him to the southern region; his adorable father gave to him the duty of protecting the world, O brahman, and the lordship over the pitṛis" (106.18–19) (Pargiter 1904, 575–6). Furthermore, as we have seen above, it is Sūrya's curse (based on Saṃjñā restraining her eyes) that causes Yama, "the restrainer" to be born to her. Yama and his role are inseparable; he was accorded this status before birth. More crucial to engaging this myth is the fact that while the myth of a primordial mother-figure causing humanity's fall from blissful immortality to tragic mortality might prevail in the Abrahamic mythic imagination, it alas, is deeply incommensurate with the myth at hand, both with respect to its specific articulation and to the cultural imagination authoring it.

Doniger's distortion results from uprooting the myth from its narrative and cultural contexts, which she does in the interest of embellishing the discourse of a "bifurcated Hindu feminine", a trope abounding throughout her work. While Doniger does indeed mention the *MkP* among the various literary spaces with which the Sūrya–Saṃjñā–Chāyā episode is furnished, she neglects to register the import of the myth's narrative context therein. We ought not to read the myth as if Chāyā were some "other" mate chosen by Sūrya and forced to contend with her husband's children of a previous marriage (as the term "stepmother" might connote). Chāyā was created by Saṃjñā through an act of self-cloning, one reminiscent of the yogic attainment (*siddhi*) of bilocation wherein the yogī is able to project a duplicate of his form, known as a shadow self (*chāyā mūrti*). We must note that shadow here does not connote nefariousness as it might in English, but merely reflection. Furthermore, this reflected self of Saṃjñā was explicitly instructed to treat the children well. The text does not indicate hatred nor ill treatment towards any of the children. Rather it indicates favouritism shown towards the younger children, which as anyone familiar with the dynamics of child-rearing in a South Asian context can readily attest, would likely have been the case, even where all of the children were of the same parents. If this sort of favouritism were unconventional, it would have in itself aroused suspicion. Chāyā is not suspected as being other than Saṃjñā through her favouritism towards the younger children, but through her very human reaction to Yama's egregious insult, a reaction which only a mother might, under ideal circumstances, have been able to suppress.

In the *MkP* account, Chāyā is not demonized as 'the wicked stepmother' – far from it. She succeeds in mothering children who are Sūrya's legitimate offspring, who have crucial cosmic roles, no less so than Sūrya's children by Saṃjñā. Despite Doniger chalking up Yama's inauspicious post as the result of Chāyā's curse, Mārkaṇḍeya informs us that envious of Chāyā's favouritism of the three younger siblings, Yama threatened to kick her due to "both anger and childishness." As inappropriate a thing this is to do in Western culture, it would be absolutely inexcusable in an Indian context not only because of one's duty to respect elders and to revere one's parents as gods on earth, but especially because it is an expression of utter disregard to touch someone with one's foot, not to mention kicking them. So stigmatized is this that injunctions persist about even displaying the soles of one's feet towards a teacher or person of respect. One would not think to kick even inanimate objects which deserve respect, such as books. Chāyā curses Yama for his atrocious "unfilial conduct" (Pargiter 1904, 566). It is clear in the text that Yama is well aware that the transgression is his, not Chāyā's; he runs to his father to beg pardon and intersession of the curse, confessing that he "lifted my foot against her, but did not let it fall on her body; whether *it was* through childishness or through foolishness, do thou, Sir, deign to pardon it" (MP 106.24; see Pargiter 1904, 568). He asks forgiveness because he has done wrong. Sūrya, in like manner, begins his response thus: "Without doubt, my son, this curse must take effect here, since anger entered into thee" (MP 106.25; see Pargiter 1904, 568). Even the overbearing Sūrya can recognize that the fault here lies with Yama's conduct. If Chāyā is faulted in this myth, it is only for falling short of exhibiting saintly compassion in the face of atrocious disrespect on behalf on the part of a haughty youth.

When Arjuna asks the Gandharva after the [patronym] Tāpatya, he relays the story of Tapatī, the resplendent daughter of the Sun. The Sun – who was concerned to marry her off – decided that King Saṃvaraṇa should be her husband due to his devotion to the Sun.

> When he saw his daughter reach the nubile age and ready for marriage, he found no peace as he worried about her marrying. Now, the son of Ṛkṣa, O Kaunteya, the powerful bull of the Kurus, King Saṃvaraṇa, was wont to worship the Sun with offerings of guest gifts and garlands, with fasts and observances and with manifold mortifications. Obediently and unselfishly and purely, the scion of the Pauravas worshiped the splendiferous Sun with great devotion as He rose. So, it came about that the Sun judged the grateful and law-minded Saṃvaraṇa on earth to be Tapatī equal in beauty. He then desired to give the maiden in marriage to that sublime King Saṃvaraṇa, O Kaurava, whose descent was glorious. Just as in the sky the fiery-rayed Sun spreads light with splendor, so King Saṃvaraṇa was resplendent on earth. And just as the scholars of the Brahman worship the rising Sun, so the brahmins and the lower subjects worshiped Saṃvaraṇa, O Pārtha. The illustrious king outdid the moon in benevolence to his friends and the Sun in fierceness to his haters. Thus the Sun himself set his mind on marrying Tapatī to the king of such great virtue and such good conduct, O Kaurava.
>
> (MBh I.11.11–20)

While hunting, the king encounters the resplendent maiden and falls madly in love. She disappears and he hits the ground, love-sick until she returns. Lovestruck – indeed "wrapped in the flames of love" (161.5; Pargiter 1904, 327) – he proposes they elope. Tapatī replies:

> I am not my own mistress, sire, for I am a girl with a father. If you have pleasure in me, ask my father for me. For if I have laid hold of your senses,

> O king, no less have you taken mine, the instant I saw you. I am not mistress of my body, therefore, good king. I cannot come to you; for women are always dependent. But what girl would not wish for her protector and loving husband a king whose descent is famous in all the worlds? Therefore, now that it has come to this, ask my father the Sun, with prostration, mortification, and observances! If he desires to give me to you, scourge of your enemies, I shall forever be yours. my king. I am Tapatī, the younger sister of Sāvitrī, the daughter of Savitar who is the torch of the world, O bull of the barons.
>
> (15–20; Pargiter 1904, 327)

Tapatī then vanishes, heavens-bound, while the king again hits the ground, losing consciousness in the wilderness. His minister (and escort) finds him in that fallen state, without his horse, "as though scorched by fire" (162.3) and raises his king from the ground. Once he comes to, the king dismisses his army,

> After the large force had departed at the king's orders, the king again sat down on that mountain plateau. He cleansed himself, and then, on that great mountain, he folded his hands and raised his arms and remained in that manner on the ground to propitiate the Sun. In his thoughts he went out to that strictest of seers. Vasiṣṭha, his house priest, did King Saṃvaraṇa, slayer of foes. Day and night the king of the people stayed in the same place, then, on that twelfth day, the brahmin seer came. When Vasiṣṭha found that the king was in love with Tapatī – the great seer who had perfected his soul knew it by divine insight-he spoke to the eminent, self-controlled prince, for being Law-minded he wished to benefit him. As the sovereign of men looked on, the blessed seer, himself of solar splendor, strode up to heaven to visit the Sun.
>
> (162.10–16; Pargiter 1904, 327)

Vasiṣṭha successfully appeals to the Sun on behalf of the king, and the two are married. The couple frolic in nature for twelve years during, and because, of which Saṃvaraṇa's kingdom endures a great drought and famine. Vasiṣṭha then appeals to the couple to return to his city, which he does, restoring order and bringing great prosperity by virtue of his royal presence. The Gandharva narrator of the Tapatī subtale concludes: "Thus the Lady Tapatī, daughter of the Sun, became your ancestress, Pārtha, so that after her you are known as Tāpatya. On Tapatī King Saṃvaraṇa begot Kuru, O greatest of burners, and hence you are a Tāpatya, Arjuna" (160.1; Pargiter 1904, 324).

The 'wicked stepmother' motif – that is, the notion that "behind this complex myth we may discern a few repeated, familiar themes [such as the dual nature of Saṃjñā expressed as] the loving mother and the wicked step-mother" (Doniger 1980, 177) – is problematic to say the least. The theme of the wicked stepmother may indeed be a "familiar" one, but only to those familiar with western fairy tales, and not necessarily their Indian mythic counterparts. In seeking to chart the "origins of evil" in Hindu mythology, one is confronted with two interconnected obstacles with respect to the conception of evil therein: first, the cosmos itself, much less any aspect of it, is fundamentally beginning-less, a notion which undercuts discourse of origins; and second, one cannot treat as a separate entity that which is conceived as an aspect of a greater whole. The lines between good and evil are incredibly (and intentionally) blurred in Purāṇic discourse where gods may behave nefariously (typically for a greater good) and demons may exhibit extraordinary piety, particular in devotional milieus, for the sake of acquiring power. For example, the gods (*suras*) and the demons (more literally, the anti-gods, *asuras*) not only share an ancestry but, as we are reminded of in the myth of the churning of the ocean, are kindred polarities which must collaborate to generate the creative tension engendering all of the universe's riches and even immortality itself. That these forces appear to oppose each other is so only from a limited perspective. From a grander perspective, these forces are like two separate hands pressed together in añjali mudrā, stemming from the same ground of being, producing a unified gesture.

In maintaining the evil stepmother motif, one silences what the MkP has to say; Doniger therefore writes,

> this transition from good mother to evil mother is highly significant in the Indian context; Indeed, some Puranic texts tried to restore a modicum of maternal spirit to Saraṇyū by stating that she turned away from the stallion because she feared that he might be some man other than her husband (MkP: 103–105). This gloss … is untrue to the original spirit of the myth.
>
> (Doniger 1980, 185)

From what perspective should we gage what is authentic? Doniger bases the "original spirit" of "the" myth upon her understanding of its earliest known incarnations and thus eclipses the authority of the composers of the MkP themselves, along with the communities which preserve, invoke and depend upon its current articulation in their religious lives. She not only reads the myth of Saṃjñā in the MkP at large through the lens of its earlier Vedic correlates, but she goes so far as to outright dismiss as inauthentic the elements which do not conform to that lens. To my mind, this outcome comprises the central hazard to uprooting Purāṇic tales from their narrative soil, intended to support, not thwart, their religious transmission; a compromise of their religious authority.

Sixteen years after her publication of the *Origins of Evil in Hindu Mythology*, Doniger produces a 1996 article dedicated to Saṃjñā/Saraṇyū (Doniger 1996) wherein she perpetuates the practice of plucking from myth cycles across vast spans of time and reading later articulations as distortions of earlier ones. She draws her data from *Ṛg Veda* 10.17.1–2, the *Harivaṃśa*, the *Mārkaṇḍeya Purāṇa*, along with an episode from the classic series Indian comics, *Amar Chitra Katha*. Rather than chart the functions of the single character of Saṃjñā across three millennia of cultural history, it is perhaps more commensurate to the Purāṇic textual transformations to study in detail how that character relates to the whole within a single articulation of the myth cycle in a given Purāṇa. It is, for example, crucial to note that the Purāṇic authors never refer to the figure in question as Saraṇyū, but only as Saṃjñā, which suggests a distancing, if not radical reconfiguring, from the figure we find in Vedic lore to the one which graces the Purāṇas. As a result of this conscious transformation, tension arises while reading Purāṇic iterations and all the while harkening to Vedic articulations in order to understand "the myth" in itself. Hence, Doniger, upon completing her discussion of Saraṇyū in the Vedic literature, refers to the articulation of this found in the Harivaṃśa and the Purāṇas as "later variants" (Doniger 1996, 158) wherein the goddess is not named Saraṇyū, but Saṃjñā (Doniger 1996, 158). This attitude of course echoes the trenchant bias towards the Purāṇas as corruptions of older texts. Keeping in line with her "variant from Vedic version" discussion, Doniger further notes that:

> Samjna's surrogate is no longer said to be of the same kind or type but is rather her chaya, her mirror image or shadow, creature who is not exactly like her but is her opposite in terms either of inversion (the mirror image) or of color (the shadow).
>
> (Doniger 1996, 158)

This note regarding colour keeps in line with her interest in questions of race (Doniger 1996, 154), yet is problematized by the fact that Saṃjñā addresses Saṃjñā as "fair one" (MkP 106.7) in her instructions prior to fleeing. Regardless, these notable developments entailing the transition of Saraṇyū and Sāvarṇā to Saṃjñā and Chāyā respectively ought not be viewed as deviations from the original Vedic myth, but as important Purāṇic articulations in their own right, whose religious vision is equally authentic to its contemporaries as the Vedic myths were to theirs.

In the section of her article discussing the MkP, Doniger translates the opening of the first account of the Saṃjñā myth as follows:

> Samjna was the daughter of Tvastr and the wife of Martanda, the Sun. He produced in her Manu, called Manu Vaivasvata, since he was Vivasvant's son. But when the Sun looked at her, Samjna used to shut her eyes, and so the Sun got angry and spoke sharply to Samjna: "Since you always restrain (samyamam) your eyes when you see me, therefore you will bring forth a twin (yama) who will restrain (samyamanam) creatures." Then the goddess became agitated by terror, and her gaze flickered; and when he saw that her gaze darted about, he said to her again, "Since now your gaze darts about when you see me, therefore you will bring forth a daughter who will be a river that darts about." And so because of her husband's curse Yama and Yamuna were born in her.
>
> (MP 74.1–7) (Doniger 1996, 164)

Doniger then proceeds to offer the following analysis: "where Manu is named after his father, and is blessed, Yama is named after his mother, and is cursed;

for he is named not after her name but after her evil deeds" (Doniger 1996, 164). First, let us be reminded that, it is not Yama who is named after his mother. Rather, it is the second Manu, Sāvarṇi, who is named after Chāyā, known also as Sāvarṇā, (i.e. She of the Likeness). Second and more importantly, the fact that this exchange is designed to paint the Sun (and not Saṃjñā) in a less than favourable light is corroborated throughout the solar myths to be found in the MkP. They unanimously warn us of the danger and disruption which ensues when the Sun is excessive in his intensity. This is unsurprising to a people born of a climate wherein when the Sun is too intense, drought ensues, hence his epithet, 'Robber of the Waters'. The aforementioned portion of the myth, accounting for Yama's birth, tells us that death (Yama) is fathered by the wrath of the Sun. Recall: that this entire episode is framed by the mythology of the Sun who is unbearable even to the creator himself and constitutes a threat to cosmic order; and that this episode (between Brahmā and Sūrya) occurs before the Sūrya–Saṃjñā episode is of course significant: the earlier serves to frame the later.

There can be little doubt that the MkP is sympathetic to the plight of Saṃjñā: for who is able to gaze at the Sun full on, in its full fury, without squinting? The text portrays an overbearing husband rather than a nefarious wife. The Sun curses Saṃjñā in this moment but the text clearly sides with Saṃjñā; hence she flees and is never once admonished for doing so, neither by her husband, her sons, her father nor the narrator of the text. Recall that Sūrya himself realizes the folly of his ways and *volunteers* to be pared down towards the conclusion of this telling. In the Sun's rash cruelty, he curses his own unborn children, but let us not forget that Yama's curse is ultimately reconfigured as a cosmic benediction insofar as Yama became the righteous-eyed judge because of it. Doniger misguidedly argues that, "as anthropogonies, these stories are saying that the primeval children, our ancestors, were abandoned by their mother" (Doniger 1996, 154). Even to entertain that this angle of inquiry as central to the contours of this myth (which, as Doniger herself admits, is probably not the case – a wise move considering Indian deities are rarely rendered as exemplars for human conduct), can we sensibly arrive at this conclusion when we are told that our primordial mother: 1) was unable to remain due to our father's excessive sharpness; 2) that she made arrangements for our care during her necessary respite, cloning herself and commanding her clone to treat us well; 3) that she engaged in religious practices in order to restore balance to our family; and 4) that she was successful in neutralizing our father's overbearing wrath and restoring balance, such that she ended up returning to us and so didn't ultimately abandon us at all? It is perhaps precisely due to the resilient faces of the feminine divine pervading the MkP, such as that of Saṃjñā, that the DM is happily at home therein.

Doniger's own words point to the incommensurability between her hermeneutic approach and the myth we find in the MkP. She states at the outset of her Saṃjñā study that she is primarily interested in "questions of gender and race" (Doniger 1996, 154), but must admit that nothing is said of the Sun's "ugliness or dark color" in the MkP's accounts of his mythology, which leave only questions of gender. With respect to such questions, she appears so intent on painting the picture of humanity's fall from grace due to the evils of a primordial stepmother (a motif familiar to anyone remotely acquainted with Abrahamic religion), that she fails to address the obvious feminist gems of this myth cycle: first, that wives and mothers are thought to hold tremendous power over the domestic sphere and thus exert great influence over their families through their religious activities; and second, rather than the typical motif of the daughter being made to succumb to the pressures of the mother-in-law, we have a shocking and refreshing reversal: a son-in-law (the Sun himself no less) who submits to the hammering down of his father-in-law for the safety and comfort of his wife, family and society as a whole. When Doniger does turn her attention to the fact that the versions of this myth cycle occurring in the MkP (along with the one occurring in the Harivaṃśa) "give new prominence to an old, silent character: the father-in-law, Tvastr" (Doniger 1996, 165), she does so in order to argue that "the aggression of the bride's father against her husband" (Doniger 1996, 166) (a statement which itself cannot be said to apply to the MkP's tellings) "lends weight, retrospectively, to the possibly incestuous connection that some Indologists have seen between Tvastr and Saranyu in the Vedic corpus" (Doniger 1996, 166).

Strangely she opts to read the father-in-law's willingness to pare down the Sun's splendour (at the Sun's behest) for the sake of the welfare of his daughter as grounds for reading into the Purāṇic telling conjecture into a possible incestuous relationship held by some Indologists in reference to myths composed two millennia earlier, rather than registering that the myth serves as a salient reminder to overbearing husbands that daughters are always welcomed (albeit temporarily) to their fathers' homes post-marriage. Not only does Doniger appear to take no interest in this dimension of the myth, she claims that Saṃjñā took the form of a mare "when her father threw her out of his house" (Doniger 1996, 163). Similarly, in *Hindu Myths* wherein she translates this same passage from the MkP, she writes that Saṃjñā's father "admonished her again and again to go to her husband" (Doniger 2004, 66). She fails to mention that the MkP tells us that Saṃjñā remained in her father's house "unreproached" (*aninditā*, 77.16), or that her father, "after praising her and prefacing his speech with love and much respect" (*stutvā ca tanayāṃ premabahumānapuraḥ saram*, 77.17), advises her to leave since it is improper for a married woman to remain among her kinsmen (i.e. away from her husband) for a long time, and that she was welcome to return in the future. The text goes out of its way to indicate that Saṃjñā was welcome in her father's home and that her father lovingly sends her back for the sake of her honour, all the while unaware that she was imperilled by her husband's overbearing nature. It is the Sun, and not Saṃjñā, who mends his ways in the MkP. In portraying this mother of the Manus, the MkP certainly does not paint a portrait of an absentee mother nor a wicked stepmother nor ultimately a disenfranchised wife. Rather it portrays a resilient feminine figure, who succeeds in softening overbearing masculinity when she is imperilled by the dangers of its sharpness.

### *3.1.2 Seminal splendour and the transmission of* tejas

Despite the richness of the term *tejas* (fiery energy, vital power, spirit), and its obvious connotations to majesty, Wendy Doniger, in her reading of this myth, favours one of its more figurative meanings: semen.[3] She therefore translates the encounter as follows:

> Then Vivasvant's body was beautiful, and had no excessive fiery energy. He went to his wife, the mare, in the form of a stallion. But when she saw him approaching she feared it might be another male, and so she turned to face him, determined to protect her hindquarters. Their noses joined as they touched, and the seed of the Sun flowed from his two nostrils into the mare and came out of her mouth, and in that way the equine twin gods called the Asvins were born.
>
> (Doniger 1996, 165)

She notes that "impregnation by drinking semen is a world-wide theme, and it is particularly well developed in India. In the Vedic story of Saṃjñā, the mare becomes pregnant by smelling or absorbing through her nostrils the seed of her husband" (Doniger O'Flaherty 1973, 276). Therefore, she reads the Sun's excessive splendour (*tejas*) as his overbearing sexuality, from which Saṃjñā must flee. She reasons that it is significant that the word for energy (*tejas*) is also a word for semen since Saṃjñā "in her anthropomorphic form avoids the Sun's energy, while in her mare form she avoids the stallion's semen" (Doniger 1996, 163). However, this comparison is lopsided: Saṃjñā does not merely avoid the Sun's energy, she flees from it out of desperation. With respect to the "strange" male, she does not flee but merely averts penetration and engages him face to face. Furthermore, Saṃjñā here does not fear Sūrya's semen but the semen of "another male". She fled from the overbearing majesty of the Sun, not his procreative proclivity, hence the begetting of three children with him prior to fleeing. This fear results not merely as a threat to her womanhood (or marehood rather) but as a threat to the celibate austerities in which she was engaged, along with a threat to her marital fidelity. In other words, she was not afraid because it was Sūrya (from whose sexuality she needed to flee) but precisely *because it wasn't Sūrya* (or so she thought), on account of her commitment to whom, sexual engagement with another ought to be avoided at all costs. These sources of anxiety may not be simplified as tantamount to fearing male sexuality at large, and particularly not her husband's.

The text could not possibly be referring to the stallion's literal semen flowing into Saṃjñā since it was emitted through his nose, not his genitals. She also received it through her nose, and receiving liquid through one's nose, as we know, is an unpleasant and dangerous experience. Saṃjñā birthed the aśvins through her mouth, and not her genitals. It is noteworthy that the verb "to drink" (*pā*) appears nowhere in this passage, despite Doniger's claim that the world-wide theme of impregnation through drinking semen has been particularly well developed in India (Doniger O'Flaherty 1973, 276). Even if seminal *fluid* was involved, Saṃjñā doesn't drink it since it would have then passed from her nose to her mouth; drinking involves swallowing. The supernormal dimension of this encounter strongly suggests that we are to literally take it that the Sun conceived the celestial twins with his literal *tejas*, his spiritual power. If the authors meant to signify physical semen, they could have easily used the term *retas*, which would very conveniently serve the prosodic demands of both meter and stress, and much better connote seminal fluid than does *tejas*. That the Aśvins were conceived with such miraculous power befits their own miraculous healing ability. We are told that the Sun and Saṃjñā in equine form "joined their noses" (Pargiter 1904, 460), an act which is bereft of physical penetration. We are soon thereafter told that Revanta was born at the end of the flow (*retaso 'ante*), presumably of the Sun's transmission. Retas, as noted above, also connotes the flow of semen. Thus, in *Hindu Myths*, Doniger translates this as "And when the seed ceased to flow [*retaso 'ante*, 'at the end of the seed'] Revanta was born" (Doniger 2004, 69). However there is only one mention of *retas*, which cannot be translated twice as both "seed" and "flow". Therefore, it may be translated as "as the end of the seed" or "at the end of the flow". It is less forced to translate *retas* as 'flow' [i.e. of *tejas*] in this context given the absence of reproductive organs or penetration involved in the encounter. Also the phrase *retaso' ante* is a play on the name Revanta, which cleverly evokes "*revato'ante*", that is, at the end of the constellation *Revati* where one finds the constellation Aśvini, the same asterism over which the Aśvin twins preside. Interestingly there is an account of a previous Manu (the fifth one) Raivata whose backstory is heavily interspersed with the constellation Revatī. Perhaps it is not without design that we hear the tale of a Manu whose backstory invokes Revatī before hearing a tale of a Manu whose backstory invokes Aśvini, at the end of Revatī (*revato'ante*).

Given the supernormal, non-penetrative, voluntary encounter between Sūrya and Saṃjñā, Doniger's claim that Saṃjñā was "raped by the Sun stallion and brought home again … [since] in the end she must submit to her husband's sexual demands, just like a human woman" (Doniger 1999, 49) is most mystifying to my mind. This reading presents the myth out of the context of its various narrative frames. Narrative frames bear tremendous thematic import, devised to ideologically orient one's reading of myth. Doniger's reading presumes that Saṃjñā attains equine form to enjoy sexual freedom. But if Saṃjñā had the gumption to devise and implement an escape plan so that she didn't have to contend with the energetic threat of her husband while in anthropomorphic form, could we really think she would hesitate to gallop away from the sexual threat of a strange male while in equine form? How can this stallion be portrayed as a threat when she turns and unflinchingly encounters him face to face? Post-encounter the MkP unambiguously informs us that Saṃjñā is *pleased* at the sight of her husband's pared down form, and describes her as the Sun's "loving wife". The passage reads: "then the Sun displayed his own peerless form, and she gazing upon his true form felt a keen joy; and the Sun, the robber of the waters, brought home this his loving wife Sañjñā restored to her own shape"

(MkP 78.25–26). One is unable to locate within this passage indications of sexual coercion of any kind, nor evidence supporting the presumption that Saṃjñā is dragged home.

That Saṃjñā opts not to flee indicates no sign of struggle, and that she voluntarily joins noses with the equine-Sun is consistent with what the text tells us: she is afraid of union with another male, intent on guarding her chastity. She attains the form of a mare to practice *chaste* austerities, rather than indulge her sexual appetite. And if the text indeed intended to portray a Saṃjñā who wished to sow her wild oats, it is doubtful that the idyllic land of the Northern Kurus[4] would be the place to do so, since it is a location where folks are born in pairs and each partner has the same lifespan so that blissful monogamy may ensue. Had they intended to invoke the theme of sexual freedom, the others of this episode would have much better served their cause by a) refraining from having Saṃjñā guard her rear, and b) choosing any of the several other regions described in the MkP than one explicitly associated with contented monogamy. The resilient and resourceful Saṃjñā of the MkP was neither raped, nor "dragged" anywhere; she left home because of her husband's overbearing *tejas*, and while we may debate about what that *tejas* might be said to represent, there is no question that the Sun had his *tejas* checked by his father-in-law. Since the cause of her discontent and flight were eliminated, what reason do we have to assume her discontent continued? She conceives the Aśvins and joyfully returns home. While Saṃjñā suffers to conceive death (Yama) when the Sun's *tejas* is overbearing, she readily receives his pared down energy to conceive health through the healer-twins. In his fierce form, the Sun fathers death. In his contained, pleasant form, he births divine medicine in the idyllic Northern Kurus. And this latter achievement is directly attributed to the equine austerities of an empowered Saṃjñā.

In addition to the discourse on *tejas* and the birth of the Aśvins, there are a number of notable themes running through the MkP's account of the mythology of Sūrya. In particular, this myth cycle is redolent with the overarching theme of mirror-images: not only does Chāyā mirror Saṃjñā but we are, as well, presented with the production of two sets of children, the second of which set mirrors the first. Manu Vaivasvata, Yama and Yamī are mirrored by their younger stepfamily Manu Sāvarṇi, Śanaiścara and Tapatī (the current Manu, the planet Saturn, and the Narmadā river respectively). Thus, we hear the tale of two Manus, two gods of human suffering, and two dark rivers. Interestingly, there is a tertiary dimension to the duality of this mythology: 1) each stepfamily consists of a threesome, not just a pair; and 2) the Sun and Saṃjñā, while in equine form, beget a third set of triple offspring comprised of the Aśvin twins and Revanta. We seem to be presented with an intriguing triplet motif comprised of 'a pair and a third entity': the daughters are the third appendage to the pairs of sons, Revanta is the third entity to be born in tandem with the Aśvins, and the entire equine family itself is a tertiary emanation of Sūrya's two anthropomorphic families. Perhaps this tertiary dynamic is fitting considering it is spawned by the threefold intertwining of Sūrya, Saṃjñā and Chāyā. An object cannot be reflected in the absence of light. Arguably, the most trenchant expression of mirroring featured in this myth consists of the interplay between shadow and light. This interplay (like the set of offspring noted above) is not merely a binary one (as might be expected in this case) but intriguingly, is tertiary. The main actors are Sūrya as emblematic of the primal, self-effulgent progenitor of the universe, along with his primary consort Saṃjñā, and his secondary consort (born of the interplay of Sūrya and Saṃjñā), that is, Chāyā. Saṃjñā casts behind her own shadow, unable to bear the Sun. For a shadow to exist before a source of light, there must be a third entity: an object to cast its shadow.

### *3.1.3 Shadow and light in the* Mārkaṇḍeya Purāṇa

In my view, the brilliance of this myth is to be found in its treatment of the interplay between shadow and light: given that it is ultimately Sūrya's brilliance (*tejas*) which causes Saṃjñā to cast behind her shadow in her stead, who is to blame for Saṃjñā's flight? When Sūrya ventures to his father-in-law's home in search of Saṃjñā (clarity), he requests that his father-in-law Viśvakarman pare down his form so that it is once again bearable (MP 106.36–38; see Pargiter 1904, 569). One sees clearly neither in the dark nor when the light is too bright. Doniger reads this as an encounter where Viśvakarman "finally mutilates [Saṃjñā's] husband in order to make him acceptable to her" (Doniger 1996, 166). Mutilation connotes forceful disfigurement resulting in unsightliness and suffering and can hardly be said to properly refer to a voluntary act of beautification and pacification, undertaken by a "mutilator" all the while full of songful praise of his object of mutilation. It is the Sun's overbearing aspect that results in Saṃjñā's flight, an aspect so overpowering that at the dawn of time, the creator himself must pare down that aspect for creation to successfully occur. Rather than fault Saṃjñā, the MkP expresses a *necessity* for Sūrya to be pared down, a task accomplished at the hands of the divine tinkerer, who is conveniently cast as Saṃjñā's father. The Sun never chastises Saṃjñā for fleeing, but rather is so much in agreement with the dangers of his overbearing nature that he *voluntarily* acquiesces to being pared down.

The Sun does not disown his children born of shadow (Chāyā); rather, he promotes them in rank to statuses parallel to those of his children born of Saṃjñā. Sūrya fathers three children with each of these wives and these step-families are parallels of one another: Saṃjñā mothers Vaivasvata (the current Manu), Yama (the god of the dead, as the shadow of that Manu), and Yamunā (a river known for turning black, also named Kālindī, Mani 1975, 894) while Chāyā mothers three children: Sāvarṇi (the next Manu), Śanaiścara (Saturn, the lord of karmic retribution), and Tapatī, who eventually receives a blessing from Sūrya whereby she becomes the Narmadā river, flowing west from the Vindhya mountains (Mani 1975, 798).

Chāyā's daughter, Tapatī, has an even far more significant role to play in the unfolding of itihāsa. The MkP sums this up in the following line: "The third of them, the daughter named Tapatī, had a son, Kuru, king of men, by king

Samvaraṇa" (Pargiter 1904, 461). In the *Mahābhārata*, Arjuna asks the Gandharva in the forest why the Gandharva not only addresses him with the matronymic Kaunteya, son of Kuntī, but also as Tāpatya, son of Tapatī. The Gandharva then dedicates a subtale to explaining that radiant Tapatī was wedded by King Saṃvaraṇa (himself a devotee of the Sun), upon whom was begotten Kuru, that great ancestor of the entire lineage. Tapatī is not only the mother of Arjuna, she is the mother of the entire line of kings populating both Pāṇḍava and Kaurava camps. The Sun is so inextricable from the symbolism of kingship that even the lunar line of kings showcased in the *Mahābhārata* attributes their lineage to the seed of the Sun. The legitimacy of both of the Sun's stepfamilies (along with the legitimacy of the solar race mothered by one branch of that family tree through Tapatī, daughter of Chāyā) bespeaks of the legitimacy of both of the *śaktis* (powers, consorts) of the Sun to whom both shadow and light must ultimately be attributed for him to retain primordial supremacy within the solar myths as the cause of all creation. Therefore rather than being a story of a wicked stepmother or absentee birthmother, a raped wife, or a mutilated son-in-law, the Sūrya–Saṃjñā–Chāyā exchange, couched in a section of the MkP dedicated to the splendour of the Sun, perhaps more directly comments on the symbiosis of light and dark.

Doniger concludes her study by confessing that questions of sociology are not the dominant questions entertained by this myth. She states that this myth cycle, rather,

> raises theological questions about the origin of the human race and of human death, about appearance and reality, about the relationship between male and female divine powers, and about the nature of the relationship between humans and the divine. … But that is yet another story, best left for another time.
>
> (Doniger 1996, 170–1)

Despite the tantalizing hope of having these seminal aspects of this myth cycle addressed, yet another eighteen years elapsed before this article on Saṃjñā reappears in Doniger's 2014 collection *On Hinduism*, relatively unaltered from its 1996 state. It is no wonder that she writes at the very outset of her discussion that despite having addressed it "variously in various books," the mythology of Saraṇyū/Saṃjñā "still accuses [her] of not even having begun to plumb its depths" (Doniger 2014a, 607, n. 1). Yet she tells the same story in this article as she did in her 1996 article and one is left wondering about this profound story "best left for another time" (Doniger 2014b, 287) as again quoted at the conclusion of the 2013 edition. This present study, at long last, begins to tell the tale of this captivating myth cycle which Doniger has broached only in passing for forty years; for it is these very issues pertaining to "the relationship between male and female divine powers, and about the nature of the relationship between humans and the divine" (Doniger 1996, 171) which the DM addresses and furthermore, why its composers opted to dovetail its narration alongside the mythology of the Sun found in the MkP. Both mythologies bespeak powerful feminine divinities whose efforts restore order in the face of peril and both bespeak the danger, which results when fiery figures, though required to preserve our world, exceed safe bounds.

Reading the story of Saṃjñā as merely a tale of an ill-treated goddess who abandons her children and whose actions are the source of the evil of death, is fundamentally incommensurate with the vision of the feminine divine that the authors of the DM present and by virtue of this, incommensurate with their understanding of Saṃjñā with whose mythology they yolk the grandeur of the Goddess to the fabric of the MkP. Saṃjñā's tale is the one which demonstrates feminine resourcefulness, faith, and tenacity of spirit which ultimately restores cosmic balance. Saṃjñā, through her austerity, causes the destructive aspect of the Sun to keep at bay and thus ensures the preservation not only of self and family, but also of the cosmos as a whole. It is primarily her efforts, and only secondarily her husband's (once he realizes the motivation for her penance), which restores cosmic balance. Doniger writes that "on the metaphysical level the myth of Saṃjñā seems to be saying that we, the descendants of Manu, are the children of the image – the children of *māyā*, not the children of the real thing" (Doniger 1996, 170) and that "these myths embody the Vedantic view that we are born into illusion, live in illusion, and can only know illusion" (Doniger 1996, 170). But in my estimation, this myth, in the context of the MkP (especially given its vital association to the DM), goes well beyond the values of Vedantic binary, succeeding in subverting them by positing a supremacy on the part of that illusion insofar as it is inextricable from anything conceived to be superior to it. We are told at the very beginning of the DM, for example, that King Suratha is made the lord of an age by the might of Mahāmāyā. To be the children of Mahāmāyā is to be children of the divine mother and arguably, to be children of the future: while the current Manu, the child of Saṃjñā, is patrilineally named Vaivasvata (after Vivasvat, the Sun), the Manu Sāvarṇi, primordial overlord of the *next* epoch, is named after his mother, Sāvarṇā, She of the Likeness. Her Likeness, through Sāvarṇi, our primordial forefather to come, shall populate an entire age. Bolstered by its Purāṇic context, the DM affirms that the diversity of this phenomenal world, along with the myriad of life forms finding homes herein, is as supreme as that dynamic feminine mystery which engenders, supports, and governs it, compelled through compassion towards colossal acts of cosmic preservation.

### *3.1.4 Saṃjñā–Chāyā symbolism*

Doniger notes the bridging between the tales of the Sun and the DM at several junctures in her work; in *Splitting the Difference*, for example, she notes that "the story of Samjna and her shadow stands at the threshold of another tradition, the beginning of the incorporation of the worship of the Goddess into Sanskrit texts" (Doniger 1999, 55). She similarly remarks in her article on Saraṇyū that the MkP "uses the story of Saṃjñā to introduce the *Devī Māhātmya* … [serving] as a bridge to, and perhaps a validation of, the new Purāṇic myth about a Goddess, Devī Mahīṣamardinī" (Doniger 1996, 163). But what is it about the story of Saṃjñā that warrants its use as a foyer into the grandeur of the great Goddess? Doniger suggests that the story of Saṃjñā would be "very important indeed, given that she is the ancestor of the human race. In the context of a Purāṇa that is so concerned with dynasties, this Ur-mother is clearly crucial" (Doniger 1996, 163). Indeed, we hear of the tale first in the *manvantara* section, detailing the origins of the succession of Manus, and hear of it again along with other myths of the Sun to kick off the genealogies section of the MkP. But one nevertheless wonders how much we read into this emphasis, given the quest for Ur-tales bequeathed to us by our scholarly forefathers. Doniger further remarks that:

> since the Markandeya Purana tells the tale of Samjna not once but twice and regards her as the mother of the Manu who rules in our age, the whole Devimahatmya is, in a sense, a footnote to the story of the shadow of Saranyu.
>
> (Doniger 1999, 55)

However, the fact that the Saṃjñā myth is told twice is not necessarily indicative of its double importance (as compared to the DM), but rather, of its framing function of the DM; it is told, as noted above, before and after the DM, and succeeds in introducing and thematically contextualizing the exploits of the Goddess, serving as preceding and subsequent narrative associates to the grandeur of the Goddess. From the perspective of the DM – which glorifies the great goddess whose might surpasses even the creator's, and whose grace is responsible for installing the next Manu – it is the story of Saṃjñā which ornaments, and echoes, the greatness of the goddess. But why would this be? What direction might we take about the exchange between Sūrya, Saṃjñā and Chāyā, which would orient us in broaching the Goddess of the DM?

That the names Saṃjñā and Chāyā were incorporated in this mythology, replacing Saraṇyū and Sāvarṇā, is surely a very significant Purāṇic development. Had the authors of the Purāṇic myths of the Sun intended to invoke only Saraṇyū and Sāvarṇā, they would have. Clearly, they intend to connote another layer of association, if not a transformation altogether, through their act of renaming. While the exchange in the Vedic mythology centred around the mortality of the Sun, this could not possibly be the case in the episodes we find in the MkP where the Sun is not only immortal, but accorded as the prime cause of all creation. It is understandable why the ancient Vedic poet-seers would be inspired to elect the Sun as a signifier for mortality, as it is born and dies with each passing day. Furthermore, its natural affinity with fire makes it readily relatable to the sacrificial fires, and the incessant ritual process whereby enjoyments are procured for the sake of ameliorating mortal existence. Yet the Purāṇic poets' laudation of the Sun modifies this model of mortality, succeeding to radically reform it, resurrecting it beyond the shadow of death in which it lies in Vedic times. This transformation befits the vision of the Sun to be found in contemporary (and lasting) astrological texts wherein the maker of day symbolizes the "the soul of all" (*sarvātmān*) (BPH 3), that is, the eternal and immortal presence which graces the bodies of all sentient life. The Sun in this context is no mortal being, to be sure. It stands to reason then, especially given the incorporation of the names Saṃjñā and Chāyā, that the Purāṇic mythology of the Sun underscores the interplay between light and dark, rather than the tension between the mortal male and the immortal female.

One readily loses sight of this transformation when one reads these accounts throughout the Vedic accounts of the goddess Saraṇyū, which is a practice no more inappropriate than measuring the use of any given word by its more ancient etymological precursors. Any given word will invariably be assigned different associations and nuances, and even entirely different concepts and applications, as it filters down through the cultural ages – and the same applies to religious symbols, deified or otherwise. We catch only a fleeting a glimmer of this interplay in the work of Wendy Doniger who, following Lommel, notes that "the alternation between light and dark, together with the relationship with the Sun, may suggest that Saṃjñā is a riddle for Sandhyā, dawn: the Doppelganger woman is then evening twilight, and the Sun has two wives" (Doniger 1980, 177). It is perhaps in invocation of this riddle of the Sun and his two consorts/powers that immediately before the Goddess is first introduced in the DM, Sage Medhas instructs Suratha (in his explication to the extent to which all creatures are under the phenomenal veil of occlusion, generated by the power of the Goddess) that "Some creatures are blind by day, while others are blind by night:/ While others still see equally by day and by night" (DM 1.35) (Balkaran 2020). Some creatures awaken at dawn (*sandhyā*), while otherwise arise at dusk (*chāyā*), both of which junctures are created by the motion of the Sun.

Doniger takes Saṃjñā to mean sign, image, or name (Doniger 1996, 158) – which of course it does, particularly in the *Mahābhārata* where, coupled with the verb to do (*kṛ*), it means to give a signal. While the abstract feminine noun Saṃjñā meaning sign, token, or signal itself makes for a fitting appellation for one signalling the presence of both shadow and light, all the more so does its deeper meaning (stemming from a time as early as the Śatapaṭha Brāhmaṇa) of "consciousness", or "clear knowledge or understanding or notion or conception".[5] In a sense, it connotes the "clear seeing" occasioned by the dawn (*saṃdhyā*), and it is thus no wonder it was accorded to the consort of the source of universal illumination, the Sun, maker of dawn and enabler of sight alike. Sight is a power[6] accompanying the Sun. The name of Saṃjñā's cloned-counterpart, Chāyā, means "shadow" or "reflection" as noted above. With respect to her role as a power (*śakti*) of the Sun, she represents his ability to cast shadows and reflections whenever anyone stands before him. It is because of the Sun's megalomaniacal magnanimity that he loses Saṃjñā (clarity) and gains Chāyā (shadow), a shadow, which he himself casts by his excessive, self-absorbed splendour. The Sun creates dawn but, ironically, also creates dusk. His movements make both day and night. In a sense, then, Sūrya possesses two *śaktis*, akin to the double faces of the Goddess of our text – the power to illumine and reveal (as personified by Saṃjñā), and the power to darken and conceal (as personified by Chāyā). The Goddess – complete and in no need of consort – must in one fell swoop represent the trinity of this self-effulgent primal being and the paradox of his oppositional powers of illumination and occlusion alike.

Occlusion, too, has a vital role to play in the cosmic sphere, for Shadow (Chāyā) not only mothers the Lord of an Age, the next Manu, but does so through the establishment of a blessing of the Goddess of the DM who represents both dark and light: both Saṃjñā, the śakti of illumination and Chāyā, the śakti of occlusion in the form of *māyā*. As such, in one of the invocatory hymns of the DM, the gods of heaven praise the Goddess as existing in all creatures as both "the *māyā* of Viṣṇu" and as the principle of "consciousness" (DM 5.12). A few verses down, she is specifically praised as residing in all creatures in the form of shadow (*chāyā*) (DM 5.17). These laudations of the Goddess occurring in the heart of the text as the occlusive power of shadow lends credence to the argument that the DM's frame narrative – exalting king Suratha to become the son of Sūrya, by Chāyā – are far from afterthought conceits contrived by śākta interpolators but, rather, are the narrative design of the DM that is symbiotically linked to the fabric of the MkP (and consciously so), particularly as manifest through its structural similitude with the stories of the Sun therein. This suggestion shall be supported in the discussion that follows. The following section of this chapter argues that the myth of the Sun and his wife Saṃjñā in fact encode the astronomical position of the Sun at the time of the Navarātra festival, when the DM is ritually chanted across India.

## 3.2 Equine exegesis

While the Purāṇas indeed make reference to the navarātra festival (Einoo 1999), it is intriguing that both the DM and MkP are silent on the matter. Or are they? Saṃjñā generates two guises: one of the same form and different essence, Chāyā, representing shadow and reflection alike, while the second guise is of another form altogether, disguised as a mare. The text gives no reason, in either telling of the myth found on the MkP, as to why Saṃjñā need chose the form of a mare. Her equine transformation is particularly perplexing given that she chooses this form in order to perform austerities. One associates neither a seated posture, nor stillness, nor yet denial with the nature of horses. Rather, one more readily associates movement, exploration, and celebration with them. Further still, we cannot perceive any cause for the Sun to engage Saṃjñā in equine form, rather than to present his splendid pared down form itself. If the purpose of Saṃjñā's mare garb was to perform austerities so that her husband might become milder, then would her form not be obsolete at that point in the story? Yet this appears to be an aspect of Saṃjñā's (and Saraṇyū's) story preserved across the millennia. Goldman, too, notes that "the point of her assuming the form of a mare is not clear aside from the etymological association with the name Aśvins. In short, the mythologist is presented with a great problem by this story. What does it represent?" (Goldman 1969, 277–8).

Interestingly enough, I believe that the answer to this question implicates yet another narrative oddity: why does Saṃjñā not merely gallop away from the strange male if she was so intent upon guarding her rear? I argue that this face-to-face equine encounter is a preconceived narrative destination, and the authors of the MkP take whatever creative turns necessary to drive us there. Saṃjñā's fear serves as an impetus for a seminal plot development: in protecting her rear, she spins around so as to enable intimate nose-to-nose engagement. At this point, one might infer that she is aware that the potentially threatening mare is her husband in the form of a stallion (particular since the narrative offers no subsequent moment wherein she makes this realization). Regardless, she appears to willingly engage a face-to-face encounter with the stallion, under the narrative pretence of guarding her rear. This movement is crucial. What Doniger refers to as a "gloss" which is "untrue to the original spirit of the myth" (Doniger 1980, 185) is more likely a clever narrative trope deployed for the sake of occasioning a crucial and lasting element of this myth cycle: the birthing of equine twins through the nostrils of the equine Sun. And this birthing is equally crucial to bridging the DM and its solar frame. In order to understand the significance of this trope, the Indian mythologist must turn to perhaps the most ancient avenue of mythic narrative: astrological mythology, that is, stories about the stars.

The Purāṇas, in their current form, are generally attributed to the flourishing of the Gupta Empire, and so too, is classical Indian astrology, Jyotiṣa (Pingree 1977, VI: 11). The MkP betrays at several junctures knowledge of, and reliance upon, the principles of Jyotiṣa with respect to: 1) ascribing categorical astrological signifiers for people and geographical locations; 2) ritual timing; 3) in conjunction with life decisions; and 4) in casting a horoscope at the time of birth (*jātaka*). With respect to the first of these, in his discourse wherein all of India is configured as resting upon Viṣṇu in his tortoise incarnation, Mārkaṇḍeya explains (in Canto 58) the various asterisms assigned to each part of the tortoise, that is, each part of India and the people thereat (MkP 58). With respect to ritual timing, Queen Madālasā schools her son Alarka on the various benefits of ancestor worship (*śrāddha pūjā*) when the moon is conjoined in the various nakṣatras (MkP 33). With respect to the third aforementioned category, the MkP presents two notable examples where astrologers were consulted by kings in order to ascertain auspicious timing for undertaking certain actions. First, when King Rājyavardhana decides to renounce his kingdom, he "enquired of the astrologers about the best days and moments for anointing his son in the kingdom" (MkP 109.38) (Pargiter 1904, 580). Second, when princess Vaiśālinī, at her *svayamvara*, did not chose any of the potential bridegrooms present, her father, the king, enquires of the astrologer for the most auspicious day for her marriage, to which query the astrologer replies: "there will be, O king, other days here, characterized by excellent conjunctures, auspicious, and after no long delay. Thou shalt perform the wedding when they have arrived, O bestower of honour. Enough of this day, wherein a great obstacle has presented itself, O noble Sir!" (MkP 123.25–27)

(Pargiter 1904, 631). Finally, with respect to the fourth of the aforementioned astrological applications to be found in the MkP (i.e. casting a horoscope at the time of birth), we find in the text a remarkable example. At the time of his son's birth, King Karandhama "asked the astrologers – who could read fate – 'I trust my son is born under an excellent constellation, at an excellent conjuncture?'" (MkP 122.4) (Pargiter 1904, 626). The astrologers reported that:

> When the moment, the constellation and the conjuncture have been excellent, thy son has been born to be great in valour, great in his parts, great in strength. O great king, thy son shall be a great king. The planet Jupiter, preceptor of the gods, has looked on him, and Venus which is the seventh and the Moon the fourth planet has looked upon this thy son and Soma's son Mercury also, which is stationed at the edge has guarded him. The Sun has not looked on him; nor has Mars or Saturn looked on thy son, O great king. Happy is this thy son! he will be endowed with all good fortune and prosperity.
>
> (MkP 122.4) (Pargiter 1904, 626)

The king, of course, was quite gladdened by his astrologers' forecast. He appears to trust completely both in the skill of his court astrologers and in the principles of Jyotiṣa themselves in order to render accurate information about the nature and destiny of an individual. He makes a most remarkable reply to his astrologers at this point:

> The preceptor of the gods has looked on him, and so has Soma's son Mercury. The Sun has not looked on him, nor has the Sun's son nor Mars. This word "Has looked upon" of that ye, sirs, have uttered often, – celebrated by reason of it his name shall be Avīkshita.
>
> (MkP 122.4) (Pargiter 1904, 626)

The faith that King Karandhama puts in his court astrologers is so central to this episode, that he ends up naming his son Avīkṣita, based on the astrological terminology. The MkP examples mentioned thus make specific references to the mechanics and usages of Jyotiṣa. For the ensuing discussion, I draw upon two standard Sanskrit treatises outlining the mechanics of classical Jyotiṣa: the *Bṛhat Parāśara Hora* (BPH) ascribed to sage Parāśara and the *Bṛhat Jātaka* (BJ) ascribed to Varāhamahira.

David Pingree (the author of the Jyotiśāstra volume of Gonda's History of Indian Luterature) places the BPH between 600–750 CE, and places the work of Varāhamihira (who was at the court of Chandragupta II) in the sixth century, and notes that his BJ "became the model for much of the subsequent Sanskrit literature on jātaka, and remains the most authoritative text-book on the subject today" (Pingree 1977, VI: 84–85). Interestingly, he traces much of its contents to Sphujidhvaja's *Yavanajātaka* in 269/270 CE during the reign of the Western Ksatrapa Rudrasena II, which itself was a versification of a Sanskrit translation of a Greek astrological text in 149–150 CE, probably at the court of the Western Ksatrapa Rudradaman in Ujjayinī. Therefore, most of the contents of the sixth-century BJ correspond to those of second-century YJ. As an aside, while Pingree's work on the historical transmission of Jyotiḥ Śāstra is indeed commendable, he does not seem to convey an appreciation for the fact that classical Indian vidyās, such as Jyotiṣa, were by and large esoteric, and transmitted orally, where the extant text was used as a prop for oral elucidation. Therefore, comments such as "it would not have been possible to compute planetary positions with only the information in the texts as extant; their original forms were presumably more complete" (Pingree 1977, VI: 11) are highly problematic.

The movements of the heavenly bodies are accompanied not only by techniques of interpretation and prediction, but also by rich and ancient narratives – narratives which, as shall be made clear, find themselves at home in Purāṇic literature. An explicit example of this is to be found in Canto 75 of the MkP, which tells of the exploits of the constellation Revatī (technically, one of the lunar asterisms, or *nakṣatras*, discussed below) which fell to earth due to Sage Ṛta-vāc's curse (see Pargiter 1904, 443–9). Similarly, the symbolism of horses is not only thematically apropos to the mythology of the Sun insofar as seven swift horses draw the chariot of the Sun across the sky "ever unwearied" (MkP 197.8), but particularly because horses symbolize the half-equine Aśvin twins whose genesis the myth relays; the same twins after which the lunar asterism (*nakṣatra*) Aśvini, is named. The use of *nakṣatras* for ritual and predictive purposes has persisted since Vedic times: these lunar mansions represent the oldest strata of Indian astrology, and quite possibly, encapsulate some of the most ancient extant South Asian narrative motifs in their mythologies. There are twenty-seven lunar asterisms, whose zodiacal arc necessarily occupy one-twenty-seventh of the 360-degree orb of the sky. Hence each asterism occupies 13 degrees and 20-arc minutes (or one-third of a degree) of zodiacal arc. We must note further that of the twenty-seven lunar asterisms, Aśvini is the first, and commences the Zodiac, occupying the first 13 degrees and 20-arc seconds of Aries, the first zodiacal sign. The 'twins' of this asterism appear in the sky astronomically as the stars β and γ Arietis. Unsurprisingly, this asterism governs all things equine in the world. For example, Queen Madālasā informs Alarka that "one attains horses when performing the śrāddha while the moon is conjoined Aśvini nakṣatra" (33.16) (Pargiter 1904, 170). That association between Aśvini and all things equine is so perennial in Indian mythology can be corroborated not only in the etymology of the very name of the nakṣatra, but, to my knowledge, all accounts of the birthing of the Aśvins (the half-equine presiding deities of this nakṣatra) entail the Sun and his wife entering equine form in order to birth them. But why must these parents be the Sun and his wife?

The BPH introduces the nine planets as the Sun, the Moon, Mars, Mercury, Jupiter, Venus, Saturn, Rahu, and Ketu (BPH 3.10). Each planet serves as signifier for a multitude of aspects of the phenomenal universe: to put it differently, each aspect of the known universe is ascribed to the sway of one of the nine planets. The BPH specifies what is foremost represented by each planet with respect to human beings, stating that "the Sun is the soul of all. The moon is the mind. Mars is one's strength. Mercury is the speech giver while Jupiter confers knowledge and happiness. Venus governs semen (potency) while Saturn indicates grief" (BPH 3.12–13) (Sharma 1994, 17). Note that while the Sun is accorded primacy, as the soul of all, it is Venus which represents sexuality and procreation. Venus is considered one of the benefic plants in Jyotiṣa, whereas the Sun is considered a (minor) malefic, probably owing to its intensity. This concept is actually encapsulated in the MkP as follows:

> When [Avīkṣita] was born, the king asked the astrologers – who could read fate –" I trust my son is born under an excellent constellation, at an excellent conjuncture? And I trust that benignant planets have looked upon my son's birth; I trust it did not pass into the path of view of evil planets? When addressed thus by him, the astrologers spake then to the king –" When the moment, the constellation and the conjuncture have been excellent, thy son has been born to be great in valour, great in his parts, great in strength. O great king, thy son shall be a great king. The planet Jupiter, preceptor of the gods, has looked on him, and Venus which is the seventh and the Moon the fourth planet has looked upon this thy son and Soma's son Mercury also, which is stationed at the edge has guarded him. The Sun has not looked on him; nor has Mars or Saturn looked on thy son, O great king. Happy is this thy son! he will be endowed with all good fortune and prosperity.
>
> (MkP 122) (Pargiter 1904, 625–6)

Venus is often personified as a goddess of fertility throughout the Indian (Lakṣmī) and Near Eastern world (e.g. Ishtar to the Babylonians, Isis to the Egyptians, Aphrodite to the Greek, and, of course, the Goddess Venus to the Romans from whence the name comes down to us). It represents not only sexual reproduction, but also sensual and aesthetic experience at large. It is telling that the most common name for this planet in Sanskrit and its derivatives is *śukra*, the word for semen itself. It is understood as a moist planet since moisture is, of course, necessary for life. The Sun, on the other hand, is a dry, hot planet. The Sun is not a suitable symbol for semen: it represents hotness and dryness, both of which threaten seminal health.

The Sun's role in fathering the foremost of these lunar mansions is definitely fitting for a myth wherein he is lauded as the primal universal principle. In the astrological myth, he seeds the beginnings of the zodiac (the universe of Jyotiṣa, the backdrop against which all heavenly action takes place), while in the myths of the MkP, he seeds creation itself (the phenomenal universe). However, his association with the Aśvins long predates the grandeur he is accorded in the Purāṇas, and was present even when he was a mere mortal in Vedic times. Jyotiṣa informs us that all of the planets acquire different degrees of strength in different signs. For example, Jupiter, being a watery planet, attains its peak performance in Cancer, the most watery of zodiacal signs. Whether or not these ascriptions were ever based on experience of the natural planets, there can be little doubt that the states accorded to the Sun as it passed through the zodiac were based on its palpable effect on the planet, particularly in an equatorial climate. The Sun, being fire itself, therefore acquires its state of peak performance (exaltation, *ucca*) in the fiery sign of Aries. The strength it acquires as it passes through Aries is expressed on earth as the coming of spring. The BPH therefore states that "Aries, Taurus, Capricorn, Virgo, Cancer, Pisces, and Libra have been spoken of respectively from the Sun on, as the signs of exaltation of the seven planets" (BPH 2.49) (Sharma 1994, 36). But given that there are twelve zodiacal signs and twenty-seven lunar asterisms, each sign will contain within it two and a fraction asterisms. Therefore, the sign of Aries would be home to three lunar asterisms: aśvinī, bharaṇī, and the first bit of kṛtikkā. Why is the Sun tied to only the first of these asterisms? The answer again lies in Indian astrological understandings. There is a particular point within the entire sign which is considered the very plexus (*yoga tārā*) of exaltation. For example, if one were to visualize a comfortable sign as warm room, the point of greatest heat would be the fireplace. This occurs at 10 degrees of Aries, which falls within the arc of aśvinī nakṣatra. The BPH states that "The deepest exaltation degrees in these planets are respectively 10, 3, 28, 15, 5, 27, 20" (BPH 2.50) (Sharma 1994, 36). Furthermore, it tell us that Aries (to which it ascribes characteristics, along with all of the other zodiacal signs), among other things, is a quadruped, possesses a bulky body, is of royal caste, and wanders through hills (BPH 4.6) (Sharma 1994, 54). As the BPH states that "The deepest exaltation degrees in these planets are respectively 10, 3, 28, 15, 5, 27, 20. And the 7th sign from the said exaltation sign each planet has its debilitation to the same degrees" (BPH 2.50) (Sharma 1994, 36).

In taking direction from ancient Indian astrological mythology, the mythologist is, perhaps at long last, equipped to understand why the Sun and Saṃjñā take equine form and encounter each other in the Northern Kurus in order to birth the Aśvins. It is a mythic representation of the annual exaltation of the Sun as it approaches 10 degrees of Aries and conjoins in the asterism of Aśvini. Furthermore, in attempting to understand why the sparse akhyāna hymns are part of the Vedic tradition, scholars such as Oldenberg posit the presence of non-Vedic "popular" traditions existing alongside the Brahmanic priestly cult. Goldman notes:

> that such "popular" cults existed cannot be very well questioned. Indeed, the evidence of the Purāṇas seems to indicate that many of the elements of Hinduism are at least as old as much of the Vedic literature. Yet, even so, the question of how and why elements of the popular mythos came to be incorporated into the sacred texts of the Vedic ṛṣis remains with all its original force.
>
> (Goldman 1969, 274)

With respect to the akhyāna hymns depicting the birthing of the Aśvins by the Sun in equine form, one answer to the question of why it was thus assembled into the Vedic corpus is because its assemblers were well aware that it represented an astronomical reality which would certainly carry significance for Vedic ritual timing. By drawing from astrological literature, we might of course explain the association with the Sun's potency, and he and Saṃjñā taking horse form and journeying into the countryside in episodes found in the MkP – but one crucial detail remains, which I promised above to account for: why must they engage face-to-face?

Corroborating the extent to which the myth of the Sun and Saṃjñā is inextricable to astrological understandings of the Sun's journey through the zodiac, we can again take direction from *jyotiḥ śāstra* with respect to why the Sun and Saṃjñā encounter each other face-to-face. Each zodiacal sign is represented by a region of the body. The BJ specifies that on the scale of the full body, Aries represents the head itself (BJ 1.4). Furthermore, each of the twelve zodiacal signs is symbolized by a part of the face.[7] The nose symbolizes the sign of Aries, in which sits the lunar asterism Aśvini. It is to embellish this nasal association that the poet has equine-Saṃjñā turn about, under the pretence of guarding her rear, conceiving the Aśvins by sniffing the *tejas* of the Sun.[8] The myth draws from the understanding that the Sun acquires its state of exaltation (*ucca*) when it sits in Aries (since this coincides with the coming of spring, around the time of the vernal equinox), conjoined the asterism of Aśvini. So, the myth encodes the cultural understanding that Aśvin twins originate in Aries (represented by the nose), powered by the Sun's exaltation therein (represented by their spawning by the Sun's stallion-form). Adding yet another dimension to the astrological associations to this myth is the character of Revanta, about which we know nothing more of than what we hear in the myth of the Aśvins' birth. This suggests to me he is merely a supporting actor in the story of the Sun and the aśvins; the name Revanta might very well be read as a pun in the form of a contraction of 'Revatī', the final asterism ending the constellation Pisces, immediately before the start of Aries, and 'anta' the termination thereof. Therefore, the Aśvins are born (where Aśvini commences) in conjunction with Revanta, at the end of Revatī.

The myths of the Sun not only serve the DM thematically but also with respect to the ritual timing of its annual recitation at the *navarātra* (nine nights) festivities dedicated to the Great Goddess. The Goddess festival takes place at two annual junctures, the first nine nights of Āśvina, when the full moon is in Aśvini (and the Sun is in Citrā), and in Caitra, when the full moon is in Citra (and the Sun is in Aśvini). To demonstrate this linkage, we again draw from texts on Jyotiṣa. The Sun attains its greatest power in Aries, conjoined Aśvini nakṣatra, in the springtime during its equine equinox. Conversely, it is at its weakest (described in a fallen state, *nicca*), six months later, at the time of the autumnal equinox. At this time, the Sun sits 180 degrees away, in the constellation of Libra. As stated in the BJ, the Sun "is most exalted in the 10th degree of Aries" and it is "considered as the most debilitated 180 degrees away from the degree of exaltation" (BJ 1.13) (Sastri 1995, 17), that is, at the 10th degree of Libra. This time of year brings with it the lunar month Āśvina, marked by the full moon in the constellation Aries (conjoined Aśvini nakṣatra) 180 degrees away from the "fallen" Sun, stationed in the constellation Libra.[9] And it is exactly at this time of year when, due to the fallen state of solar energy in the cosmos, that the grand Goddess festival takes place. It occurs on the first nine nights of the waxing moon headed towards its fullness in the asterism aśvinī, and is a time when the *Devī Māhātmya* (detailing the acts of Durgā and her reinstatement of the fallen kingship of Suratha, and her deliverance of the promise of a future Manu), is ritually chanted throughout the Hindu world. The DM, as noted, commences and concludes with invoking the Sun. Therefore, the mythologies of the Sun offer more than a narrative corollary; they serve to contextualize its ritual life, affording direction and justification for the annual juncture most auspicious for the chanting of the text.

Hillary Rodrigues traces the Sanskrit liturgy of the pan-Indic autumnal festival in honour of the Hindu Great Goddess (primarily in the form of Durgā, the Impassable, who is equated with the Goddess of the DM), which occurs during the first nine nights of the waxing moon commencing on the Indian (lunar) month of Āśvina. In many homes, the DM (also referred to as the *Durgā Saptaśatī* in ritual context) is chanted daily during the course of the festival. This study constitutes an exhaustive description of a Bengali style form of ritual worship of Durgā Pūjā, which takes place in the sacred city of Banaras. Rodrigues expounds the overt connection between the grand ritual and its mythic heritage in his discussion of the extent to which the clay image complexes erected for the festival "clearly forges a relationship between Purāṇic myth and the ritual" (Rodrigues 2003, 50). The complexes do so by enacting the demon-slaying exploits of the DM, particularly in Episode II where the Durgā slays Mahīṣāsura, an episode that also, as Rodrigues notes, echoes elsewhere in the Purāṇic corpus.[10] In the context of the gathered masses at the Goddess festival, Rodrigues designates Durgā as,

> the monarch for whom the people have gathered in a display of service, loyalty and devotion. In their numbers, and in their visible and verbalized sentiments of revelry and unity, they have a vision (darśana) of their own power, and with it, the certitude of being victorious in any undertaking. This vision of the victorious power (vijayā śakti) that permeates the community of worshippers, binding them in a union characterized by joy and fearlessness, is implicitly a view of the manifest form of the Goddess.
>
> (Rodrigues 2003, 296)

It is this spirit of motherly protection of sovereign empowerment, which characterizes the Goddess of our text, the same characterization which, as Rodrigues notes, pervades also her festival. It is quite telling that he elects the word "monarch" to describe the Goddess.

Through the chanting of the DM at this annual juncture, the waning Sun is ameliorated by the grace of the Goddess whose role it is to keep darkness (which, paradoxically, she also represents) at bay, and so, too, is the waning energy of sovereignty, of righteous regulation throughout the universe. Therefore, in invoking the majesty of the Goddess, one also invokes the majesty of the Sun. And this majesty is more than inferred, or figurative, insofar as Jyotiṣical texts specifically equate the solar and the royal. For example, according the BPH "the Sun and the Moon are of royal status" (BPH 3.14–15) (Sharma 1994, 19)[11] a notion which is echoed verbatim in Varāhamahira's BJ (2.1). Royal figures in the Indian context carry not only associations of regality and magnanimity (as, of course, in any cultural context), but equally carry sanguinary associations: to be a king in ancient India (and in the Indian literary imagination) is to necessarily be a warrior bar none. And our Jyotiṣical texts are also happy to point this out. The BPH, while assigning castes to all of the planets, unsurprisingly assigns the Sun the caste of kṣatriya,[12] a trope that is echoed at BJ 2.6. It is perhaps for this very reason that both the Sun and Mars are accorded "dark red" (*rakta śyāmaḥ*) at both BJ 2.4 and BPH,[13] whereas only Mars appears dark red to the naked eye. Thus, the majestic and sanguinary aspects of the Goddess are appropriately framed in the MkP by those of the Sun, since both Goddess and Sun are emblematic of the archetypal Indian sovereign.

Pintchman offers a lucid analysis of the role that the three feminine philosophical principles play in various Purāṇic cosmogonic accounts (Pintchman 1994, 117–84). She orders her discussion in accordance to the first two of the five Purāṇic marks (*pañcalakṣaṇas*): primary creation (*sarga*) and secondary creation (*pratisarga*) accordingly. This is unsurprising considering her emphasis on cosmogony. However, her study offers no discourse on the Goddesses' role in the remaining three of the five Purāṇic marks: the genealogies of sages and kings (*vaṃśa*), Manu-interval discourse (*manvantara*), and the dynasties of sages and kings (*vaṃśānucarita*). This absence of *manvantara* discourse is especially notable given that the DM introduces her as she by whose grace Sāvarṇi attains Manuhood. We are then told that the Manu Sāvarṇi will be an incarnation of an earthly king, Suratha. Clearly the Great Goddess plays a central cosmogonic role; however, her role as creator is as if eclipsed by her role as preserver of the cosmos. C. Mackenzie Brown, on the other hand, observes that "the frame story … serves textually to situate the glorification of the Goddess within the larger context of the *Mārkaṇḍeya Purāṇa* as a whole" wherein "the *Devī Māhātmya* is widely recognized as an interpolation" since "nowhere else in the Mārkaṇḍeya do we meet with the Śākta themes articulated so artfully and forcefully in the *Devī Māhātmya*" (Brown 1990, 157–9). Yet, both the artistry and the force of these themes are enhanced when underscored by their frame narrative, which described the making of a Manu, and this research demonstrates the significance of doing so. The commencement of the glories of the Goddess invoke the making of a Manu, and in doing so, point directly to the glories of the Sun, where from we may receive both thematic direction in how to understand the glories of the Goddess, and ritual direction on when to incant these glories. Hence, the bridge between DM and MkP is brightened by the splendour of the Sun. In light of this, it is likely that the MkP was not only deliberately selected for the placement of the DM, but that the very juncture within the MkP where it occurs was not without careful consideration. Furthermore, the term "placement" is inapt with respect to how the DM relates to the MkP as a whole: rather than constituting a discreet, self-contained composition, one mechanically inserted into the MkP by virtue of the flimsy framing conceits contrived by haphazard śākta interpolators, the DM betrays a compositional process cognizant of the content of the MkP, especially the mythologies of the Sun housed therein.

## Notes

1 Wendy Doniger has written profusely on Hindu mythology throughout her career. Hers has certainly been the most acclaimed scholarly pen of the last half-century to have drawn from the ink of Purāṇic lore. Western scholars of Purāṇa are deeply indebted to her work and as a discipline, the extent of her influence on approaches to Hindu myth is only beginning to become clear. While Doniger has written voluminously on Indian mythology, this discussion confines itself to her work on the mythology of the Sun and his wife, Saṃjñā, as appearing in the MkP.

2 The list of textual sources is as follows: *Rg Veda* 10.17.1–2: *Nirukta* 12.10: *Śatapatha Brāhmaṇa* 1.1.4.14; *Taittrīya Brāhamaṇa* 1.1.4.4; 1.1.9.10; 3.2.5.9; *Taittrīya Saṃhitā* 2.6.7.1; 6.5.6.1; 6.6.6.1; *Mārkaṇḍeya Purāṇa* 103–105; *Mahābhārata* 1.66; *Brahmāṇḍa Purāṇa* 3.59–60; *Matsya Purāṇa* 11; *Padma Purāṇa* 5.8; *Vāyu Purāṇa* 2.3; *Viṣṇu Purāṇa* 3.2; *Gopatha Brāhamaṇa* 1.1.3 (Doniger 1976, 349).

3 Corroboration of the primary meaning of the word *tejas* can be taken from its antithesis: *atejas*. The Monier-Williams entry for the antonym at hand specifies the following meanings: "n. absence of brightness or vigour"; "dimness, shade, shadow"; "feebleness, dullness, insignificance"; "not bright, dim, not vigorous". While the listlessness associated with these meanings can surely be symbolically applied to render a sense of (sexual) impotence, seminal fluid is far from the primary connotation of the term *tejas*. Furthermore, the verbal root *tij* (which, as mentioned, means to "be or become sharp", does not carry with it the connotation of 'to inseminate.')

4 Mārkaṇḍeya describes the Northern Kurus thus:

> Next I will tell thee of the Northern Kurus; hearken to me now. There the trees yield sweet fruit, they bear blossoms and fruit in constant succession; and they produce garments and ornaments inside their fruits; verily they bestow all one's desire; they yield fruit according to all one's desire. The ground abounds with precious stones; the air is fragrant and always delightful. Mankind are born there, when they quit the world of the gods. They are born in pairs; the pairs abide an equal time, and are as fond of each other as c'akravakas. Their stay there is fourteen and a half thousands of years indeed. And C'andra-kanta is the chief of the mountains, and Surya-kanta is the next; they are the two mountain ranges in that continent. And in the midst thereof the great river Bhadra-soma flows through the earth with a volume of sacred and pure water. And there are other rivers by thousands in that northern continent; and some flow with milk and others flow with ghee. And there are lakes of curdled milk there, and others lie among the various hills. And fruits of various kinds, which taste rather like amṛta, are produced by hundreds and thousands in the woods in those continents.
>
> (MkP 59.18–26) (Pargiter 1904, 389)

5 It can either be taken as the verbal root '*jñā*' (to know) conjoined with the verbal prefix '*saṃ*', – giving the sense of 'to agree with', 'to be in harmony with', or 'to understand well'. In this vein, its abstract noun correlate can also mean "agreement". Monier-Williams specifically listed: "the wife of the Sun". Furthermore, while

Saṃjñā connotes "consciousness, clear knowledge or understanding or notion or conception" from the times of the Śatapaṭha Brāhmaṇa onwards, Doniger (for the sake of her argument), tends to favour "a sign, token, signal, gesture (with the hand, eyes, etc)" as occurring in kāvya and the *Mahābhārata* (Monier-Williams *et al.* 2008).

6 The word śakti dually denotes "consort" as well as "power", and therefore the consort of any given deity functions by and large as the particular power of that deity. For example, the goddess of material comfort, Lakṣmī, is the consort of the cosmic preserver, Viṣṇu: thus, Viṣṇu is preserved through material comfort. Similarly, the goddess of creativity (both artistic and literary) is Sarasvatī, who is the śakti (power/consort) of the creator, Brahmā, himself.

7 Aries is symbolized by the nose, Leo and Cancer by the right and left eye respectively, Libra and Taurus by right and left cheek respectively, Scorpio by the mouth, Sagittarius and Pisces by right and left ear respectively, Gemini and Virgo by right and left forehead respectively, and Aquarius and Capricorn by right and left chin respectively.

8 One wonders whether or not this myth also symbolizes the Āyurvedic herb, *aśvagandha*, particularly given the association of aśvini *nakṣatra* and medicinal herbs.

9 The myth of Sūrya's hammering down is the myth of his movement from the constellation Citrā (which is owned by Aryamān, his father-in-law), to that of Aśvini, which is owned by the Aśvins.

10 The Goddesses encounter (and inevitably defeat) the demon Mahīṣa in the following Purāṇas: Kālikā Devī Bhāgavata, Skanda, Vāmana and Varāha.

11 The verse continues, "and Mars is the army chief; Mercury is the prince apparent and Jupiter and Venus are ministerial planets. Saturn is servant and Rahu and Ketu form the planetary army."

12 The caste allotments for all of the planets are as follows: Jupiter and Venus as the royal counsellors (the former sacred, the later secular) are Brahmins, the Sun and Mars are Kṣatriyas, the Moon and Mercury are Vaiśyas, while Saturn is the śūdra, that is, servant (BPH 3.21) (Sharma 1994, 24–5).

13 The entire verse reads:

> The Sun, the Lord of the Day, is blood-red, the Moon is tawny. Mars whose stature is not high is blood-red, while Mercury is akin to that of grass. O Brahmin shrestha, Jupiter, Venus, and Saturn should ne known as tawny, variegated and dark.
>
> (BPH 3.16–17) (Sharma 1994, 20)

## Works cited in this chapter

Balkaran, Raj. 2018. "The Splendor of the Sun: Brightening the Bridge between Mārkaṇḍeya Purāṇa and Devī Māhātmya in Light of Navarātri Ritual Timing". In *Nine Nights of the Goddess: The Navarātri Festival in South Asia*, edited by Caleb Simmons, Hillary Rodrigues and Moumita Sen, 23–38. Albany, NY: State University of New York Press.

Balkaran, Raj. 2019. "The Story of Saṃjñā, Mother of Manu: Shadow and Light in the Mārkaṇḍeya Purāṇa". In *The Bloomsbury Research Handbook on Indian Philosophy and Gender*, edited by Veena R Howard, 267–96. New York: Bloomsbury Publishing.

Balkaran, Raj. 2020. "A Tale of Two Boons: The Goddess and the Dharmic Double Helix". In *The Purāṇa Reader*, edited by Deven Patel and Dheepa Sundaram. San Diego, CA: Cognella Academic Publishing.

Brown, Cheever Mackenzie. 1990. *The Triumph of the Goddess the Canonical Models and Theological Visions of the Devī-Bhāgavata Purāṇa*. Albany, NY: State University of New York Press.

Doniger O'Flaherty, Wendy. 1973. *Asceticism and Eroticism in the Mythology of the Śiva*. London: Oxford University Press.

Doniger, Wendy. 1976. *The Origins of Evil in Hindu Mythology*. Berkeley, CA: University of California Press.

Doniger, Wendy. 1980. *Women, Androgynes, and Other Mythical Beasts*. Chicago, IL: University of Chicago Press.

Doniger, Wendy. 1996. "Saraṇyū/Saṃjñā: The Sun and The Shadow". In John Stratton Hawley and Donna Marie Wulff (eds), *Devī: Goddesses of India*. Berkeley, CA: University of California Press, 154–72.

Doniger, Wendy. 1999. *Splitting the Difference: Gender and Myth in Ancient Greece and India*. Chicago, IL: University of Chicago Press.

Doniger, Wendy. 2000. *The Bedtrick: Tales of Sex and Masquerade*. Chicago, IL: University of Chicago Press.

Doniger, Wendy (ed.) 2004. *Hindu Myths: A Sourcebook Translated from the Sanskrit*. London: Penguin.

Doniger, Wendy. 2014a. *On Hinduism*. New York: Oxford University Press.

Doniger, Wendy. 2014b. "Saranyu/Samjna: The Sun and The Shadow". In *On Hinduism*. New York: Oxford University Press, 269–87.

Einoo, Shingo. 1999. "The Autumn Goddess Festival: Described in the Purānas". In Masakazu Tanaka and Musashi Tachikawa (eds), *Living With Śakti: Gender, Sexuality and Religion in South Asia*. Senri Ethnological Studies 50. Osaka: National Museum of Ethnology , 33–70.

Goldman, Robert P. 1969. "Mortal Man and Immortal Woman: An Interpretation of Three Akhyana Hymns of the Rgveda". *Journal of the Oriental Institute of Baroda* 18 (4): 274–303.

Mani, Vettam. 1975. *Purāṇic Encyclopaedia: A Comprehensive Dictionary with Special Reference to the Epic and Purāṇic Literature*. Delhi : Motilal Banarsidass.

Monier-Williams, Ernst Leumann, Carl Cappeller, and Īśvaracandra. 2008. "Monier Williams Sanskrit–English Dictionary (2008 Revision)".

Pargiter, F.E. 1904. *Mārkaṇḍeya Purāṇa*. Calcutta: Asiatic Society of Bengal.

Pingree, David. 1977. *Jyotiḥśāstra*. Edited by Jan Gonda. Vol. VI. A History of Indian Literature, Part 3, Fasc. 4. Wiesbaden: Harrassowitz.

Pintchman, Tracy. 1994. *The Rise of the Goddess in the Hindu Tradition*. Albany, NY: State University of New York Press.

Rodrigues, Hillary. 2003. *Ritual Worship of the Great Goddess: The Liturgy of the Durgā Pūjā with Interpretations*. Albany, NY: State University of New York Press.

Sastri, Pothukuchi Subrahmanya. 1995. *Brihat Jataka*. New Delhi: Ranjan Publ.

Sharma, Girish Chand. 1994. *Maharishi Parasara's Brihat Parasara Hora Sastra*. New Delhi: Sagar Publications.

# 4 Mapping Mārkaṇḍeya

## Synchronic surveillance of *The Mārkaṇḍeya Purāṇa*

### 4.1 Exposition import

The manner in which the MkP is ultimately framed – the tripartite context of the questioner, the respondent, and the content of the questions themselves, herein referred to as exposition import – will necessarily grant insight into its current assembly of narrative constituent. If we look to the initial frame of the MkP, we note an expositional exchange wherein the interlocutor Jaimini asks the expositor Sage Mārkaṇḍeya four questions, questions which were apparently left unsatisfactorily addressed in the MBh. These questions constitute a four-part expositional prompt, which launches the work as a whole. In the words of R.C. Hazra, the MkP:

> commences with Jaimini, a pupil of Vyāsa, who approaches the sage Mārkaṇḍeya for the solution of some doubts raised in his mind by the study of the *Mahābhārata*. For want of sufficient time Mārkaṇḍeya does not answer the questions put to him by Jaimini but refers the latter to the four wise birds living on the Vindhyas. The beginning of the *Mārkaṇḍeya-purāṇa* agrees with its description given in the *Matsya*, which says: "That Purāṇa in which, in reply to the Muni, the duties and non-duties have been explained by the holy sages in connection with the birds and which, again, is narrated fully by Mārkaṇḍeya is called the *Mārkaṇḍeya* (-purāṇa), containing 9,000 verses."
>
> (Hazra 1975, 8)

The 'fanciful' frame inaugurating the MkP is surely not without intent. While one might choose to regard an individual textual entity as 'interpolated', one cannot exactly say the same for an initial frame. *Into what* can the inauguration of a work be said to be interpolated? Put otherwise: while one may argue that the DM was assembled into the MkP so as to be supported by the text, a frame was added to the MkP to support the MkP. But what does this initial frame hope to accomplish? Following exposition import, let us look to questionee, questioner and questions asked in the initial frame of the MkP.

DOI: 10.4324/9780429322020-5

### *4.1.1 Jaimini's questioning*

The role of the questioner is crucial to Purāṇic literature insofar as it is the nature of questions he poses, and the answers given to those questions, which succeed in advancing the narrative. Even the lengthiest of narrative passages is framed as dialogue between the questioner and sagacious respondent. We may therefore take direction from the question being asked, the nature of the questioner, and the nature of the respondent: these three elements will necessarily colour the unfolding narrative. For example, all of the various discourses in the BhG are posed as Kṛṣṇa's responses to Arjuna's questions. This conversation serves to contextualize what is being expounded. Furthermore, the exchanges between Kṛṣṇa and Arjuna are being ultimately relayed to the blind king Dhṛtarāṣṭhra by his advisor/charioteer Saṃjaya. Note that Saṃjaya had been granted the gift of *dūradarśana* (remote viewing) whereby he was able to perceive events great distances away through yogic vision. The fact that the entirely of the BhG is relayed to one who lacks the ability to view physical reality, relayed by one who is himself physically absent from the scene he describes (relaying events as they present themselves to him through his mind's eye through the grace of a supernatural gift of remote vision) serves to launch the discourse of the BhG in a transcendental, ideological space, whereby one may readily receive its inaugural locative dharma-kṣetre, 'the field of dharma', as the metaphysical, rather than physical, plane which it already implies in the absence of this ethereal framing. While, of course, Kṛṣṇa succeeds in doling out practical advice to an actual individual in a real-life scenario, the fact that he alights to the intangible realm of ethics, metaphysics – revealing his transcendental cosmic form in doing so – is foreshadowed and supported by the very non-physical, ethereal, ideational manner in which the verses themselves are framed: none of the Gītā, as relayed to the hearer, occurs within the field of direct vision. In like manner, the manner in which the MkP is ultimately framed – the context of the questioner, the respondent, and the content of the questions themselves – will necessarily grant insight into the framing process in which they partake, that is, the hermeneutic sway they hold upon that which they frame. Let us turn first to the interlocutor in question: who is this Jaimini?

The name Jaimini traditionally bears associations with the *Sāma Veda*, *Pūrva Mīmāṃsā Sūtras*, and an astrological treatise named *Jaimini Sūtras*. What is noteworthy is that Jaimini is an *expositor* in these works not an *interlocutor*. In casting Jaimini as an interlocutor, the initial frame of the MkP serves to communicate expositional mastery on behalf of Mārkaṇḍeya, whose knowledge lies even beyond that of the intellectually accomplished, such as Jaimini. Admittedly, there is no way to ascertain whether we are to understand the sūtric expositor, Jaimini, to be the same as the one questioning Mārkaṇḍeya. However, Jaimini is a reputed expositor even in itihāsa literature. Mani Vettam informs us that Jaimini was "a hermit of the highest degree of leaning" (Mani 1975, 337), being among the five foremost pupils of the great Vyāsa. He succeeds in becoming a great teacher in his own right since it is his insightful exposition to his interlocutor Hiraṇyanābha's questions in the Naimiṣā forest which comprises the *Brahmāṇḍa Purāṇa* (Mani 1975, 337). Little else is known of this figure other than his three minor appearances in the MBh: first, at Janamejaya's sacrifice to exterminate the serpents in the *Ādi Parvan* (MBh I.53.6); second, as a member of Yudhiṣṭhira's council in the *Sabhā Parvan* (MBh II.4.2); and third, as he visits Bhīṣma on his bed of arrows in the *Śānti Pārvan* (MBh XII.46.7) (Mani 1975, 337–8). Most relevant to our discussion is the reference to him in the Ādiparvan of the MBh wherein we are told that Vyāsa taught the Vedas and the MBh to Jaimini and four others (Sumantu, Paila, Śuka, Vaiśampāyana) who all "in their separate ways made public the Collections of *The Bhārata*" (MBh I.57.76) (van Buitenen 1973, I: 134). What little we do know of him – that he is a learned student of Vyāsa and mythic author of the *Brāhmāṇḍa Purāṇa* in his own right – suffices to exalt the teachings of Mārkaṇḍeya (indicative of the MkP as a whole) to a status more lofty than even the learning of the accomplished Jaimini. Now that we have registered the import of the MkP's interlocutor, let us turn to its expositor.

### *4.1.2 Master Mārkaṇḍeya*

Who is this Mārkaṇḍeya whom the knowledgeable Jaimini opts to question and what, by virtue of his unique career, might he be said to represent? The fact that Jaimini is a student of Vyāsa, the master assembler of the MhB, is certainly not inconsequential to what the MkP's frame narrative wishes to communicate about the status of the MkP. In the words of Pargiter, this dynamic "raises a presumption that there was an intention to make Mārkaṇḍeya equal with, if not superior to, Vyāsa" (Pargiter 1904, xxi). In turning our attention to the mythic progenitor of our Purāṇa, we note that various discourses of Sage Mārkaṇḍeya are to be found in MBh III.205–215, wherein he discusses

> the virtues of women (205 f.), upon forbearance towards living beings (Ahiṃsā, 206–208), upon the power of destiny, renunciation of the world and liberation, upon doctrines of the Sāṅkhya philosophy (210) and of the Vedānta (211), upon the duties towards parents (214 ff.) and others.
>
> (Winternitz 1972, 425)

From his introduction in the MBh, one gets the sense of the grandeur of Mārkaṇḍeya's presence. His massive exposition occurs while the Pāṇḍavas are in exile, visited by Kṛṣṇa and Satyabhāmā, "the beloved chief queen of Kṛṣṇa" (MBh 3.180.1) (van Buitenen 1975, II: 571). While they were speaking among themselves, the great sage Mārkaṇḍeya appears before them. The Pāṇḍava entourage welcome and honour him, extending the hospitality appropriate to so exalted a guest. They ask him to regale them with sacred tales of times long past, of sages, and women, and kings. Signalling the significance of Mārkaṇḍeya's transmission, Nārada shows up and prompts the sage to tell the Pāṇḍavas what he wishes to tell them, to which Mārkaṇḍeya invites them to make themselves comfortable given the scope of what he's about to tell. The Pāṇḍavas settled in and gave their attention to the great sage whose lustre matched the midday Sun (MBh 3.180.38–50). Mārkaṇḍeya's exalted status is clearly communicated by this exchange, even before he opens his mouth. The ensuing exposition will moreover convey the degree and calibre of his learning. Yet, what is perhaps most striking about Mārkaṇḍeya is perhaps his receipt of a very special boon – even among Purāṇic boons – granted by Lord Śiva. To appreciate this boon, we must turn to Mārkaṇḍeya's own origin: to the biographical framing of he who frames our text.

Mārkaṇḍeya's parents were childless and so his father, Mṛkaṇḍu, undertook great penance to Lord Śiva for the sake of progeny. Pleased by his penance, the great god appeared before Mṛkaṇḍu and presented him with the following choice: "Do you desire to have a virtuous, wise and pious son who would live up to sixteen years or a dull-witted evil-natured son who would live long?" (Mani 1975, 488). Valuing virtue, Mṛkaṇḍu opted for the former short-lived variety of offspring. And so he was gifted with a highly gifted son who, in accordance to the parameters of the boon, was destined to perish at the age of sixteen. Despite their joy at the receipt of such a son, as Mārkaṇḍeya's sixteenth year approached, his parents were so grief-stricken by the pending termination of the life of their wondrous son that they eventually broke beneath the weight of their turmoil and conveyed to Mārkaṇḍeya the dark secret burdening them, that is, of Mārkaṇḍeya's pending demise. The young Mārkaṇḍeya resolved to perform severe austerities to Lord Śiva before a *śiva liṅgaṃ*. He was so steadfast and devout in his worship that at the hour appointed for his death, the messengers of Yama (the lord of the departed) were unable to seize him due to the heat generated by Mārkaṇḍeya's formidable *tapas*. Angered, Yama came personally to retrieve the young Mārkaṇḍeya and cast his noose in an attempt to capture the teenaged *tapasvin*. But by the pressures of destiny, Yama's noose missed Mārkaṇḍeya and accidentally encircled the liṅgam instead. Outraged by the insult, the great destroyer Śiva himself appeared in his wrathful glory and annihilated Yama (who of course is eventually restored to life in the interest of cosmic order). Lord Śiva, having destroyed death-personified, then blesses Mārkaṇḍeya with everlasting life, forever abiding in his sixteen-year-old form (Mani 1975, 488). Hence Sage Mārkaṇḍeya, in the words of Winternitz, "though is many thousand years old, is eternally young" (Winternitz 1972, 397).

It is because of this boon that Mārkaṇḍeya, the *Mahābhārata* inform us, is the only being able to survive the end of an age and thus the only being to be graced with a direct vision of cosmic dissolution (*pralaya*) (Mani 1975, 489). This insight from the *Mahābhārata* into the career of the great sage responds to the query of how Mārkaṇḍeya could possibly know the beginnings of time (beyond of course the trans-temporal omniscience customarily accompanying sagehood, which is especially useful in relaying Purāṇic lore). Mārkaṇḍeya alone, among sages, indeed among all living beings, has lived to witness the dissolution of the universe. Once can look to Yudhiṣṭhira's questioning of Mārkaṇḍeya to get a sense of the significance of Mārkaṇḍeya's boon.

The dharma king reverently questions the illustrious Mārkaṇḍeya on the basis that he has witnessed the dissolution of many thousands of ages, and hence none but the creator, Grandfather Brahmā, has lived as long as he. Yudhiṣṭhira notes that when nothing remains of the elements, of sun, fire, wind, moon, even heaven and earth, as they are all dissolved into the primordial ocean; when all classes of beings – gods, demons, serpents – are brought to dust, Mārkaṇḍeya alone remains, beyond the grip of death, old age or sickness. Since he witnesses not only the dissolution of the age, but also the creation of the subsequent age, watching all things come into being, he is uniquely poised as one having experienced all this, as one to whom nothing in creation is unknown (MBh 3.186.1–15). Mārkaṇḍeya is personally privy to knowledge of the primordial beginnings of the universe itself. It is perhaps for this very reason that he is the mouthpiece of two myths of primordial beginnings found in the MkP, each of which is crucial to the establishment of the primacy of two deities – the Goddess and the Sun – lauded as supreme within their respective glorification. In the case of each laudation, Mārkaṇḍeya might function as a personal witness to the goings on at the dawn of time.

In light of our glimpse at the illustriousness of Sage Mārkaṇḍeya, let us turn to what Jaimini asks him; for as I argue, the Purāṇic interplay of who is speaking and what is spoken is not without ideological import.[1] The four questions asked are so central to the self-identity of the work that in its concluding chapter, it is defined as the Purāṇa containing the four questions, in the same breadth that the Purāṇic genre itself is defined: "Both creation and secondary creation, genealogy and the manvantaras and the exploits in the genealogies constitute a Purāṇa with the five characteristics. This Purāṇa which contains the four questions is indeed of the highest quality" (MkP 137.13–14) (Pargiter 1904, 685). Jaimini's four questions are as follows:

> Why was Janardana Vasudeva, who is the cause of the creation preservation and destruction of the world, although devoid of qualities, endued with humanity? And why was Drupada's daughter Krishna the common wife of the five sons of Pandu? For, on this point we feel great perplexity. Why did the mighty Baladeva Halayudha expiate his brahmanicide by engaging in a pilgrimage? And how was it that the unmarried heroic high-souled sons of Draupadi, whose protector was Pandu, were slain, as if they had no protector? Deign to recount all this to me here at length; for sages like thee are ever the instructors of the ignorant.
>
> (MkP 1.13–18) (Pargiter 1904, 2–3)

While much can be said about each of these questions, in keeping with our emphasis on framing, let us turn to the first of these framing questions which serves to frame not only the four questions, but by extension, the entire Purāṇa.

The very first of Jaimini's questions is as follows: "Why was [Viṣṇu] … although devoid of qualities, endued with humanity?" (MkP 1.13; see Pargiter 1904, 2). The authors of the MkP are grappling (through their mouthpiece,

Jaimini) with a very tension inhabiting the heart of Hinduism: the tension between world-transcendence and world-engagement, that is, between (cosmically) distal and (mundanely) proximal aims of life, as epitomized between the enterprise of the ascetic and that of the king. Indeed, why would (and how could) a supremely distal principle manifest in a mundanely proximal manner, in the garb of human flesh? The four birds which proxy for the sagacious Mārkaṇḍeya in attending to Jaimini's noble qualms explain that the aspect of Viṣṇu, which incarnates

> is assiduously intent on the preservation of creatures, always maintains righteousness on the earth. It destroys the haughty Asuras, the exterminators of righteousness; it protects the gods, and holy men, who are devoted to the preservation of righteousness. Whensoever, O Jaimini, the wane of righteousness occurs and the rise of iniquity, then it creates itself. … Thus that form, which is characterized by goodness, becomes incarnate [and] is occupied in the work of preservation.
>
> (MkP 4.51–58) (Pargiter 1904, 21)

While one may wonder why such a seemingly "non-sectarian" work would commence with a question invoking Viṣṇu's earthly incarnation, this qualm is readily assuaged when one considers that Viṣṇu's function here is more symbolic than dogmatic. Viṣṇu is invoked not necessarily in order to demonstrate his supremacy among personalities of godhead but rather for the sake of the cosmic function which he (and his incarnation) represents: the preservation of the cosmos and of this world in particular. Similarly, this "non-sectarian" Purāṇa begins with a benediction to Viṣṇu, one which specifically invokes his divine protection.[2] Furthermore, that Mārkaṇḍeya is forever preserved across cosmic cycles of destruction renders him a powerful emblem of preservation, a theme central not only to the DM but to the very question asked of him at the outset of the MkP. As a brief aside, the Padmapurāṇa (Uttarakhanda 263.81–84) details the threefold classification of the eighteen mahāpurāṇas as each corresponding the three guṇas – *sattva*, *rajas* and *tamas* – wherein the MkP is accorded the quality of rajas. According to this typology, the *sāttvika* Purāṇas are associated with Viṣṇu and lead to liberation (*mukti*), the *rājasa* ones are associated with Brahmā and lead to heaven (*svarga*), while the *tāmasa* ones lead one to hell (Rocher 1986, 20). The Vaiṣṇava bent in this statement is marked and I do not invoke this classification to lend it any particular authority or relevance to the nature of the Purāṇas as a whole, but merely as a point of contrasting the three aims given: heaven, hell and liberation. It is telling that the MkP is associated with the pursuit of heaven (enjoyment) rather than liberation. Given that all of these three spheres are construed as others to the earthly plane, what is most intriguing about the fabric of the MkP itself is it repeatedly validates life on earth, arguably even above and beyond the haven of liberation. It is the earth realm which is emphasized both by the career of Mārkaṇḍeya and by the career of the Goddess (especially as manifest in Suratha's boon), a realm requiring governance. Mārkaṇḍeya craves neither liberation nor heaven but is content to enjoy everlasting life on earth, as the only known being to survive the cosmic deluge at the end of the age. Mārkaṇḍeya's answer to Jaimini's inaugural question therefore poses as a crucial frame of context for not only the MkP as a whole but by extension, also as the central reason why the *Devī Māhātmya* and *Sūrya Māhātmya* find homes therein.

## 4.2 Making sense of the *Mārkaṇḍeya Purāṇa*

In light of this fivefold textual sediment outlined above, one may not readily look upon the MkP as a cohesive whole. However, the absence of uniformity need not be taken as tantamount to the absence of a whole: elements sometimes cohere in ways which evade initial inspection. In the words of J.Z. Smith, "map is not territory" (1978). While diachronic study may well reveal insights into the 'territory' of the MkP, synchronic study takes its cue from the MkP 'map' provided to us by the final redactors of this work. The image that comes to mind here is that of an ancient city to which growth has accrued for multiple centuries, for example, Athens. For certain purposes, with certain historical questions in mind, it might serve us to demarcate the Acropolis as part of the 'original' Athens. However it would generally be more natural – and regarding most inquiry, most fruitful – to understand the Acropolis, though ancient, as no more or less 'truly' Athens as the one which millions of people currently call home. In light of this analogy, Sections III and V, those seemingly narrated by Mārkaṇḍeya proper, might be understood as the "old city" of the *Mārkaṇḍeya Purāṇa*, while Sections I and II might be viewed as the "new city".

Such historical distinctions have little bearing on the more recent innovations which unite both the old and new city, for example, a single municipal water system or equally subject to public transit routes which pass between the two unfettered. In like fashion, there are various motifs which permeate across the apt but ultimately artificial fivefold divisions comprising the *Mārkaṇḍeya Purāṇa* which scholars such as Banerjea and Pargiter have tended to emphasize, precisely because these innovations are relatively recent. This research is in no way an exhaustive study of the themes which allow the MkP to cohere as a whole but rather to the themes common to the DM and to various other strata of the text to the extent to which grave doubt is shed on the notion that the authors of the DM haphazardly interpolated the DM into the MkP. Rather this research suggests that these Śākta 'interpolators' (along with their Saura counterparts) were well acquainted with the materials already compiled in the MkP and that those materials inspired the placement, if not the very compilation and composition, of the episodes of the DM. That we view the DM as an interpolation is not commensurate with how either the authors of these texts, or the culture which preserves them, relates to this corpus. Ironically, it is not so much that the DM as an interpolation intrudes upon the fabric of the MkP but rather that the rhetoric of 'interpolation' intrudes upon the nature and functions of the Purāṇas.

Rather than rebuke as contrived the compositional process whereby subsequent sections were "interjected" into "the MkP", this discussion embraces all narrative tributaries as proper to the MkP assemblage as a whole. This discussion proceeds on the basis that the MkP's present articulation is indicative of the most recent renovations undertaken to its structure, resulting from an organic process geared towards preserving the religious relevance of the Purāṇa. Mārkaṇḍeya makes a direct appearance in this Purāṇa for only the first three cantos. For the duration of the remaining 134 cantos, the Birds[3] usurp his role as the mouthpiece of his Purāṇa[4] – and as noted above, they do so at his behest. While a learned expounder (in whose mouth might be placed the teachings of various other figures) typically remains consistent throughout a Purāṇic assemblage, in the case of the MkP, it is only the questioner, Jaimini, who remains constant; the expository mouthpiece shifts from Mārkaṇḍeya to four birds and furthermore, they end up expositing more than merely Mārkaṇḍeya's words. We shall return to their role below. Since our interlocutor Jaimini (answers to whose crucial questions serve to advance the work) remains consistent throughout, let us plot a broad exposition guide for the MkP in order to highlight the queries to which it responds (see Table 4.1).

From the broad Exposition Guide above, we note that once the inaugural questions of Section I (originally asked in Canto 1, then recapitulated in Canto 4, since Mārkaṇḍeya defers them to the learned Birds) are satisfactorily answered in Canto 9, Jaimini launches a second barrage of questions in Canto 10, initiating Section II. And once these are answered in Canto 44, he launches his third and final barrage of questions, comprising Section III, which occupy the remainder of the Purāṇa. The final canto, constituting the Omega Section, is very much an adjunct to Section I. However, in its function as terminal frame, it explicitly harkens to all three expositional sections serving to bring closure to all of them. Thus in its final form (presumably of importance to the religious communities which have assembled it thus), the MkP is readily divisible into three expositional sections, pertaining to Jaimini's three primary expositional prompts.

It is noteworthy that the DM find itself in the middle of Section II, presented as equally a part of addressing Jaimini's third barrage of questioning. Put otherwise, that Jaimini does not interject between Cantos 45 and 137 verifies that the text does not present Cantos 81–93 as an interruption to its flow, despite diachronic scholarly emphasis to the contrary. Had the authors felt the need for interjection on the basis of thematic disjunction (as with the outset of the Father's discourse in Canto 10, for example), they certainly would have had Jaimini fulfil his role as the Purāṇas' trusty interlocutor. We might infer from the absence of such interjection that the occurrence of the DM is, in the eyes of the assemblers of the MkP, not sufficiently disjointed to warrant a separate expositional prompt on the level of discourse between Jaimini and the Birds. Similarly at the terminal frame of the MkP (the Omega Section), in their closing speech,

*Table 4.1 Mārkaṇḍeya Purāṇa* Exposition Guide

| *Sec.* | *Canto* | *Function* | *Prompter* | *Exp.* | *Verse* | *Prompt Content* |
|---|---|---|---|---|---|---|
| **1** | **1–9** | Introducing Cantos 1–3 | Jaimini | Mk | 1.4–9 | (same as below) |
| | | Introducing Cantos 4–9 (137) Inaugural Questions | Jaimini | Birds | 1.13–18 | "Why was Janardana Vasudeva, who is the cause of the creation preservation and destruction of the world, although devoid of qualities, endowed with humanity? And why was Drupada's daughter Krishna the common wife of the five sons of Panda? For, on this point we feel great perplexity. Why did the mighty Baladeva Halayudha expiate his brahmanicide by engaging in a pilgrimage? And how was it that the unmarried heroic high-souled sons of Draupadi, whose protector was Pandu, were slain, as if they had no protector? Deign to recount all this to me here at length; for sages like thee are ever the instructors of the ignorant" |
| **2** | **10–44** | Introducing Cantos 10–14 Bio-karmic Questions | Jaimini | Birds | 10.1–6 | "Declare my doubt, when I enquire, O powerful brahmans, wherein the appearance and disappearance of living beings consist. How is an animal produced? How too does it develop? How, again, is it placed when contained within the womb, pressed upon by the limbs? How, again, when it has issued from the womb, does it grow? And how at the moment of departure is it deprived of the sentient state? Every dead person also experiences the results of both his good and his bad deeds, and how then do those deeds bring about their results to him? Why does the foetus not become digested there in the stomach, as if it were converted into a morsel of food? In the female's belly, where the various foods consumed are digested although highly indigestible, how is it that the little animal is not digested there? Declare all this to me, free from doubtful terms; this very matter is a transcendent mystery, where men do err." |

*continued*

*Table 4.1* continued

| *Sec.* | *Canto* | *Function* | *Prompter* | *Exp.* | *Verse* | *Prompt Content* |
|---|---|---|---|---|---|---|
| **3** | **45–135** | Introducing Cantos 45–136 Cosmological Questions | Jaimini | Birds | 45.8–14 | "If then your mind, O noble brahmans, is favourable towards me, then deign to expound this completely; – How did this universe, both moveable and immoveable, come into existence? And how will it fall into dissolution at the proper time, most excellent brahmans? And how came the families that sprang from the gods, the rishis, the pitris, created things &c.? And how did the *manvantaras* occur? And what was the history of the families of old; and whatever creations and whatever dissolutions of the universe have occurred; and how the ages have been divided; and what the duration of the *manvantaras* has been; and how the earth remains stable; and what is the size of the world; and what are the oceans, mountains and rivers and forests according to their situation; what is the number of the worlds, the bhur-loka, svar-loka &c, including the lower regions; and what is the course of the sun, moon, and other planets, of the stars and heavenly bodies also. I wish to hear of all this which is destined to subversion; and what will be the end when this universe is dissolved." |
| **Ω** | **137*** | Closes All Sections | | | | (Close-up is discussed in Table 4.5) |

the Birds indicate that they have addressed all three avenues of Jaimini's inquiry – saying:

> And the very four questions indeed, which thou didst put to us at the very first – the conversation between the father and son, and the creation by the Self-existent One, and the administrations of the Manus, and the exploits of the kings, muni, this we have declared to thee.
>
> (MkP 137.5–6) (Pargiter 1904, 684)

There is no separate mention of the glories of the goddess since those glories comprise the third of these avenues of inquiry. One could of course argue that this verse was assembled prior to the DM's "insertion" into the MkP. However, by that same diachronic token, if this tripartite summation accounts for the "insertion" of the Sumati-Jaḍa section, then why would the assemblers of the text not alter it or compose another to follow it, to account for the additional assertion of the DM cantos? Thematically, as expressed through the answering of Jaimini's questions, the text is construed in three (and not five) constituent sections. It is from this perspective that we might begin to understand the conspicuous absence of quibbles within the tradition regarding the "interpolation" of the DM into the MkP. It is understood as an aspect of the MV section, comprising the third expositional segment of the MkP.

On the surface level of the MkP, Mārkaṇḍeya makes only a scant three-canto direct appearance during its initiation in Section I. Why then is the work named after him? Arguably, his presence at the genesis of the assemblage is necessary for the work to be ascribed to him. It is during his inaugural presence that he delegates Jaimini's questions to the Birds, ironically demonstrating his authority in authorizing the Birds to answer on his behalf. There is another very good reason that the Purāṇa at hand should be named after Mārkaṇḍeya. He is the immediate expositor of 94 of its cantos: Cantos 1–3 where he speaks directly to Jaimini, and Cantos 45–136, where the Birds serve as a mouthpiece, relaying what Mārkaṇḍeya once taught Krauṣṭuki. While the Birds operate as mouthpieces of the entire Purāṇa, save for the first three cantos before Mārkaṇḍeya passes the microphone over (in much the same way that, for example, Sañjaya does for Kṛṣṇa in the BhG), only seven cantos originate from them: Cantos 4–9 (answering Jaimini's inaugural questions) and the closing canto, 137. Over the course of the remaining cantos, they voice the teachings of other expounders: Sumati-Jaḍa's Father (Cantos 10–44) and, as mentioned, of Mārkaṇḍeya himself (46–136) which constitutes the bulk of the work. The Birds narrative ventriloquism notwithstanding, the MkP presents us with three primary expositors of knowledge: Sumati-Jaḍa's Father, the Birds and Sage Mārkaṇḍeya himself (see Table 4.2).

While the exploits of the Goddess in the DM are directly exposited by Medhas, this exposition is a component of Mārkaṇḍeya's exposition to Krauṣṭuki comprising Section III of the MkP. The same understanding applies in Section II wherein Queen Madālasā's educates her son Alarka (MkP 27–36), yet

*Table 4.2* Expositors of the *Mārkaṇḍeya Purāṇa*

| *Cantos* | *Expositor* | *Interlocutor* | *Mouthpiece* |
|---|---|---|---|
| 1–3 | Mārkaṇḍeya | Jaimini | NA |
| 4–9 | Birds | Jaimini | NA |
| 10–44 | Father | Sumati-Jaḍa | Birds |
| 45–136 | Mārkaṇḍeya | Krauṣṭuki | Birds |
| 137 | Birds | Jaimini | NA |

these teachings are placed in the mouth of the Father as part of his exposition to his son Sumati-Jaḍa. Queen Madālasā's exposition is proper to Section II of the MkP, as Medhas' is proper to its Section III.

In addition to his role as expositor proper during Cantos 45–136 of the MkP, Mārkaṇḍeya occupies the first three cantos of the Purāṇa over which he accomplishes more than merely deferring to the Birds; he presents their backstory, offering valuable exposition import towards the significance of the Purāṇa's primary mouthpiece. In response to Jaimini's astonishment at how such great learning might be found in the brains of birds – and furthermore, that birds may possess the ability to articulate such learning (MkP 1.24–25) – Mārkaṇḍeya explains that the Birds are actually reborn brāhmaṇa brothers. In their previous life, the four Birds were the four devoted sons of the great sage, Sukṛṣa, by whom they were cursed to be reborn as birds by a horrible twist of fate. In order to test the steadfastness of sage Sukṛṣa, Indra dons the guise of a tattered and greatly suffering bird (MkP 3.19–20) (henceforth avian-Indra) and begs Sukṛṣa for aid. Sukṛṣa promises aid, stating: "I will give thee the food thou desirest for the support of thy life. … What food shall I prepare for thy use?" To this avian-Indra boldly replies "My chiefest delight is in human flesh" (MkP 3.26–27) (Pargiter 1904, 13). While the sage severely chastises Indra for his brazen request, he nevertheless acquiesces to delivering the promise he made to offer the bird the meal of his desiring. Sukṛṣa's entire speech highlights the sway of *nivṛttic* religiosity as follows:

> Thy childhood is past; thy youth, too, gone; thou art assuredly in the decline of life, O egg-born. Why art thou most malign-hearted even in old age, thou in whom of all mankind every desire has ceased? What has thy last stage of life to do with human flesh? Assuredly no one is created foremost among evil-beings! Or what need hast thou to address me, being what I am? One should always give when one has promised – such is our professed opinion.
>
> (MkP 3.28–31) (Pargiter 1904, 13)

What Sukṛṣa does next is most astonishing: he calls forth his four sons (the same destined to incarnate as the Birds of our Purāṇa) and having praised their virtues, says to them: "If a father is deemed by you a guru worthy of reverence and most exalted, perform ye then my promise with cheerful mind" (MkP 3.32–36). To this, the pious and dutiful brāhmaṇa sons eagerly indicate that their father Sukṛṣa may consider already done what it is he wishes to request. This time it is the sons who, like their father a moment before, are made to unwittingly deliver a dire promise. The sage then lets them in on the horror incurred by their loyalty saying "of me has this bird sought protection oppressed with hunger and thirst; wherefore let him be straightway satisfied with your flesh, and let his thirst be quickly assuaged with your blood" (MkP 3.37) (Pargiter 1904, 13). The sons, terrified, default on their promise, which aroused the wrath of Sukṛṣa. Angered that they revoked their word, the sage curses them to be reborn as birds. He then resolves to perform his own funeral rites and offer his own body as sustenance for the wretched birds. Impressed at his resolve, Indra finally reveals the ruse, and pleased by the would-be sacrifice of the sage, offers him a blessing then departs. While the sons then propitiate their father and appeal to him to revoke his dreadful curse, as we have learned from innumerable Sanskrit tales, once a curse is issued, it cannot be undone. To do so would make a liar of the being of steadfast truth issuing the curse; hence, Sukṛṣa replies, "What I have uttered, will never become false; my voice has not spoken untruth hitherto, O sons!" (MkP 3.75) (Pargiter 1904, 16). But as we have also learned from countless South Asian tales, curses may be modified. So Sukṛṣa, remorseful that the pressures of destiny compelled him to "thoughtlessly … do a deed that ought not to be done" (MkP 3.75) (Pargiter 1904, 16), blesses his sons to attain the highest knowledge despite undergoing avian incarnation (MkP 3.75–78). Hence (concludes Mārkaṇḍeya to Jaimini in Section I of the MkP) supremely intelligent birds, minds subdued, reside within a cave in the Vindhyas (MkP 3.85) (Pargiter 1904, 17), conveniently poised to address Jaimini's queries.

Despite the richness of this episode, I touch here upon only one of its features salient to the discussion at hand; it shall be revisited in greater detail below. The Sukṛṣa episode is deeply evocative of blood sacrifice in the context of ritual. The Birds begin their tale by stating that they were reverent to their father Sukṛṣa in their last life and busied themselves producing fuel for his sacrifices, along with "whatever was needed for sustenance" (MkP 3.18). In calling upon the sons at that gruesome hour, the sage was calling upon them to produce fuel for the sacrifice at hand: oblations of human flesh and blood into avian-Indra's digestive fire. In addition to the pervasive equation with food and ritual sacrifice, the two are thoroughly blended in this episode insofar as Sukṛṣa in the same breath refers both to his own funerary sacrifice, and avian-Indra's food sacrifice as follows: "when I have performed for myself the final sacrifice, and my obsequies, according to the śāstras, do thou unhesitatingly eat me here; this my body I here grant thee for food" (MkP 3.46) (Pargiter 1904, 14). On the surface, Mārkaṇḍeya's initial discourse serves to explain the existence of the Birds and to validate the calibre of their learning; however, on a deeper level it evokes blood sacrifice. Keeping in line with our methodological process, let us now turn to Mārkaṇḍeya's terminal discourse where we shall discover a most astonishing corollary.

### *4.2.1 Insights from the astonishing story of Dama*

The episode of King Dama (MkP 133–136) is the final episode to be found in the genealogy of solar kings section of the MkP (101–136); it thus serves as the terminal frame of the genealogy section and as the terminal frame of Section III (45–136) as a whole, comprising the final episode to be conveyed by Mārkaṇḍeya himself. While the Purāṇa in fact proceeds to detail the exploits of one more king in this dynastic lineage – namely, of Dama's son Rājyavardhana[5] – we do not find Rājyavardhana's exploits directly following those of Dama, as per the patrilineal pattern typifying the section. Rather the assemblers of the MkP opt to assemble the Rājyavardhana episode immediately *before* the genealogy section proper. And this editorial decision is not without purpose. This maneuver accomplishes three tasks, all of which are significant to narrative enframement: first, it enables Rājyavardhana's exploits (in which the Sun plays a crucial role) to serve as the terminal frame of narrative tributary lauding the Sun; second, it allows that narrative within that tributary (which itself serves as the initial frame of the MkP's genealogy of kings section) to move from the heavenly sphere to the sphere of earthly kings in order to fittingly inaugurate the lineage of earthly kings comprising the section; and third and most crucially for our purposes, it enables the exploits of Dama to function as the terminal frame of Mārkaṇḍeya's discourse to Krauṣṭuki. But why would the assemblers of the MkP opt to end with the exploits of Dama? In registering elements unique to the career of Dama, we ascertain the significance of its role as the Purāṇa's episodic finale, particularly with respect to the manner in which the themes of that finale echo the themes running through the assemblage at large.

The climax of Dama's exploits occur within its final canto which details Dama extracting revenge upon his nemesis Vapuṣmān, who murdered Dama's defenseless king-turned-ascetic father, Nariṣyanta. Stemming from the verbal root '*dam*' – to tame, subdue, or control, conquer, overpower (Monier-Williams *et al.* 2008) – the Sanskrit masculine noun *dama* carries with it various interrelated connotations, all of which revolve around the notion of control: when internally directed, this word connotes "self-command, self-restraint, self-control" (Monier-Williams *et al.* 2008) and when externally directed, *dama* connotes dominion through taming, subduing, or punishing another.[6] It is clear from the events of this episode that King Dama was named after the latter. The unabashed bloodlust he exhibits during the slaughter of Vapuṣmān well surpasses all bounds of self-restraint. For in the climax of the episode, both valiant warriors, Dama and Vapuṣmān, are locked in sword-to-sword mortal combat until:

> Dama, reflecting for a moment on the king his father who had been killed in the forest, seized Vapush-mat by the hair and attacked him and felled him to the earth; and with his foot on his neck, raising his arm he exclaimed, –"Let all the gods, men, Serpents and birds see the heart also of Vapuṣmat, who is of kṣatriya caste, split open!"
>
> (MkP 136.31–33) (Pargiter 1904, 683)

Upon splitting open the heart of Vapuṣmān, Dama is so intoxicated with wrath that he was desirous of drinking (*pātukāmaḥ*) Vapuṣmān's blood but was restrained by the gods from doing so (MkP 136.34). What is even more astonishing from the perspective of Hindu ritual is what he does next: he uses Vapuṣmān's blood to offer libations to his deceased father then heads home to perform his rituals crafting the ritual cakes (*piṇḍas*) out of Vapuṣmān's flesh (MkP 136.35).

The episode adds to this explosive climax a single line, one which has been met with tremendous intrigue by Eden Pargiter. The line reads: "he feasted the brahmans who were sprung from families of Rakshasas" (MkP 136.36: *brāhmaṇān bhojayāmāsa rakṣaḥkulasamudbhavān*) (Pargiter 1904, 683). Taking his cue from H.H. Wilson,[7] Pargiter takes two aspects of the verse for granted which need to be reexamined. First, he reads the final compound of the episode (*rakṣaḥkulasamudbhavān*) as Brahmins "sprung from families of Rākṣasas", and second, as a corollary to the first notion, he presumes that the text implies that the flesh cakes are the object of the feasting. Regarding the first of these notions, the text simply states that Dama fed Brahmins who sprang from the Rakṣa clan. Rakṣa either stands for a proper noun (i.e. the Rakṣa Family) or could signify "guarding/watching", in addition to "evil being or demon" (Monier-Williams *et al.* 2008). While *rakṣa-kula-samudbhavān* could very well mean, "sprung from the clan of demons", it could also very well mean "sprung from the clan of protectors", or, quite simply, "sprung from the Rakṣa clan". What lends credence to Pargiter's reading is the polluting aspect of blood involved in Dama's ritual in which the only sufficiently polluted (or demonic) brāhmaṇas would partake. What clinches this reading for Pargiter is his assumption (following Wilson) that the verse mounts testimony of ancient cannibalism, a reading which fundamentally depends upon his second presumption: that the flesh-cakes are the object of the feasting (Pargiter 1904, xxi–xxii).

It is most likely not the case that Dama fed the *piṇḍa* cakes to living people – both from the construction of the verse and from what we know of *pitṛ pūjā*. As insulting as it would be to offer anyone food that has been polluted by another prior partaking of it, it would be atrocious to offer food that was sullied by the dead, a state of supreme pollution to living beings. Food offerings in *pitṛ pūjā* are generally discarded into running water or fed to animals. However, it is customary to feed brāhmaṇas after rituals, even ancestor rites, so one might be inclined to take the verse at face value with the piṇḍa cakes not being the object of the feeding. If the consumption of human blood or flesh were to be condoned, it is doubtful that the text would have the gods restrain Dama from drinking Vapuṣmān's blood. Given that cannibalism would be so repugnant and scandalous an affair, it is doubtful that the text would remain so scant and so ambiguous had it intended to convey this harrowing theme; one imagines it would either explicitly embellish it for the sake of making a point or telling a good story, or it would altogether dispense with any such implications. For example, given its gory affront to brahmanical ritual even in the absence of the consumption of human flesh (whether by brāhmaṇas or by some brāhmaṇa-rākṣasas hybrid), the entire encounter between Dama and Vapuṣmān has been excised from the Bengal recension of the MkP which "ends abruptly in canto 136, leaving Dama acquiescing tamely in the flight of his father's murderer Vapuṣmat" (Pargiter 1904, vii). However, Pargiter argues convincingly that, despite Banerjea's favouring of the Bengal edition, the versions to be found in the Bombay and Poona editions (whose endings conform with the above discussion) appear more genuine and he argues this on two fronts: on the bases of the intentions of would-be forgers (Pargiter 1904, vii), and – more intriguing for our study – on the basis of the world within the text, reasoning that "the pusillanimity which that ending ascribes to Dama jars with the whole tone of his threat in Canto 135 which both versions account genuine" (Pargiter 1904, vii). Pargiter's reliance here upon the synchronic coherence of the text itself is refreshing and I am left wondering what other profound insights he would have made had he directed more of his scholarly energy in this direction.

Given Pargiter's acknowledgement that it is only "implied [that Dama] gave certain degraded brahmans a cannibal feast" (Pargiter 1904, vii), and given his astonishment at this "most extraordinary passage" (Pargiter 1904, xxi–xxii), one which was "unparalleled in Sanskrit, and it is almost incredible that there should have been brahmans of any kind whatever who would have participated in it" (Pargiter 1904, xxii), it is a wonder that he doesn't read the verse more at face value: that Dama fed the Brahmins *after* performing the piṇḍa offerings not *with* the piṇḍa offerings. Certainly Wilson's reading would have held sway upon his interpretation but there would have been another crucial element at play in his psyche surrounding this textual juncture which seduced him into such intrigue: his quest for historical insight,[8] particularly within this most ancient of the strata of the MkP. As Pargiter declares in his introductory essay: "there can be no doubt that only the thirds and fifth of these parts constituted the Purāṇa in its original shape as Mārkaṇḍeya's Purāṇa" (Pargiter 1904, iv). It is for this very diachronic bias that he is bent on viewing the blood-soaked elements of the Dama episode as potential historical evidence – evidence that "savagery was not absent from the earliest memories of the Aryans in India" (Pargiter 1904, vii). He romanticizes this episode to offer ancient insight into Aryan pre-history, declaring that it "would seem to imply that it is of real antiquity, and that the account of the dynasty in which he occurred, and which is the only dynasty described, must be a purāṇa in the full meaning of the term" (Pargiter 1904, xxi–xxii). While the gore of the Dama episode is esteemed as of great historical value, the blood-soaked elements of the DM are condemned as "the product of a later age which developed and took pleasure in the sanguinary features of popular religion" wherein "the descriptions of the battles abound with wild and repulsive incidents and revel in gross and amazing fancies" (Pargiter 1904, vi–vii). Is the battle between Dama and Vapuṣmān anything less than wild, repulsive or amazing compared to what we find in the DM? It is these very elements which render the battles of the DM and of Dama's vengeance captivating literary works.

Does there truly exist such a drastic divide between the glorified gore of Dama's vengeance and the gore comprising the glories of the Goddess? Whether or not the Dama episode alludes to, or is derived from, sanguinary practices from a long lost past, we cannot know. What we can know is the spatter pattern ornamenting the MkP: Dama's offering of Vapuṣmān's blood and flesh renders explicit what is implicit (yet palpable) in the sanguinary sacrifice of Sage Sukṛṣa episode – the besmearing of ritual sacrifice with human flesh and blood[9] – and is powerfully echoed in the final verses of the DM where we learn that the king and merchant, during their steadfast worship of the Goddess, make "offerings sprinkled from the blood of their own limbs" (DM 13.9) (Coburn 1991, 83).[10] Furthermore, these sanguinary segments besmear neither the expositions of the Father nor those of the Birds, but flow forth from the mouth of Mārkaṇḍeya alone: the sacrifice of blood deliberately stains his initial and terminal exposition alike. Despite the diachronic divisions known to the *Mārkaṇḍeya Purāṇa*, its present synchronic state exalts a sage whose discourses advocate the preservation of this realm and its creatures, even when the affairs of that preservation incur the sacrifice of blood (be it physically or ritually). For as Mārkaṇḍeya tells us, it is the sacrifice of blood which earns Sukṛṣa the blessings of Indra,[11] the sacrifice of blood which appeases Dama's murdered father, and the sacrifice of blood which earns Suratha and Samādhi a vision of the Goddess. Rather than view the DM as an interpolated interruption of the Mārkaṇḍeya's Purāṇa, one might just as readily embrace it as an explicit and most articulate embellishment of a theme which is inextricable from the fabric of his discourse.

### *4.2.2 Avian exposition*

Keeping in mind the who-asks-what-of-whom tripartite thematic trail comprising exposition import, we would be remiss in not plumping for such import a most distinctive feature of the MkP: Mārkaṇḍeya's Purāṇa is primarily voiced by four mysterious birds. This expositional initiative well exemplifies the mechanics of textual framing featured in this study. Let us be sure to distinguish that the work is not primarily exposited by the Birds, for as discussed above, it is the Father, and Mārkaṇḍeya himself, who do most of the expositional legwork insofar as relaying the bulk of the teachings of the text. The Birds, on the other hand, for the most part serve as a mouthpiece mouthing the words of other teachers. Note that I refer to these birds as "mouthpiece" in the singular (verses "mouthpieces") since the Birds, though they are four in number, they are clearly intended to be taken as a single collective mouthpiece. This may be readily ascertained by the fact that they only ever speak in unison, primarily occupied with collectively mouthing the words of single speakers (the Father and Mārkaṇḍeya). No distinction is made between them and no individual contribution is accorded among them during the entire Purāṇa, even when it is they who are doing the expounding. They lack any disambiguating features apart from the fact that Mārkaṇḍeya provides four names to Jaimini upon first introducing them,[12] yet, these names appear nowhere else in the Purāṇa and despite knowing these names, Jaimini consistently collectively addresses them simply as Birds (pakṣinaḥ) throughout. Furthermore, I have not been able to locate itihāsa literature on birds possessing these specific names, whether collectively or individually. So one might be inclined to view these names as relatively inconsequential to establishing particular, individual characters, that is, bereft of particular expositor import. We are guided by the text to symbolically understand them in one fell swoop, simply as "the Birds".

That the speaker aspect of Mārkaṇḍeya's Purāṇa is bifurcated cannot be inconsequential to its thematic mechanics. Mārkaṇḍeya could have easily remained the mouthpiece of the work and relayed the teachings of the Birds (as the Birds do for the Father and for Mārkaṇḍeya himself). Yet, for whatever motive, the Birds are made to assume command of the surface level narrative, imbuing the work with their (and not only Mārkaṇḍeya's) expositor import. While the Birds themselves directly expound very little, what they do expound is quite crucial. For it is the Birds, and not Mārkaṇḍeya, who answer Jaimini's first four questions which frame the entire Purāṇa. And furthermore, this is the only direct exposition they provide wherein they serve as expositor and not merely as mouthpiece. While the Purāṇa could easily have placed Mārkaṇḍeya's answers merely in the mouths of the Birds (as it does for Cantos 45–136), it places these crucial answers within the birds themselves. It is the learning of the Birds, and not Mārkaṇḍeya himself, which appease Jaimini's burning questions, that is, the questions identified with Mārkaṇḍeya's Purāṇa. The assemblers of the MkP insist upon providing the assemblage with an expositional frame wherein there is an appropriate interplay between the four-part prompt and the expositor of that prompt: the four questions and the Birds thus enjoy a symbiotic relationship, each crafted for the other. As Pargiter notes, "the Birds, though said no doubt to be brahmans undergoing a transmigration, were inferior in education and fame to Jaimini, yet they were deemed fully capable of authoritatively answering the questions that puzzled him" (Pargiter 1904, xxi). Why should these otherwise insignificant and anonymous Birds take centre-stage in this manner?

In grappling with this textual quandary, Pargiter intriguingly theorizes that "in this construction of the story, that there was an intention to exalt the instruction given by the munis of the Vindhyas to equality with, if not superiority over, that given in Madhya-deśa" (Pargiter 1904, xxi). It certainly is tempting to read Pargiter's suggestion into the fact that the Birds are made to dwell specifically by the Vindhya mountains which is perhaps the only real-world detail accorded to them. Irrespective of the veracity of Pargiter's suggestion, it is clear that the work is intent upon according the Birds a lofty status, particularly with respect to Jaimini's vexed questions. Yet, the work is equally careful to not exalt the Birds at Mārkaṇḍeya's expense. For as Pargiter also notes:

> The prefixing of the discourses delivered by the Birds to the Purāṇa proper raised the Birds to the primary and chief position and tended to derogate from Mārkaṇḍeya's pre-eminence; but clashing was avoided and Mārkaṇḍeya's supremacy was preserved by two expedients; first, he was introduced at the very beginning in order that he might expressly declare

> the wisdom and authority of the Birds; and secondly, the original Purāṇa was interfered with as little as possible by making the Birds repeat it in its entirety as Mārkaṇḍeya's teaching, conclusive upon the subjects dealt with in it.
>
> (Pargiter 1904, v)

The status of the Birds as the mouthpiece of the Purāṇa not only refrains from trespassing upon Mārkaṇḍeya's own primacy and authority within the work but the boundaries between these two mouthpieces, Mārkaṇḍeya and the Birds, appears happily blurred within the work; not only do the Birds mouth the teachings of Mārkaṇḍeya, but it is Mārkaṇḍeya who provides the karmic biography of the Birds and during this juncture, the words of the Birds are placed in the mouth of Mārkaṇḍeya.[13]

The introduction of the Birds therefore does not appear to serve to exalt a particular figure or creed nor does it appear to implicate any particular ideological or political agenda. Furthermore, we are not presented, by their presence, with literary associations which the authors might hope to invoke; the thematic currents of other works are not made to flow into this one since, to the best of our knowledge, these Birds make their first and final appearance in the MkP itself. So in order to discover what they might represent, we must take our cue from the text itself. Pargiter notices that upon beginning the Purāṇa, the Birds

> retire from further notice, but reappear with Jaimini in the final canto to conclude their discourse and give consistency to the combined instruction. This was a termination rendered necessary by the prefixing of the first two parts to the original Purāṇa.
>
> (Pargiter 1904, v)

It cannot truly be said that the Birds "retire" beyond the introductory section of the text since they resurface at the beginning of each section in order to navigate Jaimini's subsequent lines of inquiry (see Table 4.3).

Pargiter's observation is apt insofar as if we put aside the Birds' resurfacing in Canto 10 (to receive Jaimini's second barrage of questions) and Canto 45 (to receive Jaimini's third barrage of questions), that they merely mouth the words of other expositors, all the while themselves remaining silent for the 126 cantos occurring between the first ten and final of the Purāṇa's cantos. However,

*Table 4.3* Birds in the intermediary sections of the *Mārkaṇḍeya Purāṇa*

| *SEC* | *Cantos* | *Verses* | *Content* |
|---|---|---|---|
| 2 | 10–44 | 10.7–14; 32; 45 | Introduce and Contextualize Father–Son |
| | | 44.37–40 | Closes off the Father–Son discourse; prompts Jaimini for further questions |
| 3 | 46–135 | 45.15–19 | Introduces *manvantara* discourse |

despite their 'direct' expositional presence in merely eleven cantos of the MkP, these eleven cantos very much comprise prime Purāṇic real estate, constituting the initial and terminal frame of the assemblage as a whole. It is at these most crucial framing junctures that the Birds most richly contribute to the assemblage – and this is unsurprising, since they were invented and implemented for the very purposes of framing the MkP. The assemblers of the MkP install the Birds as the primary speaker of the Purāṇa in order to reframe it through the expositor import accompanying the Birds' career. We will therefore more closely examine their role in the initial and terminal frames of the MkP. In order to obtain an overview of the way in which we will chart the presence of the Birds in the MkP, see Table 4.4.

Since (as discussed in Chapter Q) the vast majority of the import is typically derived from the initial frame, and it is in the initial frame of the MkP wherein we encounter the backstory of the Birds, let us first very briefly examine the terminal frame of the MkP. Table 4.5 presents a snapshot of the final canto of the MkP.

The Birds, of course, resurface at this point after their long silence so as to harken their presence in the MkP's initial frame, and to attend to the various frames in need of closure. They firstly provide a concluding frame for the MV section and Mārkaṇḍeya's discourse to Krauṣṭuki at large (MkP 137), a summation for all three expositional sections (MkP 137.5–6), a descriptive laudation of the Mahāpurāṇas, and then the *phalaśruti* section. The closing off of the presence of the Birds themselves occurs in the final three verses of the work, wherein Jaimini lauds the nature and the learning of the Birds, before declaring: "Let evil-minded-ness *that springs* from pain wrought by a father's curse depart from you!" (MkP 137.40–42) (Pargiter 1904, 688). The very last words escaping Jaimini's lips harkens to the Birds' curse, corresponding to the

*Table 4.4* Birds throughout the *Mārkaṇḍeya Purāṇa*

| *SEC* | *Cantos* | *Canto* | *Verses* | *Content* |
|---|---|---|---|---|
| 1 | 1–9 | See Table 4.6 | See Table 4.6 | See Table 4.6 |
| 2–3 | 10–44; 46–136 | See Table 4.3 | See Table 4.3 | See Table 4.3 |
| Ω | 137 | See Table 4.5 | See Table 4.5 | See Table 4.5 |

*Table 4.5* Birds in the final section of the *Mārkaṇḍeya Purāṇa*

| *SEC* | *Cantos* | *#Verses* | *Verses* | *Content* |
|---|---|---|---|---|
| Ω | 137 | 42 | 1–4 | Closes off *manvantara* discourse |
| | | | 5–6 | Closes off all three question-intervals |
| | | | 8–13 | Lists, describes, praises 18 Mahāpurāṇas |
| | | | 4–39 | MkP Phalaśruti |
| | | | 40–42* | Jaimini thanks Birds, lifts the curse, and returns to his āśrama. |

very first words escaping their beaks upon first setting sight on Jaimini, where they say:

> To-day has our birth become fruitful, and our lives have been well-lived, inasmuch as we see thy lotus-feet which are worthy to be praised by the gods. The blazing fire of our father's anger, which continues in our bodies, has been quenched today by the water of the sight of thee, O brahman.
>
> (MkP 4.17–21) (Pargiter 1904, 18–19)

The MkP then serves as a remedy for the Birds' curse and in order to unpack what that curse represents, let us probe the initial segment of the MkP wherein we learn the backstory of the Birds.

### 4.2.3 The plight of Pravṛtti

From the diachronic perspective discussed at the outset of this chapter, the Birds' backstory occupies what is considered (aside from the DM) the latest additions to the MkP, and thus from that perspective, an ancillary accretion to the work's most ancient core. In broaching the MkP with an eye to establishing the relative antiquity of sections or verses, one is inclined to equate antiquity with authenticity and to undermine the presence of Section I as a "later interpolation". However, given that the implementation of the Birds does not serve any particular sectarian interest, what then, is its function? This framing feature is among the MkP's most recent assemblage initiatives and in viewing it as integral to the most up-to-date articulation of the MkP, we might understand the religious ideologies occasioning and sustaining its cultural relevance. To dismiss as ancillary the framing section of the MkP is to direly devalue the craftsmanship exhibited throughout its implementation; for it succeeds, from a synchronic stance, not only in ideologically orienting the entire assemblage of tributaries but also in demonstrating an intimate intertextuality with the *Mahābharata*, artfully harkening to the inaugural framing of the great epic. This section addresses to the former of these accomplishments, while the latter achievement shall be broached in the Conclusion.

By virtue of expositor import in tracing the backstory of the Birds, we will gain insight into the nature of the MkP Purāṇa. The fact that these otherwise-unknown Birds are inventions of this work alone is corroborated by the fact that their backstory is conveniently included in the text itself. That the assemblers of the MkP were keen on imbuing the work with the Birds' import can be corroborated by the fact that they provide the backstory of the Birds within the first three cantos of the text. Also telling is the fact that all other material within the MkP is relayed by the Birds *except* the section outlining their backstory, which is the sole element which Mārkaṇḍeya relays to Jaimini himself; while the Birds tell their own story to this Sage Śamīka (who rescues, saves and raises them), this story is purposefully placed in the mouth of Mārkaṇḍeya, relayed to Jaimini before he even meets them (MkP 3.15–80) (Pargiter 1904, 12–16).

Their backstory, therefore, provides penetrating insight into Mārkaṇḍeya's role in the initial frame narrative of the MkP.

The circumstances necessitating the introduction of the Birds shall shed light upon what the Birds might be said to represent. When Jaimini asks Mārkaṇḍeya the inaugural four questions, Mārkaṇḍeya indicates that the time has arrived for him to perform his religious rites (*kriyākāle samprāptaḥ*, MkP 1.19) and refers Jaimini to the wise Vindhya-dwelling Birds (MkP 1.19–22). Pargiter remarks that Mārkaṇḍeya makes a "transparent excuse"[14] at the opening of the MkP in order to refer Jaimini to the Birds. One readily understands why Pargiter deems this to be a flimsy excuse insofar as one imagines that Mārkaṇḍeya could easily have requested Jaimini to return when Mārkaṇḍeya completed his rite (*kriyā*), for it is not as if he was about to embark upon pilgrimage or any such activity which would have incurred extended leave. And while his response to Jaimini may very well serve as a narrative conceit on the part of the text, it is probably not one which Mārkaṇḍeya disingenuously invents in that moment since he is described in the very opening line of the Purāṇa (upon Jaimini's approach) as deeply engaged in austerity and study (*tapaḥ-svādhyāya-nirata*): the inaugural verse of the MkP reads: "The illustrious Jaimini, the disciple of Vyasa, interrogated the great Muni Markandeya, who was engaged in the performance of austerities and the study of the Veda" (MkP 1.1) (Pargiter 1904, 2). One is, therefore, presented with a Mārkaṇḍeya who is *already* engaged, rather than one who excuses himself on the pretence of being engaged.

Yet, the text nevertheless insinuates something ulterior at play in Mārkaṇḍeya's deferral to the Birds. For upon doing so, the astonished Jaimini asks four additional interrelated questions about the nature of these extraordinary Birds. While it is reasonable enough that Mārkaṇḍeya defers answering Jaimini's questions on the basis that he was already engaged and couldn't spare the time, it is intriguing that he takes the time to answer Jaimini's subsequent four questions, driven by astonishment at the existence of these Birds. Given that the Birds take 91 verses (spanning Cantos 4–7) in order to address Jaimini's original questions, one presumes that Mārkaṇḍeya would have been able to answer Jaimini's questions in approximately the same number of verses. Yet, pressed for time, he defers these questions and when asked additional questions about the Birds, he willingly proceeds to take up 177 verses (spanning Cantos 1–3), to answer *those* questions. For a breakdown of Section I of the MkP, see Table 4.6.

As opposed to asking why Mārkaṇḍeya deploys a 'flimsy excuse' (which is inapt, given his bone fide engagement in religious practice), a perhaps more apt line of inquiry is: why does Mārkaṇḍeya make time for the second set of questions but not the first? It is surely significant to the assemblers of the MkP that Jaimini's first four questions are exposited by the Birds, and conversely, that the backstory of the Birds (the answer to Jaimini's second four questions) are exposited by Mārkaṇḍeya. Let us first approach the latter: what is it that Mārkaṇḍeya reveals in conveying the backstory of the Birds?

*Table 4.6* Birds in Section I of the *Mārkaṇḍeya Purāṇa*

| *Canto* | *#Verses* | *Verses* | *Content* |
|---|---|---|---|
| 1 | 54 | 1–18 | Jaimini appeals to Mārkaṇḍeya: Four Questions |
| | | 19–23 | Mārkaṇḍeya defers to Birds |
| | | 24–26 | Four Questions about Birds |
| | | 27–54 | Bird's Backstory (see Table 4.7 for close-up) |
| 2 | 65 | ALL | Bird's Backstory (see Table 4.7 for close-up) |
| 3 | 85 | ALL | Bird's Backstory (see Table 4.7 for close-up) |
| 4 | 59 | 1–35 | Jaimini meets Birds, asks questions |
| | | 36–59 | Birds answer first question (about Viṣṇu's incarnation) |
| 5 | 26 | ALL | Birds answer second question (about Draupadī's polyandry) |
| 6 | 37 | ALL | Birds third question (about Baladeva expiation for brahmanicide) |
| 7 | 69 | ALL | Birds fourth question (about Darupadi's five sons); |
| 8 | 270 | ALL | Hariścandra Episode (answering Jaimini's follow-up question) |
| 9 | 33 | ALL | Hariścandra Episode (Viśvāmitra and Vasiṣṭha Sub-Episode) |

*Table 4.7* Backstory of the Birds

| *Canto* | *Verses* | *Content* |
|---|---|---|
| 1 | 27–54 | Bird's mother's karmic antecedent curse explained |
| 2a | 1–31 | Avian Rebirth of Vapu as Tārkṣī |
| 2b | 32–65 | Birth of the Birds, and aftermath |
| 3 | 1–85 | Bird's karmic antecedent curse explained |

As discussed above, the karmic antecedent of the Birds' birth results from a curse they earned as brahmin youths from their father, Sukṛṣa, for failing to sacrifice their lives to feed Indra in avian guise. Mārkaṇḍeya ends his backstory discourse by discussing this curse. He begins his discourse by disclosing the karmic antecedent of how their bird mother, Tārkṣī, was cursed to be born a bird (see Table 4.7).

Mārkaṇḍeya sets the scene wherein Sage Nārada encounters Indra, who is being entertained by an entourage of dancing Apsaras. When asked by Indra to judge who among them was pre-eminent in "beauty, nobility, and good qualities" (MkP 1.36) (Pargiter 1904, 4), the Seer declares that it would be she who could perturb the penance-performing Muni Durvāsa. The apsara Vapu, confident that she could fit the bill, attempts to disrupt the discipline of Durvāsa. But rather than inciting the sage's lust, she provokes the passion of his wrath. Durvāsa curses Vapu to be reborn as a bird (Tārkṣī) for the span of sixteen years, begetting four offspring (namely, the Birds of our Purāṇa) but dying on a battlefield[15] without knowing their affection (MkP 1.27–54). Sage Mārkaṇḍeya's discourse, therefore, is framed by two curses, each launched by an angered ascetic.

Mārkaṇḍeya is inspired to make time for his line of questioning regarding the origin of the Birds, unlike with respect to Jaimini's first four questions. Arguably, this is the case because the Birds' backstory extols the virtue and the power of asceticism and the brahmins who hold that power.[16] Ascetics are emblematic of *nivṛtti* religiosity, of which the mighty Mārkaṇḍeya might serve as an esteemed exemplar. Mārkaṇḍeya's Section I discourse is framed by the prowess of two fellow ascetics, Sukṛṣa and Durvāsa, whose respective wrath succeeds in punishing two transgressions to *nivṛttic* ideology: sexuality and self-preservation. Broadly speaking, the former might be understood as the urge to cleave to the body of another, while the second might be understood as the urge to cleave to the body of oneself. Vapu is overconfident in her ability to allure the senses of the self-controlled Durvāsa (MkP 1.42–44), and therefore Durvāsa specifically condemns her as being drunk with pride (MkP 1.50). However, pride is her secondary vice. She takes pride in her ability to sensually allure. Being an apsara, she represents the sine qua non of apsaras and threat to asceticism bar none: sexuality. This nicely follows from chastity being the sine qua non of ascetic life. Testimony of the structural opposition between the respective function of ascetic and apsara might be found in the vast number of South Asian tales wherein apsaras are specifically deployed to distract austere adherents to celibate life, especially by Indra who fears the growing prowess being generated by their austerities. The ascetic is called to rigidly reject sensual indulgence and the apsara is called to embody and celebrate such indulgence. It is Vapu's bent towards pleasure and sexuality which ultimately earns her a curse from Durvāsa. As punishment for her joie de vivre, Durvāsa curses Vapu to be born a bird, to give birth, then to die upon a battlefield. Not only does he revoke her apsara form for the span of sixteen years (causing her to reside in avian form for that time), he curses her to procreate (a prime function of sexuality) and be denied enjoyment of her progeny.

Similarly, Sage Sukṛṣa remains staunchly detached from flesh for which he earns a boon from Indra. His detachment expresses as life-denial, enabling him to sacrifice his sons to Indra's appetite. Once his sons express their despondency, he is sufficiently detached from his own embodied existence that he proceeds to sacrifice his own life, though his hand was stayed by Indra who revealed the ruse at the eleventh hour. Once Indra reveals his identity, the remorseful Sukṛṣa bemoans the foibles of human existence which is ever subject to the power of destiny. He is emblematic of life-denial and this is portrayed as prowess. His sons' 'weakness' is that they cherish life, for which they are cursed to be reborn as birds. Both sexuality (represented by Vapu) and the self-preservation (represented by the four sons) function as threats to the ideals of *nivṛttic* religiosity; as such, they are rebuked in the framing section of the MkP by esteemed ascetic practitioners. Thus, the two episodes framing Mārkaṇḍeya's backstory discourse feature curses issued by life-denying practitioners. And perhaps it is for this reason, the great ascetic Mārkaṇḍeya takes interest in telling these tales. As for Jaimini's inaugural questions, they are, on the contrary, *pravṛttic* in scope. They are geared towards human, worldly, social concerns.

And it is perhaps for this reason that Mārkaṇḍeya does not bother to address them – they interrupt the thrust of ascetic life.

The answer to Jaimini's first question (i.e. 'Why did Viṣṇu take on a human incarnation?') pertains, in a nutshell, to the preservation of life. Conversely, it was in seeking the preservation of their own life that the Brahmins were cursed to be reborn as Birds. Moreover, the answer to this question is far from esoteric: it is very well known, emphasized as a central tenant in the most famous tributary to the *Mahābhārata*, the BhG. Therefore, Jaimini asks this question not because he wishes to know the answer, but rather, in order to underscore its importance for the sake of inaugurating the MkP. In short, the assemblers of the MkP opt to invoke *pravṛtti dharma*, as expressed through the aspect of godhead vowed to defend it, from the very inception of the work, at the outset of the MkP. Similarly, Jaimini's second question (i.e. 'Why did Draupadī have five husbands, the Pāṇḍavas?') is equally wedded to the dictates of *pravṛtti dharma* and equally obvious to anyone familiar with the *Mahābhārata*, much less the pupil of Vyāsa; for as Hiltebeitel notes that "Vyāsa, who by chance arrived" (1.187.32d), sanctions the marriage by telling Draupadī's father Drupada the *Pañcendra-Upākhyāna*" (Hiltebeitel 2010, 157). The same might be said of both Jaimini's third and fourth questions, that is, 'How could Baladeva remedy Brahman-murder through pilgrimage?' and 'How could the Pāṇḍavas' sons be murdered, as if they had no protection?', respectively.

All of Jaimini's questions are oriented towards this world and social navigation within it. It is only later on (in MkP Sections II and III) that Jaimini seeks metaphysical knowledge. The Birds represent affirmation of life and, as corroborated by the enthusiasm with which they receive Jaimini's questions (an enthusiasm juxtaposed by Mārkaṇḍeya's aloofness), they specifically represent the ethos of *pravṛtti dharma*. It is for their attachment to *pravṛttic* religiosity that they are cursed. Moreover, recall that relaying the MkP is the means whereby the Birds become free of their father's curse (*śāpa*). The MkP might therefore be said to represent a means to pacify the extent to which *pravṛtti dharma* attains an accursed hue, viewed through the lofty lens of *nivṛttic* ideology. The assemblers of the MkP therefore place its teachings to the Birds who can authentically embody the theme of life affirmation, a theme which runs throughout the assemblage.

One cannot invoke *pravṛtti dharma* in an ideological vacuum; while invoking *pravṛtti dharma*, one must in the same breath invoke its structural counterpart *nivṛtti dharma*, through contrast to which it attains its distinction. Furthermore, given the indispensability of both of these ideological apexes, the MkP cannot exalt one at the expense of the other. Rather, it exhibits great creativity in the lengths it takes to preserve the tension between the two, a tension which remains fundamentally insoluble. For example, when Sukṛṣa's sons (the Birds in their past life) beg their father's pardon, they admit to their love of life and proceed to elucidate precisely why bodily attachment is philosophically errant (MkP 3. 55–74). Likewise, in Section II of the MkP, during the conversation between the Father and Sumati-Jaḍa, Queen Madālasā educates her son, Alarka, on both these ideologies, as Hazra notes, "chapters 27–35 dealing with Pravṛtti-dharma and to chapters 39–43 dealing with Nivṛtti-dharma or Yoga" (Hazra 1975, 11). The tension between the two ideologies is presented not only in Queen Madālasā's exposition but also in the narrative cradling that exposition. Upon the completion of Alarka's education and his instalment upon the throne, she and Ṛtadhvaja (her husband and Alarka's father) depart for the forest to perform austerities. Similarly at the end of his own reign, dissatisfied with the entrapments of worldly life, Alarka follows suit.

Turning momentarily to the Purāṇic context of the DM, the fate of the merchant relates directly to the MkP's polemic against *pravṛtti* religion whereby Dattatreya (speaking to Alarka) attacks the ideology of householders. The forest exchange between King Alarka and Sage Dattatreya parallels that between Suratha and Medhas.

Dattatreya's explicit critique (implicit in the words of Medhas) asserts that the householder acts out his fundamentally insatiable desire for offspring, money, and general gain. Dattatreya attributes the householder's aspiration to selfishness dominated by the I-sense, that is, I notions of 'I' (*aham*) and 'mine' (*mama*) (Bailey 1986, 69). Greg Bailey's translation of the pertinent passage reads:

> Thinking 'it is mine' (mama) is the source of misery (duḥkha) and thinking 'it is not mine' is the source of emancipation. … With the thought 'I am' (aham) has the sprout arisen and with the thought 'it is mine', it becomes like a great trunk whose topmost boughs are houses and fields with sons, wives and other beings as its twigs. Wealth and grains are its largest leaves and it has grown up many times. Merit and demerit are its outermost flowers and its largest fruits are misery and happiness. This great tree is the knowledge of what should be done and it is opulent with bees which are the desire to act. It concerns the path to emancipation and oozes out at the touch of the perplexed. Some who are tired of the way of saṃsāra, and are anxious about happiness, knowledge and perplexity, take refuge in the shade of that tree … But there are some who cut this tree which is "mineness" (mamatā) with the axe of knowledge, sharpened on the stone of attachment to truth. They have gone by that path where, having reached the forest of Brahman, cool, dustless and free from difficulties, they, wise without activities, attain supreme bliss.
>
> (MkP 38.6–13) (Bailey 1986, 68)

This sentiment finds a direct corollary in the desire of the disenfranchisement-driven merchant of the DM: "And the wise *vaiśya*, his mind despairing of things of this world, chose knowledge/Which destroys attachment to the notions of 'I' and 'mine'" (DM13.12–13) (Coburn 1991, 84). The background of the MkP exchange is as follows: Ṛta-dhvaja (Alarka's father) becomes aged and leaves for the forest with his wife Madālasā (Alarka's mother) to practice austerities, passing the sovereignty on to Alarka. Madālasā (who had spent the previous two cantos educating her son) delivers her final teachings to him at this point "in order that her son might abandon attachment to sensual pleasures" (MkP 36.5) (Pargiter 1904, 186). She says to him:

> When intolerable pain, arising from separation from thy dear kinsmen, or caused by the opposition of thy enemies, or springing from the destruction of thy wealth, or from thy own self, may befall thee as thy rulest thy kingdom, observing the laws of a householder – for the householder depending on selfishness makes unhappiness his abode – then, my son, draw forth, draw forth and read from the ring that I have given thee the writing that is inlaid in delicate letters on the plate.
>
> (MkP 36.6–8) (Pargiter 1904, 186)

The text appears favourably to Alarka's kingly dharma, informing us that he "protected justly and like children his glad people" (MkP 37.1) (Pargiter 1904, 187) – note the parallel to Suratha who was robbed of his rule "While he was protecting all creatures well, like his own sons" (Coburn 1991, 32) – and that he prospered for many years "devoted to righteousness, wealth, and the gratification of his desires" (MkP 37.6) (Pargiter 1904, 187). Nevertheless, Alarka's forest-roaming brother, Subāhu, "heard that [Alarka] was thus besotted in his attachment to pleasure, and uncontrolled in his senses" (MkP 37.8) (Pargiter 1904, 187), and carried out a scheme in order to set him straight. Subāhu formed an alliance with the King of Kāśī who, with his retinue of forces forming alliances with neighbouring kings, attacked Alarka's domain (MkP 37.9–17). The MkP's attack on worldly engagement does not occur without a paradoxical esteem for *pravṛtti dharma*; in the words of Desai, "a reading of this text shows that the supportive role of the householder is equal to that attributed to the yajamāna in the śrauta sacrifice of the Brāhmaṇas" (Bailey 1986, 57). Similarly, the MkP declares that: "the man who has accepted householder status nourishes all the universe. The fathers, sages, gods, living being and mankind, worms, insects, and flying creatures, birds, cattle and demons subsist upon the householder and thereby become satisfied" (Bailey 1986, 57). Furthermore, we are told that before finally departing, Madālasā gives Alarka "the blessings appropriate for a man who lives the family life" (MkP 35.9) (Pargiter 1904, 186). The householder is depicted in the MkP as a crucial link in creating harmony among and linking together the beings of the triple-world by means of the performance of sacrifice, of ritual action. The *pravṛtti* world-view stresses the interdependence of humanity with other beings in the three worlds who are all bound together by reciprocal relationships, and though humanity may be privileged in this scheme, the householder's individuality is not emphasized, but rather his centrality is predicated on the centrality of sacrifice and the wealth required to uphold the sacrifice which upholds the cosmic order (Bailey 1986, 65–6).

Most intriguing is how Madālasā's teachings to Alarka are framed. Ṛtadhvaja and Madālasā had three sons before Alarka and she proceeded to offer them each a *nivṛttic* education, such that her first son, "instructed by her from his birth, having understanding and being unselfish, did not turn his mind towards family life" (MkP 36.3) (Pargiter 1904, 142). The second and third son attained a similarly *nivṛttic* bend due to their mother's influence. At last, upon the birth of their fourth (and final) son Alarka, King Ṛtadhvaja appeals to her to offer a *pravṛttic* education to Alarka, schooling him in the ways of *kṣatriya* (and kingly) duty, particularly for the sake of providing for the *pitṛs* (MkP 25.26–33). As Hazra insightfully notes:

> This request of the king to his wife Madālasā to give instructions to Alarka about the duties of the Kṣatriyas and to train him in the Pravṛtti-mārga so that the Pitṛs may not be deprived of the offerings of water and rice-balls and the gods, men and lower animals may get their respective shares, presupposes the instructions on the duties of kings, on the duties of the castes and Āśramas, and on the funeral sacrifices given by Madālasā to Alarka in chaps. 27–35.
>
> (Hazra 1975, 12–13)

Sovereignty is indispensable to *pravṛttic* religious practice; the foundational centre of the office of the king is protection, he protects the practitioners, and institutions, upholding the *pravṛttic* wheel of the world. It is sovereignty which safeguards the ideals of *pravṛtti*.

The violence of kingship is crucial for the upkeep of *pravṛtti dharma* and the affirmation of worldly, bodily life. And for this reason, blood besmears even the exploits of ascetics in Mārkaṇḍeya's Section I discourse. Paradoxically, Sage Sukṛṣa observes his vow of *satya* in honouring his words to avian-Indra; however, in resorting to violence, first to his sons, then to himself, he dispenses with his vow to ahiṃsā. The Sukṛṣa episode is representative not only of the ritualist's sacrifice of blood but also of the kṣatriya's. The steadfast sage of our episode, having sworn to protect the downtrodden bird (avian-Indra), sacrifices his vow of ahiṃsā in order to preserve the life of the wretched creature. And the violence he would willingly commit would destroy his own progeny nonetheless. While the position of the sage (who requests his sons sacrifice themselves) and the position of the sons (who refuse to do so) are at odds, they both articulate variations on the same pan-Purāṇic theme: the sons aim to preserve themselves, while the sage aims to preserve the downtrodden bird. The sage declares "of me has this bird sought protection oppressed with hunger and thirst; wherefore let him be straightway satisfied with your flesh, and let his thirst be quickly assuaged with your blood" (MkP 3.37) (Pargiter 1904, 13). The sons protest at the sage's request on the basis that one cannot perform pious acts without a body, citing holy law that "one should preserve one's self by all means necessarily" (MkP 3.39–42).

In this exchange it is not such that violence itself is lauded, which the text makes clear through Sukṛṣa's admonishment of avian-Indra, who himself refers to the consumption of flesh as a transgression. It is protection that is lauded. That Sukṛṣa's ascetic vow of *satya*, ironically, demands of him a sacrifice of human flesh suggests the virtual impossibility of adhering to *nivṛtti*'s stringent moral code, particularly where preservation is concerned. The ethos of *pravṛtti*, as manifest in the endless cycles of ritual sacrifice which serves to preserve the *pravṛttic* sphere, is inextricable to the sacrifice undertaken by Sukṛṣa. Swayed by the pressures of destiny, the sage is made to eclipse his adherence to *ahiṃsā* for the sake of a most brutal act: the sacrifice of his own sons in the name of protecting another creature. Protection – the *sine qua non* of the warrior – requires violence. His willingness to commit violence in order to preserve one who he swears to protect likens him to the *kṣatriya* in general, and the king in particular, whose sworn duty is to protect all creatures.

Violence for the sake of preservation is a theme residing not only at the heart of sovereignty but also at the heart of the MkP. The *pravṛttic* theme of preservation is invoked at the inauguration of the MkP, through Jaimini's first question pertaining to the purpose of the Preserver's incarnation; a Preserver who, unsurprisingly, takes birth in *kṣatriya* (not brāhmaṇa) ranks. The theme of lordly protection is also echoed in Jaimini's fourth question, since the first and the last question serve as the inaugural questions' initial and terminal frames, as it were. This theme is also echoed in the biography of Mārkaṇḍeya himself: through the violent destruction of Yama, Mārkaṇḍeya is preserved in a state of eternal youth, blessed by Śiva's wrathful grace. The violence of *pravṛtti* is further featured in the fury of Dama, whose *kṣatriya* wrath both punishes evil in order to protect dharma and sates his ancestors with the blood of that punishment. Furthermore, it is precisely the MkP's emphasis on the affairs of the world, represented socially by the office of the king, that constitute a fitting backdrop for the DM. But this backdrop is not fitting only insofar as it celebrates *pravṛtti dharma* alone, but in its intricate preservation of the tension between *pravṛtti* and *nivṛtti*, a tension enshrined within the framing of the DM itself. The call of *pravṛtti* is manifest in the appeal of King Suratha to the Devī to win back his kingdom by means of force. Yet, his *pravṛttic* boon is earned alongside the boon of *mokṣa*, granted to his disenfranchized merchant companion. Nevertheless, as shall be demonstrated, the pursuit of *mokṣa* is eclipsed by the grandeur of a Goddess who is inextricably bound to the cycles of creation, and the proper governance thereof. Thus, her virtues are nourished by the soil of the MkP wherein is extolled, in tandem, sovereignty, sacrifice and the blood of life; for, it is the *pravṛttic* office of preservation which must regulate its flow.

## Notes

1 As noted, the question pertains to Jaimini's confusions regarding the *Mahābhārata*. We might note further that it cannot be such that Jaimini is asking after anything new, since all available knowledge resides within the MBh. He is asking for further exposition on what the MkP already contains. By extension it would accord Mārkaṇḍeya's exposition (i.e. the MkP) as foremost among available Purāṇic compilations offering exegesis on the MBh itself.

2 Pargiter's translation of this benediction follows:

> May Vishnu's lotus-feet, which power have
>
> To dissipate the woes wrought by the fear

Of existence, and which are lauded high
By ascetics, assiduous, whose minds
From all things else are rapt – may those same feet,
Whose steps the earth, the sky, and heaven o'erpassed,
To sight appearing, purify your souls!
May He protect you, who is skilled to save
In every kind of sin impure; whose form
Within the bosom of the sea of milk
Upon the hooded snake reclines; and at
Whose touch the sea grows mountainous, its spray
Up-tossing from its waters by his breath
Disturbed, and into seeming dancing breaks.

(Pargiter 1904, 1)

3 Birds with an uppercase shall be used herein as a proper noun referring to the characters within the MkP.
4 The story of these Birds intertextually evokes the sārṅgaka birds who survive the burning of the khāṇḍava in the terminal frame of the Ādiparvan, of whom they are descendants (Balkaran 2020).
5 Pargiter notes that this same succession of solar kings (i.e. Marutta à Nariṣyanta à Dama à Rājyavardhana) are also detailed in the *Viṣṇu Purāṇa*, 4.1 (Pargiter 1904, 577).
6 What comes to mind is the take of Bharata's in the *Mahābhārata* who earns the epithet Sarvadamana during his youth at Kaṇva's āśrama, given his ability to subdue the beasts of the forest (see MBh I.68.9) (van Buitenen 1973, I: 165).
7 Wilson writes,

> a rather chivalric and curious story is told of Dama in the Márkandeya. His bride Sumaná, daughter of the king Daśárha, was rescued by him from his rivals. One of them, Bapushmat, afterwards killed Marutta, who had retired into the woods, after relinquishing his crown to his son. Dama in retaliation killed Bapushmat, and made the Pińd́a, or obsequial offering to his father, of his flesh: with the remainder he fed the Brahmans of Rákshasa origin: such were the kings of the solar race.
>
> (Wilson 1961, 353, n. 22)

8 In his introduction to the MkP, only after dedicating approximately 2,500 words speculating on the MkP's probable place of origin (Pargiter 1904, viii–xiii), and another 3,000 words speculating on the Purāṇa's dates of composition, (Pargiter 1904, xiii–xx), does Pargiter proceed (under the final heading of his introduction to the MkP is titled "Other matters of interest") to briefly remark upon issues of thematic elements of the MkP wherein he discusses the Dama episode.
9 Recall that Sage Sukṛṣa says to his sons "let [avian-Indra] be straightway satisfied with your flesh, and let his thirst be quickly assuaged with your blood" (MkP 3.37; see Pargiter 1904, 13). Sukṛṣa further specifically connects funerary rites and the sacrifice of blood and flesh speaking to avian-Indra as follows: "when I have performed for myself the final sacrifice, and my obsequies, according to the śāstras, do thou unhesitatingly eat me here; this my body I here grant thee for food" (MkP 3.46) (Pargiter 1904, 14).
10 Also while on the topic of what later tradition would deem "left-handed" religiosity devoted to the Goddess.

> … it is worthy of note that indulgence in spirituous liquor and in sensual enjoyments is viewed with little or no disapprobation in the story of Dattātreya; and meat and strong drink are mentioned as most acceptable offerings in the worship of Dattātreya (p. 106), as an incarnation of Viṣṇu (p. 99).
>
> (see Pargiter 1904, xxi).

Furthermore, from Viśvakarman's hymn to the Sun: "By reason of thy intoxication from drinking up like spirituous liquor the darkness of the world, thy body has acquired a deep red hue" (MkP 107.7; see Pargiter 1904, 573).

11 Although Indra stays Sukṛṣa's hand at the eleventh hour so to speak, he is pleased by the sage's willingness to offer blood – a blood which he himself demanded.
12 The names he gives are: Piṅgākṣa, Vibodha, Suputra and Sumukha (MkP 1.21) (Pargiter 1904, 3).
13 Mārkaṇḍeya relays the Birds' backstory verbatim as they themselves relay it to Sage Śamīka (MkP 3.15–80) (Pargiter 1904, 12–16).
14 "Markandeya does not himself explain the questions but, declining with a transparent excuse, refers Jaimini to the Birds" (Pargiter 1904, xxi).
15 The battlefield in question is none other than the field of Kuru, and the battle in question is none other than the Great War featured in the *Mahābhārata*. This is part of a highly conscious intertextual enterprise between the MBh and MkP (Balkaran 2020).
16 Similarly, "Mārkaṇḍeya narrates the story of Parikṣit Aikṣvākava and sons at Mahābhārata 3.190 in a combination of prose and verse, ostensibly to exemplify the power of the Brahmins" (see Brodbeck 2009, 227).

## Works cited in this chapter


Bailey, Greg. 1986. *Materials for the Study of Ancient Indian Ideologies: Pravṛtti and Nivṛtti*. Torino: Ed. Jollygrafica.

Balkaran, Raj. 2020. "Avian Artistry: Decoding the Intertextuality between Mahābhārata and Mārkaṇḍeya Purāṇa". *International Journal of Hindu Studies* 1 (1): 1–30.

Brodbeck, Simon. 2009. *The Mahābhārata Patriline: Gender, Culture, and the Royal Hereditary*. Farnham, England; Burlington, VT: Ashgate.

Buitenen, J.A.B. van, trans. 1973. *Mahābhārata: Volume 1: Book 1: The Book of the Beginning*. Vol. I. Chicago, IL: University of Chicago Press.

Buitenen, J.A.B. van, trans. 1975. *Mahābhārata: Volume 2: The Book of the Assembly Hall; Book 3: The Book of the Forest*. Vol. II. [Chicago, IL]: University of Chicago Press.

Coburn, Thomas B. 1991. *Encountering the Goddess: A Translation of the Devī-Māhātmya and a Study of Its Interpretation*. Albany, NY: State University of New York Press.

Hazra, R.C. 1975. *Studies in the Purāṇic Records on Hindu Rites and Customs*. Delhi: Motilal Banarsidass.

Hiltebeitel, Alf. 2010. *Reading the Fifth Veda Studies on the Mahabharata: Essays*. Edited by Vishwa Adluri and Joydeep Bagchee. Leiden: Brill.

Mani, Vettam. 1975. *Purāṇic Encyclopaedia: A Comprehensive Dictionary with Special Reference to the Epic and Purāṇic Literature*. Delhi : Motilal Banarsidass.

Monier-Williams, Ernst Leumann, Carl Cappeller and Īśvaracandra. 2008. "Monier Williams Sanskrit–English Dictionary (2008 Revision)".

Pargiter, F. Eden, trans. 1904. *Mārkaṇḍeya Purāṇa*. Calcutta: Asiatic Society of Bengal. www.wisdomlib.org/hinduism/book/the-markandeya-purana.

Rocher, Ludo. 1986. *The Purāṇas*, edited by Jan Gonda. Wiesbaden: Harrassowitz.

Smith, J.Z. 1978. *Map is Not Territory: Studies in the Histories of Religions.* Leiden: Brill.

Wilson, Horace Hayman, trans. 1961. *The Viṣṇu Purāṇa: A System of Hindu Mythology and Tradition*. Calcutta: Punthi Pustak.

Winternitz, Moriz. 1972. *A History of Indian Literature. Vol. 1.* New Delhi: Oriental Books Repr. Corp.

# Conclusion

## Paragons of preservation: Goddess, Sun, King

### 5.1 The Sun and preservation

#### *5.1.1 The Sun protects Yudhiṣṭhira*

Book II of the *Mahābhārata*, "The Book of The Forest", holds great significance for the discussion at hand. Turning to the initial frame of the book, we see Janamejaya asking how the Pāṇḍavas and their entourage survive their forest exile. Janamejaya explains that he was followed into the forest by a large number of brahmins, from whom, despite their absence of concern for their own welfare, he felt obliged to provide. He reverently approaches his wise priest, Dhaumya, asking after how to fulfil his duty and provide for the brahmins. Upon reflection, Dhaumya tells Yudhiṣṭhira that creatures all hungered when first they were created until the Sun provided for them out of fatherly compassion. He impregnated the earth with his heat for the generation of food. Dhaumya reasons that since he thus supplies the food that sustains all life, the Sun is the father of all creatures. He then exhorts Yudhiṣṭhira to take refuge in the Sun, ritually purifying himself and petitioning for aid. Yudhiṣṭhira then undertakes (*nivṛttic*) austerity – fasting, controlling his breathing, mastering his senses and makes offerings to the Sun (MBh III.3.1–15). Yudhiṣṭhira here engages in *nivṛttic* religiosity for the sake of generating the merit to harness for his *pravṛttic* aims. At this point, the narrative zooms out one frame as Janamejaya asks Vaiśaṃpāyana after the manner in which Yudhiṣṭhira placates the Sun, to which Vaiśaṃpāyana replies that Yudhiṣṭhira intoned the 108 names of the Sun as taught him by Dhaumya, who learned it from Nārada, who in turn learned it from Indra (III.3.15–30). Notable for our purposes is that the source of this ritual invocation to the Sun is not a sagacious or spiritual creature: this formula to the Sun stems from the king of the gods of heaven, incessantly engaged in the *pravṛttic* aims.

Yudhiṣṭhira's propitiation bears fruit, quite literally. The Sun, pleased by his penance and praise, appears to the dharma king in a flaming form and promises to provide ample food and water for him and his entourage for their twelve years of exile, before vanishing. The dharma king arose victorious from his penance, sought Dhaumya's blessings, embraced his brothers and joined Draupadī in the kitchen who looked on as he prepared the food himself. Their

DOI: 10.4324/9780429322020-6

rations miraculously multiplied to inexhaustible proportions, with which he fed the brahmins, his brothers, and wife (MBh III.4.1–9). Similar to the manner in which Yudhiṣṭhira propitiates the Sun, the fruits of that labour, too, are emblematic of the dharmic double helix: the Sun specifically blesses them with four foods available in the wilderness to a forest ascetic – fruits, roots, viands, and greens – yet he mentions that they are to be prepared in the Pāṇḍava kitchen. The use of fire for food preparation is evocative not of the wilderness, but of city life, where thrives the *pravṛtti* religion. As a noble king, Yudhiṣṭhira proxies for the very Sun whom he invokes insofar as he toils for the sake of preserving this world and the beings within it. This comparison is made explicit in the epic which sums up the episode thus: "So it befell that the prince, brilliant like the Sun, obtained from the Sun this boon and gave to the brahmins what their hearts desired" (van Buitenen 1975, II: 229). The Sun's blessing here is an homage to the *pravṛttic* duty of kings to protect and preserve their citizens, a duty both symbolized and enacted by the Sun.

### *5.1.2 The Sun and Mārkaṇḍeya*

The connection between Mārkaṇḍeya and solar veneration is not only made in the *Mārkaṇḍeya Purāṇa*. The *Mahābhārata*, too, makes this fascinating connection, in particular during the Pāṇḍavas' encounter with the great sage occurring in "The Book of the Forest". The Pāṇḍavas forest exile is an important juncture for our purposes, both in terms of setting and plot:

> The tension between these opposing paragons, and their opposing orientations toward the sphere of human enterprise, is poignantly preserved in the narrative motif of kings who are (temporarily) sentenced to forest exile where they commingle with, and often mimic, ascetic figures from whom they receive social and moral instruction. The most famous examples of these are the heroes of both Sanskrit epics, who inevitably quit the aristocracy to roam the forest in ascetic garb. Though the forest-teachings received by these figures often promote an ethos of ascetic detachment and introspection, these experiences paradoxically enrich the royal pupils' capacity to rule. (Balkaran 2019, 29)

It is interesting, then, that Mārkaṇḍeya – who implicitly and explicitly exposits the very dharmic double helix spun by the *pravṛtti–nivṛtti* interplay – should give by far the lengthiest discourse in *The Book of The Forest*. Moreover, beyond the inclusion of Yudhiṣṭhira's solar veneration at the very outset of the epic's forest book, there are subtle cues connecting Mārkaṇḍeya and the Sun throughout. In the words of van Buitenen, *The Book of the Forest*:

> displays in a grand manner of what the Indian epic is capable … it can be divided into two large blocks: the vicissitudes of the heroes and heroine in their forest exile and episodes relating to the main narrative on the one

hand, and, on the other, the manifold narratives to which their sojourn in the forest gives occasion.

(van Buitenen 1975, II: 174)

While Mārkaṇḍeya is a major source of these teaching narratives, even before he enters the stage to deliver his lengthy discourse, the Pāṇḍavas encounter him in a brief but symbolically laden exchange. Mārkaṇḍeya pays a visit to the Pāṇḍava entourage early on, when, we are told, he remembers the fate of Rāma while beholding the Pāṇḍava's sorrowful state. He met up with Rāma as well when he was in exile. Mārkaṇḍeya knows first-hand the tension dramatized by the king in forest exile, witnessing it now in both Sanskrit epics. Mārkaṇḍeya in fact invokes the forbearance of Rāma in counselling the Pāṇḍavas to embrace their hardship in humility, since, while it is over, they will return gloriously like the illustrious Sun (MBh III.26.4–26). It is significant that it is Mārkaṇḍeya who points us to the parallels between the fate of the Pāṇḍavas, and that of Rāma, heir to the solar line of kings. Rāma, bar none, is the face of the dharmic double helix: embracing his *pravṛttic* duty at every turn while embodying the virtues of *nivṛtti.* Owing to the intertextual richness of Sanskrit literature, Mārkaṇḍeya speaks volumes scarcely opening his mouth, by showing up at a certain juncture and pointing to its significance by invoking the story of Rāma.

After Mārkaṇḍeya's lengthy exposition occurring later in the Book, the text them returns to the main action wherein we see an exchange between Draupadī and Satyabhāmā (MBh III.222–223), the Cattle Expedition, and the abduction of Draupadī (III.248–256), directly following which Mārkaṇḍeya then tells in full the story of Rāma (III.257–275). Crucial for the study at hand is the notion that Rāma is perhaps *the* paragon of preservation along with the most prominent face of the dharmic double helix. Our sagacious exiled king oscillates between the royal and ascetic ideologies, between allegiance to both *pravṛtti* and *nivṛtti* values (Balkaran 2018a). The Story of the solar king Rāma is immediately followed by the story of Sāvitrī, the daughter of the Sun, also including Yama, son of the Sun (MBh III III.277–283). The Story of Rāma and Sāvitrī both feature separation between man and wife (which is interestingly a feature of the Sun's loss of Saṃjñā). What follows is the Story of Karṇa, son of the Sun. The transition here is rather abrupt, until you note the solar theme tying together the threads of the "Book of the Forest", commencing with Yudhiṣṭhira overt veneration of the Sun.

Karṇa's "The Robbing of the Earrings" (MBh III.284–286) functions as the closing frame of Mārkaṇḍeya's discourse. We are told that at the beginning of the thirteenth and final year of the Pāṇḍavas forest exile, Indra sets out to deprive Karṇa of his protective earrings through the ruse of appearing as a begging brahmin. The Sun appears before his son, Karṇa, also in the form of a brahmin, to warn him not to give away his earrings. The Sun is motivated by great love and compassion for his son Karṇa. He commences his address to Karṇa by declaring he speaks out of friendship. Note that Mitra, 'friend', is one of the most ancient Vedic names of the Sun. Karṇa responds by asking after the true identity of his interlocutor, who speaks to him out of such friendship. To this, the Sun reveals his identity and declares that he speaks out of affection for Karṇa and for his best interest. Karṇa acknowledges that it must be so, and replies speaking out of love for the Sun. Though Karṇa refuses the Sun's advice, the Sun tries to appeal to his status as a devotee, declaring he must protect his devotees, and that none are so devoted to him as Karṇa. While Karṇa affirms his superlative devotion to the Sun (dearer to him even than his sons or his wife) and expressed deep appreciation and honour for the care the Sun has shown him. But Karṇa nevertheless stubbornly insists that should Indra appear before him in the form of a begging brahmin that he will do his duty and supply the brahmin with his request, thereby retaining his honour and earning fame. The Sun pleads with him, indicating doing so will cost him his life, given the protective nature of his earrings, hinting at a dark secret (which, unbeknownst to Karṇa is his true parentage as the son of Kuntī and the Sun). Karṇa proudly assures his father that he will defeat Arjuna; but, knowing better, the Sun implored Karṇa to ask for an unfailing spear, if he were to give away his protective earrings.

At this point in the narrative, Janamejaya asks after Sūrya's dark secret and is told of Kuntī's unfailing year-long hospitality looking after the needs of a demanding brahmin who, in reward for her commendable service, gives her a spell whereby she may conjure up any god to father her a son. To test the spell, Kuntī conjures up the Sun, who arrives ready to impregnate her with a son. Afraid, she asks him to leave, but he refuses, since his own standing is at stake in this affair. Kuntī consents, appeased by the Sun's promise that she retains her maidenly virtue once they are done, for fear of her relatives. He promises a Sun born with armour and a breastplate. They lay together and the Sun departs (MBh III.290.10–22). Upon successfully bringing her pregnancy to term in secrecy, she gives birth to Karṇa and sends him in a basket down the river, which finds its way to the town of Campa. Karṇa is retrieved by the childless sūta Adhiratha and his wife Rādhā who gladly adopt the babe. Once he is grown, he arrives at Hastinapura, competes with Arjuna, and makes an ally of Duryodhana. Indra appears before him and demands his earrings; Karṇa eventually relents on the condition that he receives an unfailing spear, as per the Sun's advice.

That the story of Karṇa occurs at this point in the *Mahābhārata* is certainly not without significance. It serves as the terminal frame and ultimate significators of the solar thread in the *Book of The Forest*. The Sun protects his son Karṇa here as he protects Yudhiṣṭhira's entourage at the outset. The authors of the *Mahābhārata* chose to flesh out the story at this very (seemingly abrupt) juncture, though they actually summarize the story of Karṇa in Book One, the Ādiparvan (MBh I.104.1–20). In the Ādiparvan, we learn of another crucial element of Karṇa's story: his enmity with his (unknown) half-brother Arjuna. This opposition is forged at the following encounter (MBh I.124–127), as follows. The royal family and public assemble in the arena at Hastinapura to witness the Pāṇḍava princes perform a public display of their weapons skill, as suggested by Droṇa. Arjuna demonstrates his formidable skill at arms at which point Karṇa arrives and announces he can match Arjuna's skill. Karṇa's glorious entrance into the arena is described as follows, replete with solar imagery:

> His power and might were like the regal lion's or bull's or elephant's, and he was like sun, moon, and fire in brightness, beauty, and luster. Tall he stood, like a golden palm tree, this youth with the hard body of a lion. Innumerable were the virtues of this magnificent son of the Sun.
>
> (MBh I.126.1–5) (van Buitenen 1973, I: 279)

Duryodhana offers him friendship, while Arjuna insults him as an outsider to the proceedings, to which Karṇa responds by challenging him to a duel. During the duel, the heroes' celestial fathers show their support through the forces of nature: Indra rains on Arjuna, while the Sun shines down on Karṇa. So, while Arjuna is hidden in shadow, Karṇa stands in the light of the Sun (MBh I.126.24–25). When Karṇa is asked after his lineage, he hangs his head in shame, to which Duryodhana responds by installing Karṇa as king of Anga. At this point, Karṇa's foster father Adiratha enters the scene and embraces his son, to which the Pāṇḍavas berate him for his low birth as the son of a charioteer. His new ally Duryodhana defends him, reasoning:

> How could a doe give birth to this tiger who resembles the sun, with his earrings and armor and celestial birthmarks? This lordly man deserves to rule the world, not just Anga. He deserves it by the power of his arms and by me who shall obey his orders.
>
> (MBhI.127.5–20) (van Buitenen 1973, I: 281–2)

The festivities end at sundown.

Although the epic returns to the larger frame, and it is Vaiśaṃpāyana who tells Janamejaya this story, the "Robbing of the Earrings" subtale returns our attention to Mārkaṇḍeya during its terminal frame. We are told that the Pāṇḍavas are at long last at the end of their forest exile, and they leave the hermitage with their priests, cooks, retainers, chariots, etc., upon hearing the tales of old of seers and gods in all their richness from Mārkaṇḍeya (MBh III.294.42–43). The MBh insists on rendering these solar stories ultimately part of Mārkaṇḍeya's discourse. Moreover, "The Book of The Forest"'s final subtale – and thus terminal frame – is "The Drillings Woods" (MBh III.295–299) where Yudhiṣṭhira is tested by his father, the god Dharma. This encounter results from a motif carried over from the Karṇa story, that is, a Vedic god in brahmin guise visiting the Pāṇḍavas. Dharma – disguised as a brahmin whose fire-drilling woods have been caught up in the antlers of a deer – asks Yudhiṣṭhira for help, leading up to the tests in question. And his test occurs immediately after his lengthy schooling from Mārkaṇḍeya.

### *5.1.3 The Sun protects Rāma*

The only other place outside of the myths of the MkP and *Sāmba Purāṇa* where we see the Sun exalted as a supreme figure is in the Ādityahṛdaya of the Vālmīki Rāmāyaṇa. A close synopsis follows. Sage Agastya is seated among the gods as an onlooker of the important battle between Rāma and Rāvaṇa. Seeing that

Rāma is exhausted and made anxious by his battling with Rāvaṇa, Agastya approaches Rāma and implores him to:

> hear this immemorial secret teaching by means of which, my child, you shall conquer all your enemies [adding that] one should constantly intone this holy Ādityahṛdaya, which destroys all of one's enemies and brings victory [and] calms anxiety and grief.
>
> (5–10) (van Nooten 2009, 1342).

Agastya exhorts Rāma to "worship Vivasvān, bringer of light, the lord of the worlds, rising with his halo of rays, worshiped by the gods and asuras" (11–12) (van Nooten 2009, 1342). He then goes on to proclaim the exalted attributes of the Sun (13–48).

Before departing, Agastya assures Rāma that one who praises the Sun is saved from all distress, difficulty and danger. He then declares:

> Therefore, with a focused mind, you should worship that god of gods, the lord of the worlds. For, having intoned this hymn three times, you will be victorious in all your battles. This very hour, great-armed warrior, you shall slay Rāvaṇa.
>
> (49–54) (van Nooten 2009, 1343)

Upon receiving Agastya's transmission of the Ādityahṛdaya, Rāma becomes free from care. He gazes upon the Sun and intones the Ādityahṛdaya before taking up his bow, fixing his gaze on his enemy, and sallying forth to battle, with a delighted heart, determined to kill Rāvaṇa (55–60). Then the Sun, surrounded by the hosts of gods, delights in anticipation of the destruction of Rāvaṇa, gazes upon Rāma with the excited words. "Make haste!" (61–64) (van Nooten 2009, 1343).

The supremacy of the Sun is explicitly established from the very outset of Agastya's glorification, as "the essence of all the gods. Filled with blazing energy, he brings all beings to life with his rays. With his rays he protects the gods, the asuras, and all the worlds" (13–14), adding that the Sun is in essence all creatures, as the breath of life, the bringer of light, the maker of the seasons (17–18). The Sun is also presented as a manifestation of other deities. Not only does Agastya note some of the Sun's solar forms throughout – that is, as Āditya, Savitṛ, Sūrya, Pūṣan (19); Ravi (23; 42), Mārtaṇḍa (22), Āditya (34) – he equates the Sun with various other Vedic deities throughout: Brahmā, Viṣṇu, Śiva, Skanda, Prajāpati, Indra, Kubera, Kāla, Yama, Soma and Varuṇa, the ancestors, the Vasus, the Sādhyas, the two Aśvins, the Maruts, Manu, Vāyu, Agni (15–17); Viśvakarman, Agni (41), Tvaṣṭṛ (22). The Sun is even presented as the great gods of Hinduism, for example, as Śambhu, the auspicious one (22), and as master of the Ṛk, Yajur and Sāmavedas (25).

Beyond his equation with other deities, the Sun is described by his various attributes for example, as: he who moves through the sky, radiant as gold, the maker of day (19–20); the thousand-rayed lord of the tawny steeds, master of seven horses, dispeller of darkness (21); the golden embryo, the cooling one, the scorching one, the bringer of light (23); lord of the heavens, the piercer of darkness, friend of the waters, cause of torrential rains (25); the scorching one, the great orb, death, the golden one who scorches all beings (27); lord of the constellations, planets, and stars; giver of life; most radiant beings (29–30); the victorious one, he of the tawny horses, who grants victory and auspiciousness; he of the thousand rays (33–34); the eye of all the worlds (42); dispeller of darkness (42); rises on the eastern mountain and sets on the western mountain; the lord of the hosts of heavenly luminaries; the lord of day (31–32); the son of Aditi, he bears Agni in his womb (24); omnipresent, of immense blazing energy, reddish in hue, the source of all existence (28); a fierce warrior; the swift one; maker of the lotus flower (35–36); banisher of darkness; bringer of the thaw; slaughterer of enemies; destroyer of the ungrateful; lord of heavenly luminaries (39–40).

The Ādityahṛdaya ultimately exalts Sūrya even above Viṣṇu, indeed above the pantheon of Vedic gods and Hindu trimūrti of Brahmā–Viṣṇu–Śiva alike: "Homage to radiant Sūrya, who is the lord of Brahmā, Lord Śiva, and the imperishable Viṣṇu, whose radiance is that of Āditya and who, in his fierce form, devours all creatures" (37–38) (van Nooten 2009, 1343). The final verses of the Ādityahṛdaya weave together various themes to exalt Sūrya as integral to the cosmogonic functions of the great gods and Vedic sacrifice, as indeed the essence of all activity:

> He is the lord who destroys the creation and then creates it anew.
> With his rays, he dries up, scorches, and inundates the world.
> Lodged within all beings, he remains awake while they sleep.
> He is the agnihotra sacrifice as well as the reward of those who perform it. (45–46)
> He is all the vedas, all sacrifices, and the reward of all sacrifices.
> He, Lord Ravi, is everything.
> He is all actions that are done throughout the worlds (37–48)
>
> (van Nooten 2009, 1343)

Significant for our purposes is that the Sun's supremacy is inextricable from his support in Rāma fulfilling his royal duty of vanquishing his foe and protecting the realm. This makes for an intriguing parallel of Yudhiṣṭhira invoking the Goddess by intoning the Durgā Stava MBh (4.5) (Coburn 1985, 267–71).

## 5.2 Paragons of preservation

Preservation is the essence of avatāra, the very impetus of Viṣṇu's incarnation. Jaimini's question is indeed of profound significance to the Hindu world. But it begs the deeper question of why the Vaiṣṇava avatāra serves as the very inception of the *Mārkaṇḍeya Purāṇa*. While there are several unabashedly *Vaiṣṇava*

*Purāṇas*, most notably the beloved *Bhāgavata*, the *Mārkaṇḍeya Purāṇa* is not considered among them. Why then does this ultimately non-sectarian Sanskrit work pay homage to Viṣṇu's avatāric function at its outset? (for more on this, see Essence of Avatar).

The *Devī Māhātmya* celebrates the essence of the Vaiṣṇava avatāra (Balkaran 2017). Through the ambivalent function of the Great Goddess, we understand the essence of the Vaiṣṇava avatāra: to shed blood where needed in the name of compassionate protection. While the term is not used in the text, the spirit of the term is. For example, the Goddess declares "whenever there is trouble produced by demons,/Then taking on bodily form, I will bring about the destruction of enemies" (DM 11.50–51) (Coburn 1991, 78). Moreover, the *Devī Māhātmya* adopts explicit Vaiṣṇava imagery throughout. In Episode I, the Goddess wakes Viṣṇu from his yogic sleep at the end of age and helps him to slay the demons Madhu and Kaiṭabha, who emerged from his ears. Also, in Episode III the gods praised the Goddess for defeating their enemies in a hymn, the Nārāyaṇi Stuti, named for the "nārāyaṇi namostute" refrain occupying sixteen consecutive verses. She is hailed, in essence, as a feminine Nārāyaṇa, a She-Viṣṇu as it were. Once she is praised by the gods, she prophesizes to return again and again to rescue them from danger. The first of these promises specifically incorporates Kṛṣṇaite imagery:

> When the twenty-eighth *yuga* in the Vaivasvata Manu-interval has arrived,
>
> Two more great Asuras, also named Śumbha and Niśumbha, will arise.
>
> Then born in the house of the cowherd Nanda, taking birth from the womb of Yaśodā,
>
> Dwelling on Vindhya mountain, I will then slay these two.
>
> (*Devī Māhātmya* 11.37–38) (Coburn 1991, 77)

Vaiṣṇava imagery is celebrated not only in the text of the *Devī Māhātmya*, but at the very seasonal juncture when it is ritually chanted across the Hindu world. The autumnal Goddess festival:

> pays homage to the cycles of dark and light upon which the cosmos is founded, cycles expressed through the rhythms of nature, oscillating between night and day, summer and winter, full and new moon. It occurs at a time when light and darkness are equal on the earth. But, unlike its vernal counterpart (in March, on the first day of Spring), the autumnal equinox occurs when darkness overtakes light, when the days grow darker and colder. This is the most inauspicious annual juncture, the midnight of the gods, when Vishnu, the protector of the world, slumbers, fast asleep since onset of the monsoon season. It is therefore a time when even the gods are vulnerable, when the forces of darkness are at the height of their power. Protection is therefore crucial when the Sun's light starts to wane; hence the

> festival marks the consecration of kings – sworn to protect – and the invocation of the Great Goddess, protectress bar none.
>
> (Balkaran 2018b, 17)

The celebration of the Goddess is the celebration of a protective divine force, the personal descent of which we hail *avatāra*.

While the *Mārkaṇḍeya Purāṇa* may not be a "Vaiṣṇava" text proper, one can argue it concerns itself with the essence of the Vaiṣṇava avatāra: the cosmogonic function of preservation, particularly as pertains to the social and moral order here on earth. Viṣṇu unequivocally stands for world affirmation. This is unsurprising given his status as an original Vedic deity. This is in stark contrast to Rudra-Śiva who struggles to be incorporated into Vedic culture, often uninvited to Vedic sacrifices, most famously by his own father-in-law Dakṣa. This is not the case for Viṣṇu, to whom we find the dedication of five Ṛg Vedic hymns. He represents the Vedic status quo, while Rudra-Śiva represents the outlier. Such is the symbolism of this solar deity, the centre around which society revolves. In the *Ṛg Veda*, Viṣṇu is the support of heaven and earth, specifically association with the Sun, source of heat and light. Both the Vedic ethos and the function of Viṣṇu favour prosperous preservation of life on earth. Conversely, in the *Sūrya Māhātmya* section of the *Mārkaṇḍeya Purāṇa*, the Sun is praised by Brahmā as one "Who hast the nature of Vishnu" (MkP 109.10). The solar symbols of King and Goddess are therefore easily associable with Viṣṇu. I've demonstrated elsewhere the intrinsic centrality of sovereignty as an underlying theme of the *Devī Māhātmya*, showcased through the architecture of the work (Balkaran 2019, 88–123), along with the interdependence of Goddess and King, paragon of *pravṛtti dharma*, arguing that the Goddess of our text not only safeguards individual kings, she safeguards their very ideology, exalting it above and beyond the merits of ascetic idealism. Hence, the profound interconnectedness between the mythologies of the Sun and Goddess in the MkP demonstrated in this work. The discussion at hand unites this solar symbolism – that implicating Goddess, Sun and King – in light of their cosmogonic function of preservation, upon which existence depends.

The autumnal festival to the Goddess marks a time when protection is required, in social and spiritual orders alike, such that it is the time of year bar none for royal consecration. C.J. Fuller succinctly fleshes out the connection between: 1) the timing of the festival; 2) the invocation of the Goddess; and 3) the consecration of Hindu kings. He does so by drawing on two mythological traditions, one (mainly) Northern, the other (mainly) Southern. Both of these mythologize the astronomical passage through the seasons. Fuller's elucidation occur in the "The Navaratri Festival" section (Fuller 2004, 108–11) of his "Rituals of Kingship" chapter (Fuller 2004, 106–27) where he explains that in the Northern tradition, Vishnu, the protector of the cosmos, is said to slumber for four months, starting with the onset of monsoon season. Naturally, "when the great god who preserves the world withdraws from it for four months, a time of danger is heralded, when demons and other malevolent forces can become more active" (Fuller 2004, 110). Other deities are often said to slumber alongside him, "thus exacerbating the world's vulnerability [which] is consistent with the notion that Mahiṣāsura and his demon army are able to gather strength and overthrow the gods … approximately one month before Vishnu reawakens" (Fuller 2004, 110). Similarly, in the (mainly) Southern mythological tradition, "Navaratri occurs close to the autumnal equinox, the gods' midnight and middle of the dark half of the year" (Fuller 2004, 111). Therefore, according to both traditions, Navaratri occurs at a time:

> when the gods are inactive or weakened and the demons at the height of their power. But from this reversal of order and good fortune finally comes Durga's victory, and out of the chaos engendered by the demons … a new universal order, presided over by the gods under their king, is created and established. The goddess' slaying of the buffalo-demon signals the end of demonic supremacy. In this glorious victory and its aftermath, the recreation of a new kingly order, Hindu monarchs participate by celebrating royal Navaratri.
>
> (Fuller 2004, 111)

Hence, the Nine Nights festival is *the* royal festival, re-energizing the earthy office of protection at an annual juncture so dark (both literally and figuratively), that the gods themselves are left vulnerable to the forces of darkness.

That the Sun has been invoked – both explicitly and implicitly – as a protective force throughout the history of Indian religions is hardly surprising. In addition to the hymns of the *Ṛg Veda* appealing to him for protection, the fact that the Sun fathers the Vedic divine healers, the Aśvin twins, seems to corroborate this motif. His penchant for preservation is evident even in his epic and Purāṇic narrative characterization: he protects his sons Yama (modifying Chāyā's curse to save his foot) and Karṇa; he protects the Pāṇḍavas and their entourage, nourishing them during their lengthy forest exile; he protects and empowers Rāma during his cataclysmic battle with Rāvaṇa. Moreover, he fathers additional protective forces in their own right in the epic and Purāṇic literature: Sugrīva (who supports Rāma in his mission), Manu Vaivasvata (the current Manu), and Manu Sāvarṇi (the next Manu).

The DM commences as a means of elucidating the ascension of the next Manu, who shall attain his reign at the end of this age and the commencement of the next. Mārkaṇḍeya inaugurates the DM proper thus: "Sāvarṇi, the son of the Sun, will become Lord of the next Age./Hear as I relay his rise at length" (DM 1.1) (Balkaran 2020). In like fashion, Mārkaṇḍeya concludes the DM by declaring: "Thus receiving a boon from the Goddess, Suratha, best of rulers,/ Will receive another birth from the Sun, and/Will become Sāvarṇi, Manu of the next Age" (DM 13.18) (Balkaran 2020). The Goddess here becomes as if an afterthought. In light of the DM's intrinsic frame narrative, the exploits of the Goddess are mere means for King Suratha firstly to regain his earthly regime, and second, to secure sovereignty over an entire age as the future *Manu*,

Sāvarṇi. The DM, then, is the story of Sāvarṇi, who is destined to be the future Manu of the next age of this cycle of creation. The tales of the Goddess are therefore part of the story of Sāvarṇi, who is destined to be the future Manu of the next age of this cycle of creation. But what is the significance of transforming the glories of the Goddess to the making of a Manu in this manner?

The most obvious answer, in my view, as to why the glories of the Goddess are implicate in the making of a Manu is so as to underscore the central tenant to Indian religious thought, common to the work of Goddess, Sun and Manu alike: preservation. This theme is moreover personified in the Indian king. Therefore, the DM's outer intrinsic enframement (connecting the DM to the fabric of the MkP's MV discourse) wherein Suratha is granted cosmic rulership as a Manu is commensurate with its intrinsic inner enframement wherein Suratha's earthly kingdom is restored through his encounter with Sage Medhas. It is not by chance that the most popular face of cosmic preservation (Viṣṇu) is associated with earthly kings, since preservation is arguably their staunchest duty, if not the sine qua non of the Indian king. Frame narratives are not haphazard entities: they necessarily import significance to the tale they attempt to didactically contextualize. Unsurprisingly, the work of preservation is squarely shouldered by the Goddess throughout her exploits in the DM, and utterly underscored by the cosmic impetus behind the relaying of these episodes, for Suratha to secure a subsequent birth as the next Manu, who will be the son of the Sun. The DM's making of a Manu is therefore also the tale of solar succession, which may be understood as the lineage of the function of preservation within this realm.

The invocation of the Sun constitutes fitting symbolism for a narrative preoccupied by themes of preservation; like the Goddess, both sovereign and Sun are charged with supporting this realm. As Richard Lannoy writes:

> With the consolidation of the universal empire under the Mauryas, the idea of the *chakravartin*, or universal emperor, was introduced and became the commonest ideal of kingship for orthodox Hinduism. The *chakravartin* was a kind of temporal *avatār*, somewhat resembling the Mahāyānist Buddhas and the *avatars* of Vishnu (viz. Krishna and Rāma), born at auspicious times to proclaim the universal empire and righteous government within the grand cosmic scheme.
>
> (Lannoy 1971, 219)

In accounting for why both the *Sūrya Māhātmya* and *Devī Māhātmya* find homes in the MkP, we need look no further than Mārkaṇḍeya's core teachings on *pravṛtti dharma*. When we take the time to take at face value the fabric of the MkP, we see great method to the interpolational madness: the patchwork quilt has a story to tell. It depicts the glories of Goddess and Sun, singing the praises of great Manus and kings, all of whom partake in the MkP's ideological ecosystem tilted towards *pravṛtti*, preservation, and the affirmation of life.

## Works cited in this chapter

Balkaran, Raj. 2017. "The Essence of Avatāra: Probing Preservation in The Mārkaṇḍeya Purāṇa". *Journal of Vaishnava Studies* 26 (1): 25–36.

Balkaran, Raj. 2018a. "The Sarus' Sorrow: Voicing Nonviolence in the Vālmīki Rāmāyaṇa". *Journal of Vaishnava Studies* 26 (2): 143–61.

Balkaran, Raj. 2018b. "The Splendor of the Sun: Brightening the Bridge between Mārkaṇḍeya Purāṇa and Devī Māhātmya in Light of Navarātri Ritual Timing". In *Nine Nights of the Goddess: The Navarātri Festival in South Asia*, edited by Caleb Simmons, Hillary Rodrigues, and Moumita Sen, 23–38. Albany, NY: State University of New York Press.

Balkaran, Raj. 2019. *The Goddess and The King in Indian Myth: Ring Composition, Royal Power, and the Dharmic Double Helix*. London: Routledge.

Balkaran, Raj. 2020. "A Tale of Two Boons: The Goddess and the Dharmic Double Helix." In *The Purāṇa Reader*, edited by Deven Patel and Dheepa Sundaram. San Diego: Cognella Academic Publishing.

Buitenen, J.A.B. van. 1973. *Mahābhārata: Book 1: The Book of the Beginning*. Vol. I. Chicago, IL: University of Chicago Press.

Buitenen, J.A.B. van. 1975. *Mahābhārata: Book 2: The Book of the Assembly Hall; Book 3: The Book of the Forest*. Vol. II. Chicago, IL: University of Chicago Press.

Coburn, Thomas B. 1985. *Devī Māhātmya: The Crystallization of the Goddess Tradition*. Columbia, Mo.: South Asia Books.

Coburn, Thomas B. 1991. *Encountering the Goddess: A Translation of the Devī-Māhātmya and a Study of Its Interpretation*. Albany, NY: State University of New York Press.

Fuller, Christopher John, ed. 2004. *The Camphor Flame: Popular Hinduism and Society in India*. Princeton, NJ: Princeton University Press.

Lannoy, Richard. 1971. *The Speaking Tree: A Study of Indian Culture and Society*. London: Oxford University Press.

Nooten, Barend A van. 2009. *The Rāmāyaṇa of Vālmīki an Epic of Ancient India. Volume VI: Yuddhakāṇḍa*. Edited by Robert P Goldman. Princeton, NJ: Princeton University Press.

# Bibliography


Adluri, Vishwa P. 2011. “Frame Narratives and Forked Beginnings: Or, How to Read the Ādiparvan”. *Journal of Vaishnava Studies*, The Critical Edition and its Critics: A Retrospective of Mahabharata Scholarship, 19 (2): 1–21.

Agrawala, Vasudeva Sharana. 1963. *Devī-Māhātmyam: The Glorification of the Great Goddess*. Varanasi: All-India Kashiraj Trust.

Arora, R.K. 1971. “The Magas Sun-Worship and the Bhaviṣya Purāṇa”. *Purāṇa* 13 (1): 47–76.

Atkins, Samuel D. 1938. “A Vedic Hymn to the Sun-God Sūrya: (Translation and Exegesis of Rig-Veda 1. 115)”. *Journal of the American Oriental Society* 58 (3): 419–34.

Bailey, Greg. 1986. *Materials for the Study of Ancient Indian Ideologies: Pravṛtti and Nivṛtti*. Torino: Ed. Jollygrafica.

Bailey, Greg. 1999. “Intertextuality in the Purāṇas: A Neglected Element in the Study of Sanskrit Literature”. In Mary Brockington, Peter Schreiner, and Radoslav Katičić (eds), *Composing a Tradition: Concepts, Techniques and Relationships: Proceedings of the First Dubrovnik International Conference on the Sanskrit Epics and Purānas, August 1997*. Zagreb: Croatian Academy of Sciences and Arts, 179–98.

Bailey, Greg. 2005. “The Pravṛtti/Nivṛtti Chapters in the Mārkaṇḍeyapurāṇa”. In P. Koskikallio (ed.), *Epics, Khilas and Purāṇas. Continuities and Ruptures*. Zagreb: Croatian Academy of Arts and Sciences, 495–516.

Bailey, Greg. 2016. “Introductory Notes on the Literary Structure of the Mārkaṇḍeyasamāsyāparvan”. In Vishwa Adluri and Joydeep Bagchee (eds), *Argument and Design: The Unity of the Mahābhārata*. Leiden: Brill.

Bain, F. W. 1906. *The Descent of the Sun: A Cycle of Birth*. London: James Parker.

Balakrishnan, R., Rashtriya Lalit Kala Kendra (Bhubaneswar, India), and Alice Boner Institute (Varanasi). 2004. *Genesis of Sun Worship: The Sun Gods of Tribal Orissa*. Bhubaneswar; Varanasi: Rashtriya Lalit Kala Kendra; Alice Boner Institute.

Balkaran, Raj. 2017. “The Essence of Avatāra: Probing Preservation in The Mārkaṇḍeya Purāṇa”. *Journal of Vaishnava Studies* 26 (1): 25–36.

Balkaran, Raj. 2018a. “The Safeguard of Sovereignty: Focusing the Frame of the Devī Māhātmya”. In Raj Balkaran and Taylor McComas (eds), *Purāṇa Studies: Select Papers from the 16th World Sanskrit Conference (Bangkok, 2015)*. Delhi: DK Publishers, 67–95.

Balkaran, Raj. 2018b. “The Sarus’ Sorrow: Voicing Nonviolence in the Vālmīki Rāmāyaṇa”. *Journal of Vaishnava Studies* 26 (2): 143–61.

Balkaran, Raj. 2018c. “The Splendor of the Sun: Brightening the Bridge between Mārkaṇḍeya Purāṇa and Devī Māhātmya in Light of Navarātri Ritual Timing”. In

Caleb Simmons, Hillary Rodrigues, and Moumita Sen (eds), *Nine Nights of the Goddess: The Navarātri Festival in South Asia*. Albany, NY: State University of New York Press, 23–38.

Balkaran, Raj. 2019a. *The Goddess and The King in Indian Myth: Ring Composition, Royal Power, and the Dharmic Double Helix*. London: Routledge.

Balkaran, Raj. 2019b. "The Story of Saṃjñā, Mother of Manu: Shadow and Light in the Mārkaṇḍeya Purāṇa". In Veena R. Howard (ed.), *The Bloomsbury Research Handbook on Indian Philosophy and Gender*. New York: Bloomsbury Publishing, 267–96.

Balkaran, Raj. 2019c. "Visions and Revisions of the Hindu Goddess: Sound, Structure, and Artful Ambivalence in the Devī Māhātmya". Edited by Patricia Dold. *Religions*, Special Volume: "On Violence: Voices and Visions from the Hindu Goddess Traditions". 10 (5): 322.

Balkaran, Raj. 2020a. "A Tale of Two Boons: The Goddess and the Dharmic Double Helix". In Deven Patel and Dheepa Sundaram (eds), *The Purāṇa Reader*. San Diego, CA: Cognella Academic Publishing.

Balkaran, Raj. 2020b. "Arjuna and Acyuta: The Import of Epithets in the Bhagavad-Gītā". In Ithamar Thedor (ed.), *The Bhagavad-Gītā; a Critical Introduction*. Delhi: Routledge.

Balkaran, Raj. 2020c. "Avian Artistry: Decoding the Intertextuality between Mahābhārata and Mārkaṇḍeya Purāṇa". *International Journal of Hindu Studies* 24 (2).

Balkaran, Raj, and McComas Taylor (eds) 2018. *Purāṇa Studies: Select Papers from the 16th World Sanskrit Conference (Bangkok, 2015)*. Delhi: DK Publishers.

Balkaran, Raj, and McComas Taylor (eds) 2019. *Purāṇic Studies: Proceedings of the Purāṇa Section of the 17th World Sanskrit Conference (Vancouver, 2018)*. Vancouver: University of British Columbia.

Banerjea, Jintendra Nath. 1952. "Myth Explaining Some Alien Traits of the North-Indian Sun-Icons". *Indian Historical Quarterly* 28: 1–6.

Bhattacharya, G. 2003. "A Unique Narrative Stone Panel Illustrating Revanta". In *Proceedings of the Seventeenth International Conference of the European Association of South Asian Archaeologists*. Bonn, Germany.

Biardeau, Madeleine. 1997. "Some Remarks on the Links Between the Epics, the Purāṇas and Their Vedic Sources". In Gerhard Oberhammer (ed.), *Studies in Hinduism: Vedism and Hinduism.* Vienna: Austrian Academy of Science Press, 74–177.

Boileau, J.T. 1833. "Description of a Sun Dial in the Court of the Motí Masjíd in the Fort of Agra". *The Journal of the Asiatic Society of Bengal* 2: 251.

Bonazzoli, Giorgio. 1983. "Remarks on the Nature of the Purāṇas". *Purana* 25 (1): 77–113.

Bowles, Adam. 2006. *Mahābhārata: Book 8: Karṇa*. Vol. 1. Clay Sanskrit Library. New York: New York University Press.

Bowles, Adam. 2008. *Mahābhārata: Book 8: Karṇa*. Vol. 2. Clay Sanskrit Library. New York: New York University Press.

Brockington, John. 1998. *The Sanskrit Epics*. Leiden: Brill.

Brodbeck, Simon. 2009. *The Mahābhārata Patriline: Gender, Culture, and the Royal Hereditary*. Farnham: Ashgate.

Brodbeck, Simon. *Krishna's Lineage: The Harivamsha of Vyāsa's Mahābhārata*. New York: Oxford University Press.

Brodbeck, Simon, and Brian Black (eds) 2007. *Gender and Narrative in the Mahābhārata*. London: Routledge.

Brown, William Norman. 1968. "Agni, Sun, Sacrifice, and Vāc: A Sacerdotal Ode by Dīrghatamas (Rig Veda 1.164)". *Journal of the American Oriental Society* 88: 199–218.

Buitenen, J.A.B. van. 1973. *Mahābhārata: Book 1: The Book of the Beginning*. Vol. I. Chicago, IL: University of Chicago Press.

Buitenen, J.A.B. van. 1975. *Mahābhārata: Book 2: The Book of the Assembly Hall; Book 3: The Book of the Forest*. Vol. II. Chicago, IL: University of Chicago Press.

Buitenen, J.A.B. van. 1978. *Mahābhārata: Book 4: The Book of Virāṭa; Book 5: The Book of The Effort*. Vol. III. Chicago, IL: University of Chicago Press.

Burgess, Ebenezer. 1858. "Translation of the Sūrya-Siddhānta, A Text-Book of Hindu Astronomy; With Notes, and an Appendix". *Journal of the American Oriental Society* 6: 141–498.

Chaudhuri, Nanimadhab. 1941. "The Sun as a Folk-God". *Man In India* 21 (1): 1–14.

Chemburkar, Jaya. 1992. "Significance of the Description of Dissolution in the Viṣṇu Purāṇa and the Mārkaṇḍeya Purāṇa". *Journal of the Oriental Institute* 41 (3–4): 225–31.

Coburn, Thomas B. 1985. *Devī Māhātmya: The Crystallization of the Goddess Tradition*. Columbia, MO: South Asia Books.

Coburn, Thomas B. 1991. *Encountering the Goddess: A Translation of the Devī-Māhātmya and a Study of Its Interpretation*. Albany, NY: State University of New York Press.

Collins, Richard. 1887. "Krishna, and Solar Myths". *Journal of The Transactions of the Phiosophical Society of Great Britain* 21: 155–94.

Coomaraswamy, A.K. 1940. "The Sun-Kiss". *Journal of the American Oriental Society* 60 (1): 46–67.

Creel, Austin B., Vasudha Narayanan, and J. Patrick Olivelle. 1990. "Village Vs. Wilderness: Ascetic Ideals and the Hindu World". In Austin B. Creel and Vasudha Narayanan (eds), *Monastic Life in the Christian and Hindu Traditions: A Comparative Study*. Lewiston, NY: Edwin Mellen Press, 125–60.

Dandekar, R. N. 1992. "Vedic Mythology: Rethinking Some Dual Divinities in the Rgveda." In A.W. van den Hoek, D.H.A Kolff, and M.S. Ort(eds), *Ritual, State, and History in South Asia: Essays in Honour of J.C. Heesterman*. Leiden: E.J. Brill, 65–75.

Dandekar, R.N. 1995. "Heretical Doctrines in the Purāṇas". *Purāṇa* 37 (1): 3–20.

Dange, Sindhu S. 1994. "Sun-Soul in the Vedic Ritual Tradition". In Biswanath Nath Banerjee (ed.), *Cultura Indica: Tributes to an Indologist, Professor Dr. Asoke Chatterjee Sastri*. Delhi: Sharada Publishing House, 34–37.

Dass, Ayodhya Chandra. 1981. "Pre-Puranic Form of Sun-Worship in Atharvaveda-Saṁhitā". *Vishveshvaranand Indological Journal* 19: 20–29.

Dass, Ayodhya Chandra. 1984. *Sun-Worship in Indo-Aryan Religion and Mythology*. Delhi: Indian Book Gallery.

De, S.K. 1931. "Bhāgavatism and Sun-Worship". *Bulletin of the School of Oriental Studies, University of London* 6 (3): 669–72.

Derrett, J. Duncan M. 1976. "Rājadharma". *The Journal of Asian Studies* 35 (4): 597–609.

Desai, Nalini. 1992. "Padmini Vidyā in the Mārkaṇḍeya Purāṇa". *Journal of the Oriental Institute* 41 (3–4): 297–303.

Desai, Nileshvari Y. 1968. *Ancient Indian Society, Religion, and Mythology as Depicted in the Mārkaṇḍeya-Purāṇa: A Critical Study*. Baroda: Faculty of Arts, M.S. University of Baroda.

Desai, Nileshvari Y. 1979. "Glimpses from Astrology and Chiromancy in the Mārkaṇḍeya Purāṇa". *Purāṇa* 21 (2): 100–107.

Deshpande, Indu C. 1985. "Sun-Worship in the Āraṇyakas". *Journal of the Asiatic Society of Bombay* 60–61: 37–43.

Dhaky, Madhusudan. 1963. "The Date of the Dancing Hall of the Sun Temple, Modhera". *Journal of the Asiatic Society of Bombay* 38: 211–22.

Dhand, Arti. 2002. "The Dharma of Ethics, the Ethics of Dharma: Quizzing the Ideals of Hinduism". *The Journal of Religious Ethics* 30 (3): 347–72.

Dhand, Arti. 2007. "Paradigms of the Good in the Mahābhārata: Śuka and Sulabha in Quagmires of Ethics". In Simon Brodbeck and Brian Black (eds), *Gender and Narrative in the Mahābhārata*. New York: Routledge, 258–78.

Dhand, Arti. 2008. *Woman as Fire, Woman as Sage Sexual Ideology in the Mahābhārata*. Albany, NY: State University of New York Press.

Dhillon, Dalbir Singh. 1980. "Sun Worship in Ancient Punjab". *Proceedings of the Punjab History Conference* 14: 77–82.

Diserens, Helene. 1997. "Two Stone Reliefs of Sūrya from Gum: A Study of the Sun-Chariot and Its Teams". *Silk Road Art and Archaeology* 5: 329–51.

Doniger O'Flaherty, Wendy. 1976a. "The Paradox of the Good Demon: The Clash Between Relative and Absolute Ethics". In *The Origins of Evil in Hindu Mythology*. Berkeley, CA: University of California Press, 94–198.

Doniger O'Flaherty, Wendy. 1976b. *The Origins of Evil in Hindu Mythology*. Berkeley, CA: University of California Press.

Doniger O'Flaherty, Wendy. 1984. *Dreams, Illusion, and Other Realities*. Chicago, IL: University of Chicago Press.

Doniger, Wendy. 1980. *Women, Androgynes, and Other Mythical Beasts*. Chicago, IL: University of Chicago Press.

Doniger, Wendy. 1984. "The Shifting Balance of Power in the Marriage of Śiva and Pārvatī". In John Stratton Hawley (ed.), *The Divine Consort: Radha and the Goddesses of India*. Delhi: Motilal Banarsidass, 129–43.

Doniger, Wendy. 1993a. "Echoes of the Mahabharata: Why Is a Parrot the Narrator of the Bhagavata Purāna and the Devibhagavata Purāna?" In *Purāna Perennis: Reciprocity and Transformation in Hindu and Jaina Texts*, edited by Wendy Doniger, 31–57. Albany, NY: State University of New York Press.

Doniger, Wendy. 1993b. *Purāna Perennis: Reciprocity and Transformation in Hindu and Jaina Texts*. Albany, NY: State University of New York Press.

Doniger, Wendy. 1996. "Saraṇyū/Saṃjñā: The Sun and The Shadow". In *Devī: Goddesses of India*, edited by John Stratton Hawley and Donna Marie Wulff, 154–72. Berkeley, CA: University of California Press.

Doniger, Wendy. 1999. *Splitting the Difference: Gender and Myth in Ancient Greece and India*. Chicago, IL: University of Chicago Press.

Doniger, Wendy. 2000. *The Bedtrick: Tales of Sex and Masquerade*. Chicago, IL: University of Chicago Press.

Doniger, Wendy, ed. 2004. *Hindu Myths: A Sourcebook Translated from the Sanskrit*. London: Penguin.

Doniger, Wendy. 2005. *The Woman Who Pretended to Be Who She Was: Myths of Self-Imitation*. Oxford: Oxford University Press.

Doniger, Wendy. 2009. *The Hindus: An Alternative History*. New York: Penguin Press.

Doniger, Wendy. 2014. "Saranyu/Samjna: The Sun and The Shadow". In *On Hinduism*. New York: Oxford University Press, 269–87.

Dumont, Louis. 1971. "The Conception of Kingship in Ancient India". In *Religion, Politics and History in India; Collected Papers in Indian Sociology. [Ecole Pratique Des Hautes Études, Sorbonne. 6. Section]*, 62–88. The Hague: Mouton.

Eco, Umberto. 1994. *Six Walks in the Fictional Woods*. Cambridge, MA: Harvard University Press.

Eco, Umberto. 1997. *The Role of the Reader: Explorations in the Semiotics of Texts*. Bloomington, IN: Indiana University Press.

Einoo, Shingo. 1999. "The Autumn Goddess Festival: Described in the Purānas". In *Living With Śakti: Gender, Sexuality and Religion in South Asia*, edited by Masakazu Tanaka and Musashi Tachikawa, 33–70. Senri Ethnological Studies 50. Osaka: National Museum of Ethnology.

Farquhar, J.N. 1920. *An Outline of the Religious Literature of India*. London: H. Milford, Oxford University Press.

Fox, Hugh. 1989. *The Mythological Foundations of the Epic Genre*. Lewiston, NY: E. Mellen Press.

Fuller, Christopher John, ed. 2004. *The Camphor Flame: Popular Hinduism and Society in India*. Princeton, NJ: Princeton University Press.

Gail, Adalbert J. 2001. *Sonnenkult in Indien: Tempel und Skulpturen von den Anfängen bis zur Gegenwart* [*Sun Worship in India: Temples and Sculptures from the Beginning to the Present*]. Berlin: Reimer.

Ganguli, Kalyankumar. 1965. *Some Aspects of Sun Worship in Ancient India*. Calcutta: Abhedananda Academy of Culture.

Giri, Kamal. 1987. "The Cultural Life as Depicted in the Sculptures of the Sun Temple of Moḍherā". *Journal of Asiatic Society of Bengal* 62–63: 48–58.

Goldman, Robert P. 1969. "Mortal Man and Immortal Woman: An Interpretation of Three Akhyana Hymns of the Rgveda". *Journal of the Oriental Institute of Baroda* 18 (4): 274–303.

Gonda, Jan. 1959. "The Sacred Character of Ancient Indian Kingship". In *The Sacral Kingship*, edited by International Congress for the History of Religions. Leiden: E.J. Brill.

Gonda, Jan. 1969. *Ancient Indian Kingship from the Religious Point of View*. Leiden: Brill.

Gonda, Jan. 1977. *A History of Indian Literature. Volume II, Fasc. 1*. Wiesbaden: O. Harrassowitz.

Griffith, Ralph T. 1895. *Hymns of the Samaveda*.

Guha, Abhijit. n.d. "Sun-Worship Amongst the Aboriginal Tribes of Eastern India". *Journal of the Department of Letters*, 11:87–94(1924). Accessed May 13, 2019.

Gupta, Shakti M. 2008. *Surya, the Sun God, Its History, Iconography, Mythology, His Family, and Surya Temples*. Mumbai: Somaiya Publications.

Hawley, John Stratton, and Thomas B. Coburn (eds) 1984. "Consort of None, Śakti of All: The Vision of the Devī-Māhātmya". In *The Divine Consort: Radha and the Goddesses of India*. Delhi: Motilal Banarsidass, 153–65.

Hazra, R.C. 1939. "The Upapurāṇas". *Annals of the Bhandarkar Oriental Research Institute* 21 (1/2): 38–62.

Hazra, R.C. 1955. "The Sāmba-Purāṇa, a Saura Work of Different Hands". *Annals of the Bhandarkar Oriental Research Institute* 36 (1.2).

Hazra, R.C. 1958. *Studies in the Upapurāṇas Vol. 1 (Saura and Vaiṣṇava Upapurāṇas)*. Calcutta: Sanskrit College.

Hazra, R.C. 1962. "The Purāṇas". In Haridas Bhattacharyya, Suniti Kumar Chatterji, and Sarvepalli Radhakrishnan (eds), *The Cultural Heritage of India*, 2nd edn. Calcutta: Ramakrishna Mission, Institute of Culture, 2:240–70.

Hazra, R.C. 1963. *Studies in the Upapurāṇas Vol. 2 (Śākta and Non-Sectarian Upapurāṇas)*. Calcutta: Sanskrit College.

Hazra, R.C. 1975. *Studies in the Purāṇic Records on Hindu Rites and Customs*. Delhi: Motilal Banarsidass.

Heesterman, J.C. 1973. "India and the Inner Conflict of Tradition". *Daedalus* 102 (1): 97–113.

Heesterman, J.C. 1982. "Householder and Wanderer". In Louis Dumont and T.N Madan (eds), *Way of Life: King, Householder, Renouncer: Essays in Honour of Louis Dumont*. New Delhi: Vikas, 251–72.

Heesterman, J.C. 1998. "The Conundrum of the King's Authority". In John F. Richards (ed.), *Kingship and Authority in South Asia*. Delhi: Oxford University Press, 13–40.

Hiltebeitel, Alf. 1976. "The Burning of The Forest Myth". In Bardwell L. Smith (ed.), *Hinduism: New Essays in the History of Religions*. Leiden: E.J. Brill, 208–24.

Heesterman, J.C. 2001. *Rethinking the Mahābhārata: A Reader's Guide to the Education of the Dharma King*. Chicago, IL: University of Chicago Press.

Heesterman, J.C. 2007. "Among Friends: Marriage, Women, and Some Little Birds". In Simon Brodbeck and Brian Black (eds), *Gender and Narrative in the Mahābhārata*. London: Routledge, 110–43.

Heesterman, J.C. 2010. *Reading the Fifth Veda Studies on the Mahabharata: Essays*. Edited by Vishwa Adluri and Joydeep Bagchee. Leiden: Brill.

Hornell, James. 1944. "The Ancient Village Gods of South India (4 Plates)". *Antiquity; Gloucester* 18 (January): 78–91.

Jacob, Alexander. 2012. *Brahman: A Study of the Solar Rituals of the Indo-Europeans*. Hildesheim: Olms.

Jai, Prakash. 1996. "Inscriptional Reference to the Worship of Sun-God in the Chandella Period". *Gauravaṁ: Recent Researches in Indology (Prof. B.K. Gururaja Rao Felicitation Volume)*, 192–4.

Jamison, Stephanie. 1991. *The Ravenous Hyenas and the Wounded Sun: Myth and Ritual in Ancient India*. Ithaca, NY: Cornell University Press.

Joshi, K.L. 2004. *Mākaṇḍeya Purāṇa: Sanskrit Text, English Translation, Notes and Index of Verses*. Translated by F.E. Pargiter. Delhi: Parimal Publications.

Joshi, P.B. 1921. "Side Lights on the Past History of the Parsis: The Revival of Sun-Worship and Its Connection with the First Advent and Settlement of the Zorastrian Priests in India". *The Journal of the Bombay Branch of the Royal Asiatic Society* 26: 177–94.

Kasturi Iyer, N. 1931. "When the Sun Enters Aries in Modern India". *The Aryan Path* 2: 158–60.

Kinsley, David. 1978. "The Portrait of the Goddess in the Devī-Māhātmya". *Journal of the American Academy of Religion* 46 (4): 489–506.

Kinsley, David. 1987. *Hindu Goddesses: Visions of the Divine Feminine in the Hindu Religious Tradition*. Motilal Banarsidass Publ.

Kinsley, David. 1989. "Durgā, Warrior Goddess and Cosmic Queen". In *The Goddesses' Mirror: Visions of the Divine from East and West*. Albany, NY: State University of New York, 3–24.

Kisari, Ganguli Mohan, trans. 1883. "The Mahabharata, Book 1: Adi Parva: Astika Parva: Section XXIV". In *The Mahabharata of Krishna-Dwaipayana Vyasa*. sacred-texts.com.

Kuppana Shastri, T.S. 1955. "The Vāsiṣṭha Sun and Moon in Varāhamihira's Pañcasiddhāntikā". *The Journal of Oriental Research Madras* 25: 19–41.

Lobo, Wibke. 1982. *The Sun Temple at Modhera: A Monograph on Architecture and Iconography*. Munich: C.H. Beck.

Malville, J. McKim, and Rana P.B. Singh. 1995. "Visual Astronomy in the Mythology and Ritual of India: The Sun Temples of Varanasi". *Vistas in Astronomy* 39 (4): 431–49.

Malville, J. McKim, and R.N. Swaminathan. 1996. "Surya Puja Temples of South India". *Archaeoastronomy; College Park, Md.* 12 (January): 310–18.

Malville, J. McKim, and R.N. Swaminathan. 1985. "Sun Worship in Contemporary India". *Man In India* 65: 207–21.

Mangalam, S.J. 1977. "Sun-Worship in Andhra Pradesh". *Sri Venkateswara University Oriental Journal*, no. 20: 61–7.

Mani, Vettam. 1975. *Purāṇic Encyclopaedia: A Comprehensive Dictionary with Special Reference to the Epic and Purāṇic Literature*. Delhi : Motilal Banarsidass.

Matsunami. 1977. "A Preliminary Essay in Systematic Arrangement of the Purāṇas – with Special Reference to the Legend of Yama's Birth". *Purāṇa* 29 (1): 214–32.

Mevissen, Gerd. n.d. "The Lost Sūrya Temple of Pātharghāṭā (Bihar)". In Vincent Lefèvre, Aurore Didier, and Benjamin Mutin (eds), *South Asian Archaeology and Art 2012. Vol. 2: South Asian Religions and Visual Forms in Their Archaeological Context*. Turnhout: Brepols, 2016 (Indicopleustoi: Archaeologies of the Indian Ocean, 12).

Mevissen, Gerd. 2008a. "Surya in Bengal Art". *Sculptures in Bangladesh. An Inventory of Select Hindu, Buddhist and Jain Stone and Bronze Images in Museums and Collections of Bangladesh (up to the 13th Century), Eds. Enamul Haque; Adalbert J. Gail. Dhaka: International Centre for Study of Bengal Art (Studies in Bengal Art Series No. 8).*

Mevissen, Gerd. 2008b. "A Group of Strange Surya Images from Gajole in the Malda Museum: Some Remarks on the Bare Feet of Surya and His Attendants". *Journal of Bengal Art* 13 (14) (September): 89–108.

Mevissen, Gerd. 2009. "Three Noteworthy Surya Fragments from North Bangladesh". *Abhijñan: Studies in South Asian Archaeology and Art History of Artefacts – Felicitating A.K.M. Zakariah.* Edited by Shahnaj Husne Jahan. Oxford: BAR International Series 1974, 99–112.

Mevissen, Gerd. 2012. "Figurations of Time and Protection: Sun, Moon, Planets and Other Astral Phenomena in South Asian Art". In Dietrich Boschung and Corinna Wessels-Mevissen (eds), *Figurations of Time in Asia*. Munich: Fink Wilhelm Verlag, 82–147.

Mevissen, Gerd. 2013. "Revanta Images Mainly from Bihar and a Special Type of Three Equestrian Deities from North Bengal". *Journal of Bengal Art* 18: 61–86.

Mirashi, V.V. 1966. "Three Ancient Famous Temples of the Sun". *Purāṇa* 8 (1): 38–51.

Mitra, Sarat Chandra. 1932. "Sun-Worship in Bengali Nursery-Rhymes". *Man In India* 12: 181–3.

Mitra, Sarat Chandra. 1986. *The Cult of the Sun God in Medieval Eastern Bengal*. New Delhi: Northern Book Centre.

Monier-Williams, Ernst Leumann, Carl Cappeller, and Īśvaracandra. 2008. "Monier Williams Sanskrit–English Dictionary (2008 Revision)".

Morihiro, Oki, and Bettina Baumer. 2007. *Konārka: Chariot of the Sun God*. New Delhi: D.K. Printworld.

Nooten, Barend A van. 2009. *The Rāmāyaṇa of Vālmīki an Epic of Ancient India. Volume VI: Yuddhakāṇḍa*. Edited by Robert P. Goldman. Princeton, NJ: Princeton University Press.

Olcott, William Tyler. 2008. *Sun Lore of All Ages*. Charleston, SC: Bibliobazaar.

Oldham, Charles Frederick. 1905. *The Sun and the Serpent: A Contribution to the History of Serpent-Worship*. London: A. Constable & Co.

Olivelle, Patrick. 1993. *The Āśrama System: The History and Hermeneutics of a Religious Institution*. New York: Oxford University Press.

Pandey, C.D. 1984. "The Magian Priests and Their Impact on Sun-Worship". *Purāṇa* 26 (2): 203–5.

Paradkar, M.D. 1979. "Sun Worship in Indian and Other Cultures". *Journal of the Asiatic Society of Bombay* 54–55: 103–17.

Pargiter, F.E. 1904. *Mārkaṇḍeya Purāṇa*. Calcutta: Asiatic Society of Bengal.

Parpola, Asko. 2014. "Beginnings of Indian and Chinese Calendrical Astronomy". *Journal of the American Oriental Society* 134 (1): 107–12.

Parpola, Asko. 2016. "Rudra: "'Red' and 'Cry' in the Name of the Young God of Fire, Rising Sun, and War". In Dieter Gunkel, Joshua T. Katz, Brent Vine, and Michael Weiss (eds), *Sahasram Ati Srajas. Indo-Iranian and Indo-European Studies in Honor of Stephanie W. Jamison* . Ann Arbor, MI: Beech Stave Press, 322–32.

Perry, William James. 1923. *The Children of the Sun: A Study in the Early History of Civilization*. London: Methuen & Co.

Pingree, David. 1977. *Jyotiḥśāstra*. Edited by Jan Gonda. Vol. VI. *A History of Indian Literature*, Part 3, Fasc. 4. Wiesbaden: Harrassowitz.

Pintchman, Tracy. 1994. *The Rise of the Goddess in the Hindu Tradition*. Albany, NY: State University of New York Press.

Pollock, Sheldon. 1984. "The Divine King in the Indian Epic". *Journal of the American Oriental Society* 104 (3): 505–28.

Pollock, Sheldon. 1986. *The Rāmāyaṇa of Vālmīki: An Epic of Ancient India. Volume II: Ayodhyakāṇḍa*. Edited by Robert Goldman. Princeton, NJ: Princeton University Press.

Pollock, Sheldon. 1993. "Rāmāyana and Political Imagination in India". *The Journal of Asian Studies* 52 (2): 261–97.

Pontillo, Tiziana (ed.) 2015. "The Ekavrātya, Indra and the Sun". In *The Volatile World of Sovereignty. The Vrātya Problem and Kingship in South Asia*. New Delhi: DK Publishers, 33–64.

Poston, Charles D, and P.V.N Myers. 1877. *The Sun Worshipers of Asia*. San Francisco, CA: A. Roman & Co.

Quackenbos, George Payn. 1917. *The Sanskrit Poems of Mayūra*. New York: Columbia University Press.

R.D.M. (Ramabai). 1887. "Rescuing the Sun and Moon". *The Indian Antiquary* 16: 288–90.

Raghavan, V. 1970. "Worship of the Sun". *Purāṇa* 12 (2): 205–30.

Rajaram, K. 1977. *The Genealogical Tables of Solar & Lunar Dynasties*. Bangalore: Sri Ramakrishna Bhaktha Mandali.

Ram, Rajendra. 1990. "Heretic Motifs in Mārīchī: The Sun Goddess of Buddhism: A.D. 700–1400". *Journal of the Bihar and Orissa Research Society* 76–78: 231–38.

Ramesh, K.V., and S Subramonia Iyer. 1981. "An Incomplete Eulogy of the Sun at Udaipur". *Journal of the Epigraphical Society of India* 8: 97–100.

Ranade, H.G. 1974. "Sun-God and His Associates in the Rigveda". *Bulletin of the Deccan College Post-Graduate and Research Institute* 34: 143–46.

Rao, Velcheru Narayana. 2004. "Purāṇa". In Sushil Mittal and Gene R. Thursby )eds), *The Hindu World*. New York: Routledge, 97–115.

Rocher, Ludo. 1986. *The Purāṇas*, edited by Jan Gonda. Wiesbaden: Harrassowitz.

Rodrigues, Hillary. 2003. *Ritual Worship of the Great Goddess: The Liturgy of the Durgā Pūjā with Interpretations*. Albany, NY: State University of New York Press.

Rodrigues, Hillary. 2009. "Fluid Control: Orchestrating Blood Flow in the Durgā Pūjā". *Studies in Religion/Sciences Religieuses* 38 (2): 263–92.

Rohlman, Elizabeth Mary. 2002. "Textual Authority, Accretion, and Suspicion: The Legacy of Horace Hayman Wilson in Western Studies of the Purāṇas". *Journal of the Oriental Institute* 52 (1–2): 55–70.

Sahu, Rusav Kumar. n.d. "Sun Worship in Odisha". *Odisha Review*. Accessed May 13, 2019.

Sahu, Rusav Kumar. 2011. "Iconography of Surya in the Temple Art of Odisha". 7.

Sankaranarayana, N. 1990. "Sun Cult in India". In Bhubaneswar Duḥkhiśyāma Paṭṭanāẏak (ed.), *Mahamahopadhyaya Samanta Chandrasekhara Commemoration Volume*, 187–8.

Saran, Anirudha Behari, and Gaya Pandey. 1992. *Sun Worship in India: A Study of Deo Sun-Shrine*. New Delhi: Northern Book Centre.

Sarkar, Guru Das. 1918. "Alleged Buddhist Influence in the Sun Temple at Konarak". *The Indian Antiquary* 47: 209–20.

Sastri, Hirananda. 1933. "Akbar as a Sun-Worshipper". *Indian Historical Quarterly* 9: 137–40.

Sastri, Pothukuchi Subrahmanya. 1995. *Brihat Jataka*. New Delhi: Ranjan Publ.

Satchidanandan, K. 1984. "The Blind Man Who Discovered the Sun: Transl. from Malayalam by the Poet". *Indian Literature* 27 (2): 10.

Sengupta, B.K. 1959. "A Short Note on the Antiquity of the Sun-Cult of Orissa." *Orissa Historical Research Journal* 8 (1): 62–4.

Sewell, Robert. 1917. "The True Longitude of the Sun in Hindu Astronomy". 14: 1–67, 241–64.

Sewell, Robert. 1921. "The First Arya-Siddhanta". *Epigraphica Indica* 16: 100–221.

Sewell, Robert. 1923. "The Brahma-Siddhanta of Brahmagupta (A.D. 628)". *Epigraphica Indica* 17: 123–87, 205–90.

Sharma, Girish Chand. 1994. *Maharishi Parasara's Brihat Parasara Hora Sastra*. New Delhi: Sagar Publications.

Shimkhada, Deepak. 1984. "The Masquerading Sun: A Unique Syncretic Image in Nepal". *Artibus Asiae* 45 (2/3): 223.

Sick, David H. 2004. "Mit(h)Ra(s) and the Myths of the Sun". *Numen: International Review for the History of Religions* 51: 432–67.

Siddheshwar, Varma. 1931. "Burushaskī Texts I. Story of the North Wind and the Sun". *Indian Linguistics* 1–4: 256–82.

Siṃha, Rañjana Kumāra. 2010. *Surya: The God and His Abode*. Patna, Bihar, India: Parijat.

Simson, Georg von. 2007. "Kṛṣṇa's Son Sāmba: Faked Gender and Other Ambiguities on the Background of Lunar and Solar Myth". In Simon Brodbeck and Brian Black (eds), *Gender and Narrative in the Mahābhārata*. London: Routledge.

Singh, Madanjeet. 1993. *The Sun: Symbol of Power and Life*. New York: H.N. Abrams: UNESCO.

Singh, Sb. 1994. "The Universal Sun God Surya". *Arts of Asia* 24 (6): 83–87.

Spottiswoode, William. 1863. "On the Súrya Siddhánta, and the Hindú Method of Calculating Eclipses". *Journal of the Royal Asiatic Society of Great Britain and Ireland* 20: 345–70.

Srivastava, V.C. 1969. "The Purāṇic Records on the Sun-Worship". *Purāṇa* 11 (2): 229–72.

Srivastava, V.C. 1972. *Sun-Worship in Ancient India*. Allahabad: Indological Publications.

Srivastava, V.C. 1979. "The Kuṣānas and the Sun-Cult". *The Journal of the Ganganatha Jha Research Institute* 35 (3–4): 115–46.

Srivastava, V.C. 1987. "Tantricism and the Sun-Cult in India: A Historical Perspective". *Purāṇa: Bulletin of the Purāṇa Department* 29: 166–84.

Srivastava, V.C. 1988. "Two Distinct Groups of Indian Sun-Priests: An Appraisal". *Purāṇa* 30 (2): 109–20.

Srivastava, V.C. 1989. "Indian Sun-Priests". *Purāṇa* 31 (2): 142–58.

Srivastava, V.C. 1992. "Continuity and Change in the Purāṇic Sun-Worship". *Purāṇa* 34 (1): 14–25.

Srivastava, V.C. 1996. *Revision in the Purāṇic Sun-Cult*. Varanasi: Department of Ancient Indian History, Culture, and Archaeology.

Srivastava, V.C. 2013. *Sāmba Purāṇa: An Exhaustive Introduction, Sanskrit Text, English Translation, Notes and Index of Verses*. Delhi: Parimal Publications.

Stietencron, Heinrich von. 1966. *Indische Sonnenpriester: Sāmba Und Die Śākadvīpīya-Brāhmaṇa.* Wiesbaden: Harrassowitz .

Tagare, G.V. 1992. "Polity in the Viṣṇu Purāṇa (VP) and the Mārkaṇḍeya Purāṇa (MP)". *Journal of the Oriental Institute* 41 (3–4): 203–12.

Taylor, McComas. 2008. "What Enables Canonical Literature to Function as 'True'? The Case of the Hindu Purāṇas". *International Journal of Hindu Studies* 12 (3): 309–28.

Tilakasiri, J. 1971. "Imagery in Vedic Mythology". *Archív Orientální; Praha* 39 (January): 76–83.

Warrier, Krishna. 1991. *The Sāmānya Vedānta Upaniṣads*. Madras: The Adyar Library and Research Centre.

Wilkins, W.J. 1900. "Hindu Mythology, Vedic and Puranic: Part I. The Vedic Deities: Chapter VI. Sun or Light Deities". In *Hindu Mythology, Vedic and Puranic*. Calcutta: London Missionary Society.

Wilson, Horace Hayman. 1961. *The Viṣṇu Purāṇa: A System of Hindu Mythology and Tradition*. Calcutta: Punthi Pustak.

Winternitz, Moriz. 1972a. *A History of Indian Literature. Vol 1*. New Delhi: Oriental Book.

Winternitz, Moriz. 1972b. *A History of Indian Literature. Vol 2*. New Delhi: Oriental Books.

# Index

Page numbers in **bold** denote tables, those in *italics* denote figures.


Achaemenian invasion, of 6th–5th century B.C 22–23
Acyutya (Viṣṇu) 44
Aditi (mother of gods) 70; cāndrāyaṇa penance 45; effort to propitiate the Sun 43–44, 58; grant of boon from the Sun 45, 58; hymns in praise of Sun 42–44; Suṣumna incarnation 45
Āditya 15, 19, 40, 60, 136–137
Ādityahṛdaya 19, 135–137
*Āditya Purāṇa* 22
Agastya, Sage 19, 21, 135–136
*Agni Purāṇa* 20, 22
*ahiṃsā* (non-violence) 5, 126–127
alpha–omega principle 29–30
*Amarakośa* 56
*Amar Chitra Katha* 75
ancestor worship (*śrāddha pūjā*) 88
añjali mudrā 75
anti-gods *(asuras)* 75
Arjuna 19, 27, 73, 83, 100, 134–135
Aruṇa (Sun's charioteer), story of 21, 61
asceticism, ideology of 5, 70, 122
*aśvagandha* (Āyurvedic herb) 97n8
Aśvini constellation 80, 90, 92–94, 97n8
Aśvin twins (Nasatya and Dasra) 49, 79–80, 87; akhyāna hymns depicting the birthing of 92; appointment as celestial physicians 64; birth of 15, 48, 70, 90
*Atharva Veda* 15, 21, 40
*avatāra*, of Vishnu 17, 137–139, 141

Bailey, Greg 6, 124–125
Bāṇa's Caṇḍī-Śataka 7
*Bhagavad-Gītā* (BhG) 7, 26, 138; alpha–omega principle 29; alpha principle 29; Kṛṣṇa's responses to Arjuna's questions 100; plane of dharma 29; plane of Kuru 29
*Bhāgavata Purāṇa* 12, 23
Bhāskararāya 62
*Bhaviṣya Purāṇa* 20, 21, 23
bifurcated Hindu feminine, discourse of 72
Birds, in *Mārkaṇḍeya Purāṇa:* avian exposition 115–119; backstory of 120, **121**, 122; curse of Sukṛṣa 121; introduction of 120; karmic antecedent of 121; origin of 122; in section I **121**; Tārkṣī (bird mother) 121; Vindhya-dwelling 120
blood sacrifice, in context of ritual 111, 115, 126
*Book of The Forest, The* 18, 131–135
Bowles, Adam 19
Brahmā, Lord 40–41, 53, 58–60, 137; creation of the world 42; hymns in praise of Sun 41–42, 139
brāhmaṇa-rākṣasas hybrid 113
*Brāhmāṇḍa Purāṇa* 101
Brahmanism: ideology of 2; paradoxical allegiance to *pravṛttic* and *nivṛttic* religious impulses 6; Sanskritic Brahmanism 24
*Bṛhad Saṃhitā* 23
*Bṛhat Jātaka* (BJ) 89
*Bṛhat Parāśara Hora* (BPH) 89–90, 95
Brown, C. Mackenzie 95

Caṇḍī, Goddess 62; Caṇḍī-Śataka 7, 21; iconography of 20
caste allotments, for planets 97n12
*chakravartin* (universal emperor), idea of 141
Chandragupta II, King 89

chariot of the Sun 19, 90
Chāyā (a reflection/shadow-form of Saṃjñā) 34, 46, 63, 70, 82, 86; curse to Yama 34–35, 46, 70–73; favouritism of three younger siblings 72; hatred of her stepson 70, 72
cosmic cycle (*kalpa*) 56; of creation and destruction 59, 104
cosmic dissolution (*pralaya*) 2, 24, 102
Cosmic Man (*puruṣa uttama*) 40
cosmic protection and governance, acts of 58

daityas 42–43, 58
Dakṣa 15, 39, 42, 44, 139
Dama, King 66n5, 112–115, 127, 128n7
dānavas 43, 45, 58
Dattatreya, Sage 124
demonic beings, classes of 43
demons–gods battle 45
Desai, Nileshvari 8, 125
*devarṣayaḥ* 35
devas 43, 58
*Devī Māhātmya* (DM) 1, 6–9, 12–13, 24, 68, 94–95, 105; chanting of 94; connection with *manvantara* discourse of the *Mārkaṇḍeya's Purāṇa* 8; demon-slaying exploits of 94; destruction of enemies 138; on essence of Vaiṣṇava avatāra 138; glorification of the Goddess 6; on Goddess as sovereignty incarnate 61, 64; "heavenly throne" episode 58; imagery of the Sun 61; *manvantara* section 85; Nārāyaṇi Stuti 138; parallels with *Sūrya Māhātmyas* **37**; restoration of earthly sovereignty of King Suratha 64; Saṃjñā, story of 84; Vaiṣṇava imagery 138
Devī–Mahīṣa battle 61
Devī Mahīsamardinī 85
*dharma* 1, 29, 48, 131; dharma-kṣetre 100; *dharmopadghāthāya* 50; *nivṛtti* dharma 1–2, 5, 53, 123; *pravṛtti* dharma *see pravṛtti* dharma
dharmic double helix 6, 132–133
*dharmopadghāthāya* 50
Dhṛtarāṣṭhra, King 100
Doniger, Wendy 8, 68–87, 96n1; article dedicated to Saṃjñā/Saraṇyū 75; *On Hinduism* (2014) 83; *Origins of Evil in Hindu Mythology, The* (1976) 69, 75; *Splitting the Difference* 84; theory of good and the bad mother 70

Draupadī 103, 123, 131, 133
*dūradarśana* (remote viewing) 100
Durgā Goddess 62, 94; as Devī Mahīsamardinī 85; victory over Mahiṣāsura 94, 140
Durgā Pūjā 3, 68, 94
*Durgā Saptaśatī* 94
Durvāsa, Muni 121–122; curse to apsara Vapu 121

Eco, Umberto 25
epics, in Vedic literature: *Mahābhārata* 17–19; *Rāmāyaṇa* 19

fire sacrifice 15, 51
food offerings, in *pitṛ pūjā* 113
forest hermits–exiled kings relations 6
Fuller, C.J. 139–140
funeral sacrifices 12, 126

*Garuḍa Purāṇa* 20, 23
Garuḍa, story of 20, 22, 61
Gāyatrī hymn 15
*gītā see Bhagavad-Gītā* (BhG)
Goddess: association with *tejas* 61–62; Caṇḍī 62; celebration of 139; Devī–Mahīṣa battle 61; Devī Mahīsamardinī 85; Durgā 62, 94; feminine Nārāyaṇa 138; glorification of 6, 95; as Great Demoness 64; as Great Goddess 64, 68, 93, 138–139; Kālī 61; Lakṣmī 91; Mahādevī 64; Mahāsurī 64; mythologies of 8; relation with Sun 59, 61; Venus 91
*Goddess and The King, The* 1, 5–6
gods *(suras)* 75; as Kāśyapa's sons 43
Goldman, Robert 71, 87, 92
Gonda, Jan 20, 89; discourse on *māhātmya*s 7
Gupta Empire 88

*Harivaṃśa* 65n2, 75–76, 78
Hazra, R.C. 9, 12, 21–24, 99, 124, 126
healing power, of the Sun 15–16
heavenly bodies, movements of 51–52, 90
heaven–Sun relationship: Aditi hymns 42–44; birth of Mārtaṇḍa 44–46
Hindu trimūrti of Vedic gods 137
*History of Indian Literature, A* 7, 20

Indian astrological mythology 92
Indian Saura cult 23
Indra (chief of the gods) 18–19, 36, 44, 45, 63, 110–111, 115, 121–122, 126, 131, 133–136

interpolations, mechanics of 5, 8–11, 13, 95, 105–106, 109, 119
Islamic invasion of Afghanistan 23

Jaimini 109, 116, 119–120; questioning to Mārkaṇḍeya 100–101, 120; as student of Vyāsa 101
*Jaimini Sūtras* 100–101
Jambudvīpa, origin of sun worship in 23
Janamejaya 28, 131, 134, 135; sacrifice to exterminate the serpents 101
*jyotiḥ śāstra* (classical Indian astrology) 88–91, 90, 93

Kālī, Goddess 61, 63; battle with demons Caṇḍa and Muṇḍa 61
Kāmarūpa Mountains 51
Karandhama, King 89
Karṇa, story of 4, 18–19, 133–135, 140
Kaśyapa, Sage 39, 42–43, 45, 61
kingship: ideology of 5; Indian discourse of 60; *pravṛtti dharma* and 126; violence of 126
kingship–asceticism dichotomy 5
Krauṣṭuki 9, 13, 38–39, 49, 57, 109, 112, 118
Kṛṣṇa, Lord 17, 28–29, 101; lunar associations of 54; responses to Arjuna's questions 100
*kṣatriya* 112, 126–127; caste of Sun 95

Lakṣmī, Goddess 91, 97n6
Lannoy, Richard 141
*Lord of the Rings* 27
lunar asterisms 90, 92–93

Madālasā, Queen 88, 90, 109–110, 123–124; teachings to Alarka 125
Magi Sun-priests 22–24
*Mahābhārata* (MBh) 6, 25, 60, 83, 86, 99, 119, 123, 131; abduction of Draupadī 133; *Ādi Parvan* 101; as allegorical battle of dark and light 17; birth of Dṛṣyadyumna 26; Cattle Expedition 133; destruction of Kṛṣṇa's entire clan 54; Drapadī's *svayamvara* 26; Duryodhana–Karṇa friendship 135; exchange between Draupadī and Satyabhāmā 133; Hiltebeitel notes of Kṛṣṇa in 29; Indian Saura cult 23; Janamejaya's sacrifice to exterminate the serpents 101; Karṇa–Arjuna rivalry 19, 134–135; Karṇa, story of 18, 133–134; Kuntī's curse 54; on Magian priests of Iran 23; mythologization of the Sun in 17–19; Pāṇḍava's encounter with Mārkaṇḍeya 132–135; *Sabhā Parvan* 101; Sāmba, story of 54; Sāvitrī poem of 11; story of Sāmba's birth 54; on Sun protection of Yudhiṣṭhira 131–132; tale of the co-wives of Kaśyapa 61
Mahādevī 64
*Mahā-Purāṇas* 19–20; classification of 104
Mahāsurī 64
*māhātmyas* 63; Gonda's discourse on 7; literature on 7; of *Mārkaṇḍeya Purāṇa* (MkP) 2, 6, 34, 55
Mahāyānist Buddhas 141
Mahiṣāsura 94, 140
majesty of the Sun 7, 37, 48–49, 79, 95
male and female divine powers 83
Māninī, Queen 49, 52–53, 58
Manu-intervals *(manvantaras)* **55**, 56, 95, 138
Manu Sāvarṇi 1, 13, 46, 81, 84, 95, 140
Manu Vaivasvata (son of Sun God) 1, 34, 46, 48, 76, 81, 140
*manvantara* 56, 60, 85, 95, 103
Marīci (son of Brahmā) 42
*Mārkaṇḍeya Purāṇa* (MkP) 1, 5, 75; account of Manu-intervals *(manvantaras)* **55–56**; association between *māhātmyas* of 59; attack on worldly engagement 125; avian exposition of 115–119; backstory of the birds **121**; birds in section I of **121**; compilation of solar myths in 7–8; connection between DM and *manvantara* discourse of 8; Dama, story of 112–115; *Devī Māhātmya*'s "insertion" into 109; diachronic dissection of 7–14; English translation of 8, 11; ethos of preservation 5; exposition guide **107–108**; exposition import of 99–105; expositors of **110**; glorification of the Goddess within 95; on greatness of the Sun 38–40; historical strata of **10**; *māhātmyas* of 2, 6; making sense of 105–127; *manvantara* section of 55; *phalaśruti* section of 56; on plight of Pravṛtti 119–127; polemic against *pravṛtti* religion 124; royal dynasties (vaṃśānucarita) of **56**; Saura–Śākta symbiosis 68; sections of **8**; shadow and light in 82–84; solar family tree of *36*; solar sources of mapping 14–25; story

of Saṃjñā 68; *Sūrya Māhātmya* section of 139; Sūrya–Saṃjñā–Chāyā epsiode 72, 83; on Vaiṣṇava avatāra 137, 139; Wilson's summation of quality of 12
Mārkaṇḍeya, Sage 5, 24, 39; austerities to Lord Śiva 102; biography of 6, 127; birth of 44–46; blessings from Lord Śiva 102; classes of born of Kāśyapa 42–43; description of Northern Kurus 96n4; description of the Sun 39–40; discourses of 101–105; interaction with Yudhiṣṭhira 11; Jaimini's questioning to 100–101, 120; Pāṇḍava's encounter with 132–135; on parallels between Saura *māhātmya* and its Śākta counterpart 55; story of Sāvitrī (Patrivratāmāhātmya) 11; Sun's power 45, 132–135; teachings of 101; Yudhiṣṭhira's questioning of 102–103
*Matsya Purāṇa* 20, 99
*māyā* 84, 87; of Viṣṇu 87
Mayūra 21; Sūrya-Śataka 7, 20–21
Medhas, Sage 9, 57, 86, 109–110, 124, 141
Mitra 15–17, 133
*mokṣa*, boon of 127
moral and social order, preservation of 2
Mṛkaṇḍu (father of Mārkaṇḍeya) 102

*nakṣatras* 88, 90, 92–94
Nārada, Sage 22, 54, 101, 121, 131
Nārāyaṇi Stuti 138
Nariṣyanta 112, 128
Narmadā river 81–82
Navaratri Festival 87, 93, 139–140
*nibandhakāras* 22
*nivṛtti* dharma 1–2, 5, 53, 123–124; austerity of 131; religiosity of 122

*oṃ*, utterance of 40
*On Hinduism* (2014) 83
*Origins of Evil in Hindu Mythology, The* (1976) 69, 75

Padmapurāṇa 104
*pañcalakṣaṇas* 38, 56, 95
*Pañcendra-Upākhyāna* 123
Pāṇḍavas 17–18, 26, 83, 101, 102, 123, 131–135, 140
pan-Indic autumnal festival 94
Parāśara, Sage 89
Pargiter, Eden 7–14, 113, 116
*piṇḍa* cakes 113
Pingree, David 89
*pitṛ pūjā* 113
*pitṛs* 126
*pratisarga* (secondary creation) 56, 95
*pravṛttic saura-śākta* symbiosis 2
*pravṛtti* dharma 1–2, 25, 34, 50, 53, 123, 139, 141; ethos of 123, 126; function of preservation 5; glorifications of Goddess and Sun 6; ideology of 2; *Mārkaṇḍeya Purāṇa* polemic against 124; plight of 119–127; of preservation 127; prioritization of 50; royal work of 2; sovereignty, notion of 126; violence of kingship and 126; work of kings in their homage to the Sun 2, 6
*pravṛtti-nivṛtti* interplay 6, 132
preservation, ethos of 84; cosmogonic function of 139; essence of avatāra 137; in *Mārkaṇḍeya Purāṇa* 5; of mortal beings 64; paragons of 137–141; *pravṛttic* theme of 127; Sun and 131–137; supreme power and 61
primordial king, birthing of 61
protective divine force, celebration of 139
Ptolemy 22
Purāṇas 70; cross-generational assemblage 8; on function of preservation 5; *Mahā-Purāṇas* 19–20; mythologization of the Sun in 19–25; *pañcalakṣaṇas* 56; on relationship between myth and the ritual 94; as sectarian Brahmanical corruptions 7; study of 2; translation into English 7; Western Purāṇic scholarship 7, 11
Purāṇic marks (*pañcalakṣaṇas*), types of 95
*Pūrva Mīmāṃsā Sūtras* 100
Pūṣan 15, 136

Rājyavardhana, King 49, 52–53, 58–59, 66n5, 88, 112
*rakṣaḥkulasamudbhavān* 113
rākṣakas 43
*rakṣa-kula-samudbhavān* 113
Rāma, Lord 133; battle with Rāvaṇa 135–136; protected by Sun 135–137; royal duty of vanquishing his foe 137; worship of Vivasvān 136
Rāmānuja's Viśiṣṭādvaita philosophy 7, 20
*Rāmāyaṇa:* mythologization of the Sun in 17–19; Rāma–Rāvaṇa battle 135–136; story of Rāma 133; on Sun protection of Rāma 135–137; *Vālmīki Rāmāyaṇa* 19, 135
religious ideologies 119; dissemination of 12

Revanta 93; as Lord of the Guhyakas 49; as son of Sun God 48
*Revati* constellation 80, 90, 93
*Ṛg Veda* 40, 45, 75, 140; hymns dedicated to Lord Viṣṇu 139; myth of Saraṇyū and her husband in 71
ritual sacrifice 111; cycles of 127; with human flesh and blood 115
Robber of the Waters 45, 48, 77, 80
Rocher, Ludo 8, 13, 20–23
Rodrigues, Hillary 94
royal dynasties *(vaṃśānucarita)*, of *Mārkaṇḍeya Purāṇa* 38, **55–56**
Ṛtadhvaja 124–126
Ṛta-vāc, Sage 90
Rudra (Śiva) *see* Śiva, Lord
Rudradaman, King 90
Rudrasena II, King 89

sacrificial fires, in Vedic religion 15, 85
Śākadvīpa 20, 22–23
Śākta 'interpolators' 105
*Sāma Veda* 35, 40, 100
*Sāmba Purāṇa* 20, 22–25, 55, 135; English translation of 24; Goddess, the Sun and the story of Sāmba 53–55
Sāmba, story of 22, 53–55; associated with leprosy 55; association with lunar mythology 55; blessing of Lord Śiva 55
Śamīka, Sage 119
Saṃjaya (Dhṛtarāṣṭhra' advisor/ charioteer) 100
Saṃjñā (wife of Sun) 63; act of self-cloning 72; articulations of 70; birth of Aśvin twins 15, 48, 70, 90; birth of Yama and Yamī 70; Chāyā 34, 46, 70; debunking Doniger on 68–87; dual nature of 74; equine exegesis 87–96; flight from marriage and motherhood 71; as mother of Manu 68; nasal association 35, 48, 79–81, 88, 93; pacification of her destructive husband 71; practice of *chaste* austerities 81; seminal splendour and the transmission of tejas 79–82; sexual coercion of 80–81; structuralist sleight of hand 69–78; Sūrya–Saṃjñā–Chāyā epsiode 72, 83; threat to her marital fidelity 79; Vedic story of 34–35, 46, 68, 79; 'wicked stepmother' motif 74
Saṃjñā-Chāyā symbolism 72, 84–87
saṃsāra, bondage of 24, 124
Saṃvarṇa, King 18, 73–74, 83
Sāṅkhya philosophy, doctrines of 101
Saraṇyū, Goddess 16, 70–71, 75–76, 84–87
*sarga* (primary creation) 56, 95
Śatapaṭha Brāhmaṇa 86
Satyabhāmā 101, 133
*satya*, vow of 126
*Sauradharma upa-Purāṇa* 21
*Sauradharmottara upa-Purāṇa* 21
*Saura Purāṇa* 22, 55
Saura–Śākta ideological symbiosis 54, 55–65, 68
*Saurasamhitā* 20
Saurasaṃhitā 21
Saura upa-Purāṇas 21–22
Sāvarṇi, story of 1, 13, 46, 56, 77, 140–141
Sāvitrī (Patrivratāmāhātmya), story of 11, 133
"sectarian" *versus* "non-sectarian" spirit 14
semen, symbol for 91
sexual freedom, theme of 80–81
shadow self (*chāyā mūrti*) 72
sharpness (*tejas*), of the Sun 34, 79–82
*śiva liṅgaṃ* 102
Śiva, Lord 40, 44, 53, 102, 137, 139; annihilation of Yama 102, 127; blessings to Mārkaṇḍeya 102
*Śiva Purāṇa* 54
*Skanda Purāṇa* 20
Smith, J.Z. 105
solar deities, in Vedic literature 15; grouping of 15
solar family tree, of *Mārkaṇḍeya Purāṇa 36*
Solar iconography, foreign influence on 23
Solar icons (*mūrtīs*), in the Purāṇas 19
solar kings: exploits of 66n5; genealogy of 112; Rāma, story of 133; succession of 128n5
solar myths: compilation of 7–8; in *Mārkaṇḍeya Purāṇa* 7
solar sources, of *Mārkaṇḍeya Purāṇa* 14–25; in epics 17–19; in Purāṇic literature 19–25; in Vedic literature 14–17
solar symbols, of King and Goddess 139
solar veneration 14; Aryan and non-Aryan 15; connection with Mārkaṇḍeya 132; epic expressions of 17–19; Magian influences on 24; sectarian movement dedicated to 24; Yudhiṣṭhira's 132
sovereign empowerment, protection of 94
sovereignty, notion of 1, 58–59, 61, 66n5, 95, 126–127, 139–140
Sphujidhvaja's *Yavanajātaka* 89
*stava* 7

*stotras* 7
Sudāman 51
Sugrīva (vānara) 19, 140
*śukra* 91; *see also* Venus (goddess of fertility)
Sukṛṣa, Sage 115, 121–123; admonishment of avian-Indra 126; vow of *satya* 126; vow to ahiṃsā 126
Sun and creation: Brahma hymns the Sun 41–42; greatness of the Sun 40
Sun–earth relationship 49–53; citizens hymn the Sun 49–52; King Rājyavardhana hymns the Sun 52–53
Sun in Purāṇic sources: *Mahā-Purāṇas* 19–20; in Minor Saura texts 20–21; *Sāmba Purāṇa* 22–25; *Saura upa-Purāṇas* 21–22
Sun, mythology of 1, 8; advice to Karṇa 133–134; an instrument of spiritual purification 17; beginnings of the zodiac 91; as deity to Vedic religion 14; destructive aspect 20; healing power 15; iconography and chariots 19; known as Āditya 19; kṣatriya caste 95; in *Mahābhārata* 17–19; protection of Rāma 135–137; protection of Yudhiṣṭhira 131–132; in *Purāṇic* sources 19–25; in *Rāmāyaṇa* 19; Saura vratas and rites 19; solar forms of 136; spiritual power 15; as spiritual symbol of the self 17; synchronic study of 25–31; in Upaniṣadic literature 17; in Vedic sources 14–17; worship of Sun 16, 18–20; Yama–Sun relationship 19
Sun's family: majesty of the Sun 48–49; paring down of the Sun 46–47; Viśvakarman hymns 47–48
Sun, splendour of 34–55, 95; Agastya's glorification of 136; attributes of 136–137; Brahma hymns on 41–42; Chāyā, story of 34–35; creation of 40–42; earth and 49–53; greatness of 40; heavens and 42–46; identity as Vivasvat 60; incarnation of 45; majesty of 48–49; in *Mārkaṇḍeya Purāṇa* 38–40; Mārkaṇḍeya's description of 39–40; paring down of 46–47, 60; Purāṇic myths of 85; Saṃjñā (wife of Sun) and 34–35; seminal splendour and the transmission of tejas 79–82; Viśvakarman hymns on 47–48
Sun's *tejas*, paring down of 35, 59–60
Sun temple 22, 53
Sun worship 16, 18–20; arghya offerings 51; iconography and rituals 20; means of 51; origin of 23; Sun-priests 22–23; Vedic and Epic religiosity 23; *vratas* for 20
Suratha, King 58, 140–141; encounter with Sage Medhas 141
Sūrya 15–16, 137; cosmogonic functions of 137; dark secret 134; excessive power in the form of his *tejas* 60; *śaktis* of 86–87; sectarian supremacy of 24; themes to exalt 137
*Sūrya Gītā* 7, 20
*Sūrya Māhātmya* (SM) 1, 6–7, 37, 63, 105, 139; episode chart **65**; in Jan Gonda's discourse on *māhātmya*s 7; on myth of the Sun and his family 7; parallels with *Devī Māhātmyas* **37**; on *pravṛttic saura-śākta* symbiosis 2; Rājyavardhana episode 58–59; structure of **38**
*Sūrya Purāṇa* 21–22
*Sūrya-Śataka* 7, 20–21
*Sūrya Upaniṣad* 21
Suṣumna (incarnation of Sun) 45
*svayamvara* 26, 88
synchronic study, of Sanskrit Saura and Śākta narratives 25–31; enframement import 27; expositional import 27; framing import 27; guiding principles of 29–31; inception import 28–29; narrative's (intrinsic) framing of 26–29; prompting import 27

*tapaḥ-svādhyāya-nirata* 120
*tapas* 54, 62, 102
Tapatī, story of 3, 18, 34, 36, 46, 73–74, 81–83
Tārkṣī (bird mother) 121
*tejas:* assembly of gods derived from 61; association of Goddess with 61–62; *atejas* (anti-thesis) 96n3; concept of 60; and Indian discourse of kingship 60; transmission of 79–82
*tīkṣṇa* 60
Time, concept of 16

Upanishads 70; associated with Atharva Veda 21; *Sūrya Upaniṣad* 21

Vaiśālinī 88
Vaiśaṃpāyana 131, 135
Vaiṣṇava avatāra, essence of 137, 138–139
*Vaiṣṇava Purāṇas* 137–138
Vaivasvata Manu 35, 138
*vaivasvata-manvantara* 56, 60

*Vālmīki Rāmāyaṇa* 19, 135
*vaṃśa* 56, 95
*vaṃśānucarita* 56, 95
Vapu, Apsara 121–122
Varāhamihira 22–23, 89, 95
Vasiṣṭha, Sage 74
*Vāyu Purāṇa* 20, 66n6
Vedic religion: ethos of 16; mythologization of the Sun in 14–17
Vedic ritual timing, significance for 93
Vedic sacrifices 137, 139
Venus (goddess of fertility) 89–91
victorious power (vijayā śakti) 94
Vipaścit, story of 10–11
virtues of the Sun 7, 21
Viṣṇu, Lord 15, 17, 40, 53, 137; dedication of Ṛg Vedic hymns to 139; incarnation of 104, 137; *māyā* of 87; on preservation of life on earth 139; protector of the cosmos 139; purpose of taking on human form 65; slaying of demons Madhu and Kaiṭabha 138
*Viṣṇu Purāṇa* 22; descriptions of the Sun 20; English translation of 12; on Magian priests of Iran 23
Viśvakarman (divine architect-tinkerer) 35, 65n1; forging of protective weapons for the gods 50; hymns in praise of Sun 47–48; paring down of the Sun 46–47, 82
Vivasvat (Lord of Rays) 15–16, 46, 49, 79; Sun's identity as 60
von Simson, Georg 54–55
Vṛṣṇis 54
Vyāsa, Sage 99–101, 120, 123

'wicked stepmother' motif 68, 72, 74, 78, 83
Wilson, H.H. 7, 11, 113; Western Purāṇic scholarship 7, 11
Winternitz, Moriz 8–11, 13, 102
World Sanskrit Conference 2

*Yajur Veda* 40
Yama 76–77, 133; annihilation by Lord Śiva 102, 127; attempt to kick Chāyā 70; cursed by Chāyā 34–35, 46, 70–73; as king of virtue (*dharmarājā*) 48; as regent of the departed souls 49; as son of Sun God 19, 34, 46, 48
Yamunā 34–35, 49, 82
*yoga tārā* 92
yogic attainment *(siddhi)* of bilocation 72
yogic meditation 35
Yudhiṣṭhira 11, 18, 101; protected by Sun 131–132; questioning of Mārkaṇḍeya 102–103; solar veneration 132–133

zodiac: Aries 92; beginnings of 91; zodiacal signs 92–93

Printed in the United States
by Baker & Taylor Publisher Services